WHY NOT LE

LEANING TOWER

COLLAPSE?

WHY NOT LET THE LEANING TOWER COLLAPSE?

and other essays examining what we think of as 'history'

Daniel Snowman

BROWN DOG BOOKS

First published 2024

Published under licence by Brown Dog Books and
The Self-Publishing Partnership, 10b Greenway Farm,
Bath Rd, Wick, nr. Bath BS30 5RL

www.selfpublishingpartnership.co.uk

ISBN printed book: 978-1-83952-815-6
ISBN e-book: 978-1-83952-816-3

Cover design by Kevin Rylands
Internal design by Tim Jollands

Printed and bound in the UK

This book is printed on FSC® certified paper

Contents

Introduction   11
  1. **Mahler's Second Symphony** *(Resurrection)*   14
     (*Jewish Chronicle,* 30 September 2005)
  2. **Where is the Jewish Pavarotti?**   16
     History contains a multitude of outstanding musical Jews but there is
     one glaring gap. Why? (*Jewish Chronicle,* 8 October 2010)

Heritage, History and Historians
  3. **On the Heritage Trail**   18
     Tracking down what Britain's 'Historic Heritage' means to some of
     those in charge of it. (*History Today,* 9 September 2004)
  4. **'Historians' Today: why historians are 'Very Important People'** 29
     Introduction to book about the life and work of 28 leading historians,
     published by Palgrave Macmillan in 2007.
  5. **Is Biography 'History'?** (*History Today,* 11 November 2014)   44
  6. **'IFS' of History**   47
     Could the past have been different? (Based on the Introduction to my
     book *If I Had Been: Ten Historical Fantasies*, Robson Books, 1979)

History and the BBC
  7. **Wireless is More: From** *The Long March of Everyman* **to**   52
     Fins de Siècle. (*BBC History Magazine,* August 2002)
  8. **BBC Centenary**   56
     This essay was first drafted in 2021 with the approach of the centenary
     of the creation of the BBC. Versions of the essay were subsequently
     published in a variety of journals, and it was also used as the basis for
     a number of different lectures.

History and the Institute of Historical Research (IHR)
  9. **'History Now and Then'**   71
     The title was adopted for a series of six public seminars held at the IHR
     over the course of academic year 2015/16 and aimed at examining
     ways in which we use (and abuse) the past. This article was published
     by the *BBC History Magazine* in January 2016. 'History' had never
     been more popular, I suggested. Yet many people seemed to live in a

bubble of the immediate present. Did this matter – and if so, why?

10. **'History Now and Then'** (continued)　　　　77
The following is taken from a blog written in August 2016 to help promote the second series of IHR seminars (2016/17). It first appeared under the heading Talking Humanities on the website of London University's 'School of Advanced Study' (SAS) of which the Institute of Historical Research was, and remains, an integral part.

IHR Website

11. *A Promised Land* by Barack Obama　　　　80
Review of Volume 1 of the former US President's Memoir. (*Reviews in History*, February 2021)

12. **IHR blogs**　　　　87
A series of four essays, all raising and illustrating provocative issues about how we regard and memorialise what we think of as 'history'. The first three were issued monthly on the IHR Website in May, June and July 2022, and the fourth in September 2023.

1. **Leaning Tower of Pisa** (May 2022)
We all seek what we think of as 'historical authenticity'. In which case, shouldn't the famous Tower of Pisa be restored to its original perpendicular form? Or allowed to collapse with the passage of time? The one thing that isn't historically authentic, surely, is to use modern technology to retain its (otherwise temporary) leaning position.

2. **Telling History Backwards** (June 2022)
In the second of my IHR blogs examining provocative issues about how we regard and memorialise what we think of as 'history', I suggested that instead of starting at the beginning of the story and going forwards we might start in the present and unravel the story backwards.

3. **Should we concrete over 'dark tourist' monuments?** (July 2022)
Is there a danger that a powerful historical memorial (and place of pilgrimage) like Auschwitz might, with time, morph into a monument to a distant, forgotten past and, eventually, become just another historical museum?

4. **Is it the job of the historian to judge the past?** (September 2023)
In August 2023 the IHR asked Senior Research Fellows to say something about what they had been reading over the summer break. I cited a new book by Julian Jackson about Philippe Pétain: the French military leader widely known as the victor of the Battle

of Verdun in World War I – and the man who collaborated with the Nazis in World War II as ruler of Vichy. Was Pétain a good guy or a bad guy? More profoundly, is it the job of the historian to judge the past?

Britain, Germany, War and the World

13. **Prussia 1701: A European Affair:** a new exhibition in Berlin.   108
    (*History Today*, May 2000)
14. **World War II: Forty Years On: Is the War 'just history'?**   111
    (*The Listener*, 30 August 1979)
15. **Dresden: What do you do if your city has been destroyed?**   117
    Rebuild the past – or move with the times? (Drafted in February 2004 for adaptation in a variety of lectures and publications)
16. *The Bauhaus Group: Six Masters of Modernism*   122
    by Nicholas Fox Weber (*Literary Review*, March 2011).
17. *Final Solution: The Fate of the Jews, 1933–49*   125
    by David Cesarani (*History Today*, May 2016).
18. **The 2003 IHR Scouloudi Lecture: *'The Hitler Emigrés': The Cultural Impact on Britain of Refugees from Nazism'***   128
    This lecture was delivered in Beveridge Hall, Senate House, London on 12 June 2003 at the invitation of the Director of the Institute of Historical Research, David Cannadine. Here is an expanded version of the text that was subsequently published (and sourced) by the IHR where, in 2004, I became a Senior Research Fellow.
19. *Insiders/Outsiders*: **Introduction**   153
    This article is based on my introduction to the book accompanying the *Insiders/Outsiders Festival* (created by art historian Monica Bohm-Duchen) published by Lund Humphries in 2019.
20. **President Truman's decision to drop the atomic bomb in 1945**   157
    Was Hiroshima a 'good thing' (it brought World War II to a rapid end with minimum loss of life) or one of the most abhorrent decisions in history? I spoke to Truman about this a few years later.

History and the Arts

21. **From the Pulpit: History and the Arts should get together more often** (*Literary Review*, June 2010)   163
22. **'Historians and the Arts, 1950–2010'**   165
    (*History Today*, February 2011)

Contents

23. *'Guerra! Guerra!'* – War and the Arts, 1800–2000   172
    Reflections on the historical relationship between war and the arts
    since Napoleonic times. This essay was published in a variety of forms
    (and magazines) and became the basis of a frequently commissioned
    lecture for the Arts Society (formerly 'NADFAS').

...and Music in Particular
24. **Vauxhall Gardens: A History** by David Coke and Alan Borg   182
    (*Literary Review,* June 2011)
25. **Nuremberg Chronicles: In search of Mastersingers**   187
    and Minnesingers
    An historically-based piece which I drafted (with the detailed help of
    Lucie Skeaping). (*OPERA* magazine, February 2015)

Matters Operatic
26. **Introducing** *The Gilded Stage*   195
    Most histories of music concentrate on composers and their works. I
    tried to suggest a different approach. (Article from *NADFAS Review*,
    Winter 2009)
27. **Let's Get Together: Daniel urges musicologists and**   197
    historians to join forces.
    The Gilded Stage: A Social History of Opera was published in autumn
    2009. By way of anticipation, I drafted this article. (*OPERA*
    magazine, November 2009)
28. **Opera in America: New World Overtures**   207
    Opera has flourished in the USA, several American companies
    rated among the world's finest. But how did this 'elite' art form
    become deep-rooted in a nation dedicated to popular culture and
    the proposition that all men are created equal? This article combines
    material from an excerpt in *Opera Now* in 2007 with a longer essay
    published in *History Today* in January 2010.
29. **The ROH Collections**   222
    Essay about the Covent Garden Archives, commissioned in 2011 by
    the ROH.
30. **Callas as Catalyst: Memories of Maria Callas to mark**   228
    her centenary
    (*OPERA* Magazine, January 2024)

Composers: Handel, Verdi, Wagner and Puccini — 232

31. Handel: Introduction to *Solomon* — 234
(*ROH programme*, October 2018)
32. 'Viva Verdi!' — 239
For *OPERA* Magazine, January 2011 – the 150th anniversary of
Italian statehood.
33. *Winifred Wagner: A Life at the Heart of Hitler's Bayreuth* — 246
Review of the biography written by Brigitte Hamann. (*Opera Now*,
Sept/Oct 2005)
34. Wagner (*Compass* magazine, 2012) — 249
35. At home with Puccini: Torre del Lago — 252
(*Opera Now*, May/June 1999, including brief updatings)

Life and Times: Past, Present and Future
36. Pepys and the Covent Garden piazza — 261
Based on lecture to the Samuel Pepys Club in June 2023 and later
adapted as introduction to an all-day tour of the Covent Garden
piazza undertaken for the Institute of Historical Research (May 2024).
37. *Virgins: A Cultural History* by Anke Bernau and *Rape: A* — 268
history from 1860 to the Present by Joanna Bourke
(*History Today*, October, 2007)
38. *Pole Positions: The Polar regions and the future of the planet* — 270
From the Foreword to the book, first published in 1993 by Hodder &
Stoughton.
39. *21 Lessons for the 21st Century* by Yuval Noah Harari and — 274
Denial: The Unspeakable Truth by Keith Kahn-Harris
(*The Jewish Chronicle*, 31 August, 2018)
40. Obituary. Yet to be published! — 276

Afterword — 285

Introduction

I have always enjoyed writing, speaking – communicating and exchanging my ideas with others. As a schoolboy, and later a student at Cambridge and then Cornell in the USA, I regularly had to write essays on some subject of my recent research. As candidate for an Open Scholarship to Cambridge in autumn 1957, I relished being faced with an exam paper that offered something like fifteen different historical topics from which I had to choose just three on which to write brief essays. A day or two later we had to sit a 'general' paper for which candidates were invited to compose a more substantial essay. The one I chose focused on the differences between what we called 'the arts' and 'entertainment'. I plunged straight in. And in some ways I have been drawn to this and equally provocative topics ever since.

Looking over some of the articles and essays I have written over the years I find myself forever asking potentially awkward questions. I began doing so when growing up after the war as a little Jewish boy in Edgware. Why (I would ask my parents) can't we have milk after meat? Or eat pig meat? If we hated the Nazis because of their murderous, anti-Semitic racism, shouldn't a young Jewish boy like myself be encouraged to cross the boundaries and befriend girls who are not Jewish?

I didn't want to upset my beloved parents. But then, and ever since, I have enjoyed engaging with thoughtful people who might have interesting answers to the quasi-philosophical questions I found myself posing. Especially concerning our views about the past. If 'the past' is everything that has ever happened, why does what we call 'history' keep changing? What causes historical change? Could aspects of the past itself have been different? Is there an argument for telling 'history' backwards, starting with the present? What do we (and don't we) choose to retain as part of our 'heritage', and why? Are 'the arts' part of history or merely illustrative of it?

And more specifically, what do we mean by 'opera', for example? Was there anything 'Jewish' about the cultural impact of the refugees from Nazism? Was Pétain (or Napoleon) a good guy or a bad guy? Is Auschwitz in danger of becoming just another historical museum? Should the leaning Tower of Pisa be allowed to fall in the interests of 'historical authenticity'?

Then there was (or is) the future. Why, I've often wondered, are historians supposedly brilliant at explaining everything that has ever happened in the past – yet useless at predicting the future? I am reminded of the wise words of the great French historian Marc Bloch (who was executed by the Nazis in 1944): 'Misunderstanding of the present is the inevitable consequence of ignorance of the past.'

***

This book is not an autobiography. Much about my life and times is chronicled in a recent memoir: *Just Passing Through: Interactions with the World, 1938–2021.* Here, I recounted something about my time in the academic world and the BBC, watching Churchill making one of his last public speeches, interviewing Harry Truman about Hiroshima, staying with a black family in the American South while working on a Civil Rights project and spending a week in Bayreuth with Wagner's daughter-in-law. I wrote of my near-half-century singing in the London Philharmonic Choir, of visiting the polar regions and writing about climate change, of meeting Pope John-Paul II, Isaiah Berlin and the enigmatic Lord Snowdon and getting to know many of the most famous among the 'Hitler Emigrés' and that operatic superstar Plácido Domingo.

Some of this is reflected in the essays that follow. But this book is essentially a collection, or a selection, of some of the more meditative essays I have written over the years. Many concern history, or our shifting attitudes towards aspects of the past. Others focus on particular issues: the similarities and differences between British and American social attitudes and values, or historical attitudes towards Germany and the rise and fall of the Third Reich and the cultural impact on Britain of migration and in particular the refugees from Nazism. Much of my writing and research has concerned the socio-political history of the arts, especially that most ambitious and multimedia form we call 'opera'. And I've periodically found myself addressing various aspects of what we think of as Jewish history. What do we mean by 'Jewish'? Or 'the arts'? Or, indeed, 'history'?

Almost all the essays reproduced here were, as indicated, originally published elsewhere and all the earlier sources I have managed to contact have agreed they could be reproduced here. A punctilious reader might spot one or two carefully considered overlaps between the content of one essay and another, while some articles have been slightly edited and updated. The collection as a whole is far from comprehensive, most of the pieces included here having been aimed at a wide, general but not necessarily academic readership. And I have excluded all but a handful of the countless reviews of books and operas I have written over the decades.

So let's start with a couple of brief pieces in which, somehow, I managed to incorporate an interest in history, German history, music, culture and the apparent universality of matters Jewish.

I hope you enjoy a good browse!

Daniel Snowman, November 2024

Mahler's Second Symphony *(Resurrection)*

This was published by the Jewish Chronicle *(30 September 2005) in a special supplement to mark the Jewish New Year. I was one of several writers who had been asked to try and pinpoint an artwork or artefact that conveyed an essential aspect of 'Jewishness'.*

The first of many articles and reviews I wrote for the JC was in autumn 1964 after I had spent the summer working on a Civil Rights project in the American South. The following article, written over forty years later, was about the supposed 'Jewishness' of Mahler.

I tend to look at things from as cosmopolitan a perspective as I can. Do I 'feel' Jewish? Of course I do. But I 'feel' lots of other things too. We all have multiple identities, and so did people in the past. I have no difficulty, therefore, in being seduced by the genius of Wagner despite aspects of his personality I find despicable and the longueurs in even his most inspired operas.

In Mendelssohn, I hear echoes of the German Enlightenment and of early-Victorian optimism just as Mahler evokes for me *fin-de-siècle* Vienna – in tandem with my knowledge about the Jewish roots of each. To think of them as 'Jewish' composers is to diminish them, as it is to describe Jane Austen as a 'woman' novelist, Verdi as an 'Italian' composer or Chagall as a 'Jewish' artist.

But to understand the world we need labels, however reductionist. So is there a sense in which we might legitimately regard a figure like Mahler, through his work, as 'Jewish'? I'd like to suggest that Mahler was Jewish in a paradoxically 'non-Jewish' way. Like Marx, Freud and many other figures to emerge from the German Enlightenment, Mahler gained part of his strength from the fact that he crossed cultural borders, dwelt on the frontiers of various civilisations, religions and nations.

Listen to (or better still, get a chance to sing!) the final section of his Second Symphony and I think you'll hear what I mean. It begins, after an evocation of the graveside Last Post, with an almost inaudible pianissimo entry for the chorus reasserting the eternity of life. As momentum builds, Mahler adds a wonderfully insistent passage about the need to believe: what is created will die – but what dies will live again. And the 'Resurrection' symphony ends with a thunderous final acclamation of indestructible faith in God.

The very attempt to reach out to all humanity by transcending boundaries of mind and place has resonances deep within Jewish history and tradition. After all, if anything unites 'Jewish' achievement, perhaps it is that of a scattered diaspora linked by the shared legacy of settlement, upheaval, flight, resettlement – and hope for the future. To me, it is this optimistic universalism of Mahler that is most characteristic of his post-Enlightenment Jewishness.

Where is the Jewish Pavarotti?

History contains a multitude of outstanding
musical Jews but there is one glaring gap. Why?
Jewish Chronicle, 8 October 2010.

When I was a child, shortly after the war, I remember asking why so many
famous violinists were Jewish and being told that Jews had often been on
the run and that you could always take your fiddle with you. There was
some truth to this. The *Yidl Mitn Fidl*, like the fiddler on the roof, was the
stuff of Jewish legend, and it became reality when (for example) three of
the future members of the Amadeus Quartet fetched up in London from
Nazi Vienna with no special aptitude other than the ability to play the
violin.

But if the violin was portable, surely the voice was even more so?
When my parents took me to my first opera, and to Gigli concerts at the
Royal Albert Hall, I wondered why there were so few famous Jewish opera
singers. Sixty-odd years later, it's about time I tried to answer the question.

Think of a famous Jewish 'classical' musician over the past century
or two. Hordes of names spring to mind: pianists such as Rubinstein,
Horowitz, Schnabel and Barenboim and violinists from Joachim, Kreisler
and Heifetz to Menuhin, Stern, Perlman and beyond. The list is endless, as
is that of celebrated composers and conductors with Jewish backgrounds
(Mendelssohn, Meyerbeer, Offenbach, Mahler, Walter, Klemperer,
Gershwin, Bernstein etc).

But what about top opera singers? A handful of starry names suggest
themselves: a few recent Americans (Merrill, Peerce, Tucker, Sills), some
Central and Eastern Europeans from a little earlier (Kipnis, Schorr,
Schmidt, Tauber) and one or two from further back still. Opera history
has of course been graced by far more Jewish singers than this. But among
the absolutely stellar figures those from Jewish backgrounds form an
appreciably smaller cohort than those excelling in other forms of musical
performance. Caruso, Gigli, Patti, Melba and Callas were not Jewish, nor
Sutherland, Pavarotti, Domingo, Fleming or Flórez.

In the Jewish Pale a couple of centuries ago, a talented young man's
sense of identity would have been wrapped up with his Jewishness. If he
was blessed with a good voice, the place to use it would have been the shul.
Here, chazanut flourished: a vocal genre that drew upon many elements
but was little touched by opera.

Later, as Jews moved west to cities such as Vienna, Prague and Berlin, or further (London, New York), some went on to become doctors, lawyers, scientists and writers. And musicians: by the later 1800s, music was widely regarded as something of a sanctified art. Especially 'absolute' music: Beethoven quartets and the like. Listening to these was ennobling, morally uplifting, and playing them more so. By contrast, popular operas by Rossini or Verdi were highly crafted entertainments.

Many Jews shared this romantic view. It was one thing to enjoy a night out at the opera, but you wouldn't want your son (much less your daughter) to enter the profession. Nor would many Jewish singers have found it comfortable working with the one figure who tried to unite these disparate worlds into a transcendent combination of the arts: the notoriously antisemitic Richard Wagner.

Perhaps there was something, too, about the institutional nature of opera production that discouraged Jewish entry. The 18th-century Romanov or Habsburg courts were hardly natural magnets for Jewish singers. By the late 19th century, when it was easier for a talented Jewish violinist or pianist to choose when and where to perform, an opera singer was in effect an employee of a large factory, with work schedules handed down from management: not the kind of ambience in which it was easy to ask leave of absence on Shabbat or Yomtov!

In the 20th century, as many Jews became assimilated into the wider culture, opera houses came to include on their roster a number of singers from Jewish backgrounds. Tragically, most in Central Europe lost their jobs, and many their lives, with the advent of Nazism. But now opera has become an attractive and welcoming profession to Jewish singers. So next time you go to the opera you may see (and hear) a Jewish superstar in the making!

Heritage, History
and Historians

On the Heritage Trail

Tracking down what Britain's 'Historic Heritage'
means to some of those in charge of it.
History Today, 9 September 2004.

It is five o'clock in the morning. A relentless sun peers up over the horizon as an army of sturdy English soldiery lies abed under canvas awaiting the day's campaigning. You could be forgiven for thinking this the dawn of Agincourt. Indeed, you would not be far wrong. Except that this tent city lies on an anonymous 200-acre spot of greenery close to the heart of England, and the dormant army will soon materialise not only as sturdy longbowmen but also as Roman centurions, medieval knights and falconers, Tudor yeomen, Georgian fops, sappers from the Somme, the odd cooper, wheelwright, barber-surgeon, ropemaker, ratcatcher and Green Man, and happy hordes of equivalently costumed girls and women led by a peripatetic Queen Victoria. We are on the site of a giant Festival of History run by English Heritage. Before this weekend has come and gone, hundreds of re-enactors will have donned their togas and tabards, chain mail and periwigs, tilted their lances, played their sackbuts and citterns, roasted boar and rabbit over a spit, polished bayonets, checked field hospitals and come within a musket shot of winning the Battle of Edgehill for King Charles. Even greater numbers will have watched the displays, learned the skills, sung the songs, bought the craftware and logged into the websites.

Simon Thurley, Chief Executive of English Heritage (2002–2015), likes to joke that the only thing wrong with the organisation he heads is the two words in its title, both of which have lately been suffering a bout of political incorrectness. 'English' is (among other things) a description of the extent and limits of Thurley's bailiwick. But 'Heritage'? Everybody I spoke to in the course of my researches heaved a cross between a sigh and a smile when asked to define this slippery term. It's like the proverbial elephant, laughed one; impossible to describe but you know it when you

The Sealed Knot: a British historical association dedicated to costumed re-enactment of battles and events surrounding the English Civil War.

see it. Another paraphrased what Churchill said about democracy: the word 'Heritage' is pretty awful – but better than any of the alternatives. Our 'Heritage', suggested a third helpfully, is anything of significance we've inherited from the past – but that immediately got us into knotty debate about what is meant by 'significant', who 'we' are and which 'past' we were talking about.

Until a few years ago, few in Britain talked about history as 'Heritage'. The past was interesting and there were doubtless lessons to be learned from it. But as London came to be rebuilt in the wake of the wartime Blitz, much that had been regarded as historical was modernised, or elbowed aside by a new shopping mall or pedestrian precinct, while fading aristocrats were often forced to vacate their country houses and see their crumbling townhouses replaced by concrete tower blocks. Paternoster Square around St Paul's Cathedral aroused controversy for a while, Euston station lost its classical arch and nearby St Pancras was only reprieved from total demolition at the last moment. History, it has been said, becomes especially important at times of danger. Here, it was the very physicality of the past that was under threat – or so it seemed to those who talked anxiously of 'Heritage'. Pressure groups and governmental authorities began to take action (English Heritage was set up by the National Heritage Act of 1983). Who could quarrel with the idea that, while there was still time, the nation's 'Heritage' had to be saved?

A number of influential writers, while sympathetic to the fundamental idea of preserving the legacy of the past, were disturbed by the way they saw it being done. Historian and broadcaster Patrick Wright, returning to Thatcher's Britain after a number of years in California and Canada, found a modernising nation whose historic past was in danger of becoming enwrapped in mere quaintness and antiquarianism. In 1985 he published *On Living in an Old Country* in which he sensed that a sanitised narrative of national history had been harnessed for political purposes while the nation's richer, more authentic core culture, instead of being nurtured, was being systematically undermined. David Cannadine, who had made the opposite journey and gone to live in America, looked back across the Atlantic that same year to warn his compatriots against the very idea of a national heritage, a concept that he thought was in danger of encouraging 'a neo-nostalgic, pseudo-pastoral world of manufactured make-believe, a picture-postcard version of Britain and its past, titillating the tourist with tinsel "traditions".' In 1985, too, David Lowenthal produced his ground-breaking study of the uses and abuses of history, *The Past is a Foreign Country* (at one point quoting Marghanita Laski to the effect that the word 'heritage' had come to sound either pompous or twee). Then, a couple of years later, Robert Hewison came out with a powerful polemic about the 'Heritage Industry', arguing that the past was becoming commercialised and commodified by self-appointed curators to whom every ancient site had to be endowed with theme-park prettiness and an obligatory lavender-tinted retail outlet. Meanwhile, Raphael Samuel, incomparable guardian of the minutiae of the popular past, was penning a series of pieces which, while documenting the postwar transition to modernism, also noted the emergence of its kitsch nemesis, 'retrochic'.

The critique came from many quarters. Heritage, said some, was essentially a form of sentimental conservatism, a middle-class, rearguard movement that overvalued the aristocratic past and set its collective face against social and aesthetic change, a symptom perhaps of resurgent nationalism, a consolation for loss of empire (there were few black or brown faces among the crowds who went to celebrate the kings and queens of England at Warwick or Windsor castles). 'Heritage' also had critics on the right, arguing against increasing subsidies for historic sites and disturbed at how 'living museums' would elevate the importance of ordinary people in the past and endow the daily grind of farming, soldiery or industrial work with a romantic patina it did not warrant. The critics attacked each other, too; thus Wright noted that Hewison's phrase, the 'Heritage Industry', had in fact first been used by the writer and campaigner Colin Ward, while Samuel upbraided Wright and Hewison as 'heritage-baiters'.

In time, the attack on 'Heritage' took root. Today, twenty years later, the ground has moved, the climate warmed and 'Heritage' has flowered in more fertile soil. How healthy is the garden today, in 2004?

***

The nation's head of heritage is the Secretary of State for Culture, Media and Sport, Tessa Jowell. Jowell (who held this position from 2001 to 2007) had an unusually wide remit – but to all of it, she insisted, Heritage was central. In addition to being a shorthand term for the management of notable historic sites, the idea of Heritage also provided a point of reference for the shaping of personal, local and national identity. Heritage is currently a hugely popular brand, says Jowell, a growth industry whether measured in visits to historic and heritage sites, sales of history books, people researching their family history or involved in historical re-enactment or audiences for radio and TV programmes (e.g. the BBC's *Restoration* series in which viewers decide on which listed buildings in need of remedial work should win a grant from the Heritage Lottery Fund). Liz Forgan, chair of the HLF, agrees. Every year, she tells me, the number of applications for grants continues to climb while National Trust membership has evidently doubled in the previous fifteen years.

There is nothing novel in people being interested in earlier times. Simon Thurley, who remains a practising historian as well as running English Heritage, points to the Victorian revival of medievalism, for example, while the National Trust historian Merlin Waterson recalls that 18th-century gentlemen liked their houses to contain columns and porticos redolent of classical Greece. What's new, suggests Thurley, is today's mass engagement with the legacy of the past. Why? Many point to the rapid and unpredictable speed of change in the environment in which most of us live. Traditional indicators of identity (nation, religion, family, school, etc.) have lost some of their earlier authority while many feel subjected to threats over which they have no control. In such a world it is tempting to seek identity in what seem to be the greater certainties of the past.

Demography plays a part too; there are more elderly people with disposable time and income than ever before, and they tend to be drawn to history. Computers and cheap travel, likewise, have helped stimulate and feed the appetites of people interested in knowing more about the history of both the wider world and their own more immediate surroundings. The establishment of the National Lottery in 1994 led to large amounts of money flowing into the building and restoring of museums, galleries and historical sites (some £300 million enters the HLF's coffers every year), while broadcasters, publishers and curators have found new and imaginative ways of presenting and portraying the past to a sizeable public. The 'Heritage' constituency is larger than ever before.

It is also more socially mixed. One of the requirements imposed upon Tessa Jowell's ministry is to show that they've made efforts to attract a new public, particularly from among the nation's ethnic communities and other more deprived segments of society. As a result, something like 25 per cent of the increase in numbers attending regional museums are people who have never been to a museum before. Liz Forgan's Heritage Lottery Fund helps finance 'Young Roots', a scheme that enables teenagers to explore their local heritage while the largest recent shift in the profile of National

Trust membership, says its Director-General Fiona Reynolds, has been the increase in younger members through family membership schemes. Nowadays, it seems, some 400,000 schoolchildren visit NT properties annually on educational visits.

***

What of the nature of the 'Heritage' that is purveyed? In some ways, little has changed. The nation's most popular sites still tend to be its castles and palaces, monuments and museums, and the majority of visitors (other than school parties) to be older, well-heeled and white-skinned while the press can always stir up a lather of outrage if some great work of art is in danger of being 'lost to the nation' or a country house collection dispersed. Much TV history continues to concentrate on the deeds and misdeeds of the great, and biographies of monarchs and warriors still fill the bookshelves. The National Trust has recently acquired William Morris's Red House and Tyntesfield, a Victorian Gothic country house in Somerset, while a visit to Blenheim or Hampton Court remains essentially a privileged opportunity for ordinary folk to walk, with reverence and lowered voices, through art-filled rooms set in a magnificent estate once inhabited by the rich, famous and powerful.

But a broader definition of Heritage has come to incorporate a more diverse view of the legacy of the past. Not just ancestral estates and great art but individual, anecdotal connections to the past: domestic memorabilia, a local pub, shop, custom, dialect or beauty spot. To Thurley, Heritage can mean anything that people value about the historic environment in which they happen to live. 'Power of Place' was the evocative name of an English Heritage document produced in 2000 which provided a key statement of current heritage thinking. Heritage must be socially 'inclusive' too, adds Liz Forgan, something that people of all kinds will want to visit, engage with, campaign about, look after, feel that it's theirs.

In its current Strategic Plan, the Heritage Lottery Fund outlines three potential recipients. There are 'Traditional Conservers' primarily concerned about protecting historic and traditional sites, 'Diversity Celebrants' who emphasise Britain's multi-cultural society and the heritage of the disadvantaged, and 'Grass Roots Activists' who campaign for greater recognition of the history of 'ordinary' people. In caricature, the first are the castles and cathedrals brigade, the second campaign for ragas and ramps and the third for a working-class view of the past. These are not warring perspectives, Liz Forgan emphasises. On the contrary, she believes there is a clear continuum between them, which it is her job, and that of others in the field, to find.

This is not easy. If your dad was a coalminer or granddad came to Britain from the Caribbean in the 1950s, for example, it might be hard to feel that an art-packed Restoration palace was part of your heritage. A recent MORI poll revealed that 75 per cent of black respondents thought the heritage of ethnic minorities was inadequately represented. But things have been changing. Today, English Heritage has installed Blue Plaques to mark the homes of Paul Robeson, Mahatma Gandhi and Jimi Hendrix and is helping to develop a 'Sikh Heritage Trail' to highlight 150 years of Anglo-Sikh history. The National Trust's Sutton House, in the heart of Hackney, home of a highly successful Black History programme, was recently shortlisted for the Gulbenkian Museum of the Year Prize. Meanwhile, historians are revealing that there were far more people of African and Asian origin in Britain in earlier centuries than we used to think. The idea of a continuous, more or less stable and ethnically homogeneous historical narrative reaching back over the centuries no longer holds up. On the contrary, British history has been marked by recurrent political, economic and military disruption and conflict, social mobility (downwards as well as upwards) and migrations (outwards as well as inwards). The history of Britain, more than that of most countries, has been intimately integrated with that of the wider world. In any case, most people can respond to a historic heritage that embraces more than merely their own bloodlines. Part of the appeal of 'family history' is the unexpected twists and turns people discover once they have traced their ancestry back a generation or two, while many are discovering the joys of researching the history of their locality. Ultimately, it is the sheer diversity of British history, over both time and place, not its homogeneity, that is most striking and this enables its complex heritage to embrace everyone.

One way in which this is reflected is in the methods by which the legacy of the past is portrayed. People today don't simply want to look at a historic site, says the National Trust's Fiona Reynolds. They want to know the whys and wherefores of the past and, if they can, to mix their own labours with what they encounter – to 'interrogate the past'. Hampton Court still offers a breathtaking glimpse of Henry VIII's chapel and Mantegna's incomparable 'Triumphs of Caesar'. But it also, like many historic sites, provides 'interpreters' in period costume trained to engage with the visitor and explain details about the palace and its historical occupants. At Warwick Castle, a suite of rooms reproduces an aristocratic soirée in late Victorian times, complete with waxwork figures of identifiable people (young Winston Churchill among them) placed in authentically furnished rooms. Outside on the lawns, a mounted horseman tells the crowds of his adventures fighting for Warwick the Kingmaker in the Wars of the Roses.

Where a site has no such aristocratic baggage, curators have felt free to present a more 'inclusive' view of the past. Jorvik, site of the Viking settlement in York, was one of the first of the many 'dark rides' through history now on offer, complete with the sights and sounds (and smells) of yesteryear, while 'living museums' encourage the visitor to step into the past and interact with the ordinary people – women and children as well as men – who inhabited it and the lives they led. You can walk through 'authentic' streets, watch ancient skills being practised, enter traditional shops, dress in historic garb and enjoy the 'experience' of living in earlier times. Today, as the management jargon puts it, heritage is about 'process' as much as 'product'.

This can still result in a prettified view of the past. The official remit of the National Trust (founded in 1895) has long remained to care for places of 'Historic Interest' and 'Natural Beauty', almost as if to suggest an organic link between the two. Moreover, 'Heritage' was widely acknowledged as important to the tourist industry, visitors clearly happy when going to places that made them feel good. A great hall full of swords or guns was fine, especially if they were aesthetically displayed, and everyone could enjoy a clash of lances in a tiltyard or the predatory flight of a falcon, confident that all they saw conformed to the latest health and safety regulations. Grisly historic murders continued to draw the crowds, from the Princes in the Tower to those committed by Jack the Ripper, while the occasional ghost was always good for business. But the real nastinesses of history, particularly perhaps of more recent times, were harder to present and tended to be avoided. Should some of Britain's more oppressive, asbestos-filled factories, schools, hospitals or prisons be 'saved for the nation'? Should smouldering slag heaps be retained above obsolete Rhondda coalmines (or a plaque mark the site where Crippen – or Fred and Rosemary West – once lived)? Perhaps not. Or not yet.

But things are changing. Some of the genuine horrors of war (and of the Holocaust) are on display at the Imperial War Museum while the Bristol

Museum of Empire,* for example, includes an impressive presentation of the history of slavery. The National Trust, for all its reputation as squeaky clean guardian of the nation's aristocratic houses, has of late been acquiring historic slums, suburban houses (including the one in which John Lennon was raised) and an Oliver-Twist-style workhouse in Nottinghamshire. Nobody pretends that a visit to a slavery exhibition or workhouse site will in itself give the visitor a full sense of the past that is represented; authentic re-enactment would be impossible and an approximation to it tasteless. But a series of what/why/how questions alongside such exhibitions can help stimulate the visitor's historical imagination. All this amounts to a modest revolution in the presentation and management of what is still called our 'Heritage'.

Is there a danger of over-management? Not so long ago, people could roam freely among ancient sites and historic ruins (like Gibbon in Rome or Hardy's Tess across Stonehenge) – doubtless ruining them further in the process. Sometimes this further ruination was deliberate, as visitors carried off statuary and carved their names on objects too large to loot. More often, it was the sheer tramp of feet, the sweaty touch and the hot breath that gradually did the damage. That didn't matter too much when the great palaces and temples were the preserve of the few. Today, with a broader definition of the historic environment and huge visitor numbers, careful management is essential if the legacy of the past is not to be ruined as a result of its very popularity. Patrick Wright worries that virtually every fragment of history is being squeezed into a management format, programmed, packaged and presented to maximise visitor numbers and till turnover. There is some truth in this, acknowledges Fiona Reynolds, though the National Trust tries as far as possible to display its properties without formal guidance. Simon Thurley, too, believes in heritage management with a long leash; you don't have to create a fixed stage and then herd a passive audience in and out before they can spoil everything, he says. To Thurley, the best way of learning is by doing and this can mean anything from trying a spot of jousting or a sip of mead to the studious re-creation of a pre-Reformation Latin Mass in the Chapel Royal at Hampton Court.

***

In a sense, everything that has survived from the past is part of the 'historic heritage'. A reductionist view would lead to the destruction, demolition

---

* The Museum was closed in 2013.

or replacement of nothing. But what to retain? This waste bin or that lightbulb, your old scout card or abandoned longjohns, a deserted garden shed, overgrown scrubland, a derelict bicycle, an audiocassette of granny's schoolgirl reminiscences? People talk of retaining traditional skills, too. Should that include cranking up the old jalopy, handwashing the laundry, shaving with a naked razor, bloodletting with leeches? Yes, perhaps, in some cases, just as resources should go into the teaching of Manx or Cornish or the maintenance of ancient religious practices recently arrived in Britain from Africa or the Caribbean. But if we were to decide everything is heritage, no object would ever be thrown away, no land site developed, no new parks, buildings or artworks encouraged and we would sink into a deadening morass of antiquarian sentimentality. Why does it matter if a particular archive or painting is sent abroad, a minority language or plant species allowed to die a natural death, or an old church or school demolished and replaced?

You need a bit of distance before deciding. Priorities and tastes change over time. Eighty years ago, few people valued Georgian art and architecture. In the 1950s, it was almost *de rigueur* to dismiss the Royal Albert Hall (and probably Tyntesfield) as ugly Victorian wedding-cakery, while a decade later we learned to be excited by steel-and-concrete modernism. Today, such attitudes have been largely reversed. When Battersea Power Station was decommissioned, many thought it hideous and argued for its demolition; twenty years later, it had acquired the patina of 'industrial archaeology'. When Liz Forgan came to the HLF, the fund would not, as a rule of thumb, finance anything less than twenty years old; today, the figure is down to ten. But it can't be yesterday. And attitudes to 'Heritage' itself have also changed. In the 1980s, the historic heritage was still often viewed primarily through the prism of aesthetics. Nowadays, those charged with deciding which building, artefact, beach or dialect to help save also have to consider tourist interest, job opportunities and a greatly broadened definition of historical significance, and must take serious account of what visitors say to them.

For all the forward-looking stance of Britain's Heritage-managers, the nation is still often portrayed as 'living in the past', what with all those tourist posters of Beefeaters, castles and Tudorbethan inns. In the late 1990s, some argued not only that Britain's historical heritage was too sentimentalised but that its real history was once again being marginalised for political reasons. The enthusiasm with which Blair's Britain embraced a glossy image of the nation's present and future seemed to run in tandem with a blatant disregard for its past. Venerable institutions such as the House of Lords and Lord Chancellorship were placed under threat without serious thought as to what they should be replaced with, while the Millennium Dome contained scarcely a reference to the previous 2,000 years whose passing it was presumably intended to mark. Tony Blair liked to be photographed against new buildings not historic ones and when he did mention history it was often in the future tense rather than the past. 'This is something I am confident history will forgive', he told the US Congress when acknowledging the anti-Iraq coalition may have been wrong about WMDs. New Labour, itself a radical break from its own socialist roots, saw 'Heritage' as the rearguard preserve of a discredited elite.

Nonsense, ripostes Tessa Jowell, who talks with transparent enthusiasm about how an understanding of the past opens doors to who we are, where we have come from, the kind of society we live in today. The politics have evidently shifted, with New Labour claiming the political centre and expropriating much on the right of the spectrum. A decade ago, it was still perhaps legitimate to think of 'Heritage' as conservative by its very nature, an inherent inhibition to progress or modernity; as Hewison put it, the real past was about change, while 'Heritage' was about wishing change had never happened. Today, Fiona Reynolds likes to talk of the National Trust as in part a regeneration agency, pumping money into the redevelopment of derelict sites. For every new job the NT creates, she reckons, a further half-dozen or so are created in the local economy. Simon Thurley, too, sees 'Heritage' as a progressive force, a way of managing change, of harnessing a rich, variegated past for the cultural (and economic) enrichment of those enjoying it today and tomorrow. Liz Forgan plucks from the air the example of a Joseph Paxton park. You try to revive the beauty of Paxton's original intentions, she says; but you also include modern amenities and children's play areas (and don't reproduce archaic planting schemes requiring armies of paid gardeners!). All have come to agree that you can no longer go about simply pickling the past in aspic. But few people talk nowadays, either, of wanting to uproot everything and start again from scratch. The road to future development must start by tapping into pre-existing physical and psychological roots and building up organically from there. In this sense, our 'historic heritage' is an important ingredient in the regeneration of 21st-century Britain.

'Historians' Today

Why historians are 'Very Important People'.

In 2007 Palgrave Macmillan published a collection of essays I had written over the preceding few years about the life and work of twenty-eight leading historians of the time. The essays had all originally been published in the magazine History Today *and included pieces about David Cannadine, Eric Hobsbawm, Peter Burke, Theodore Zeldin, Asa Briggs, Eric Foner, John Keegan, Geoffrey Hosking, Antonia Fraser, David Starkey, Ian Kershaw, Roy Foster, Lyndal Roper, Christopher Dyer, Peter Stansky, Natalie Zemon Davis, Linda Colley, Orlando Figes, Felipe Fernández-Armesto, Lisa Jardine, Richard J Evans, John Brewer, Simon Schama, Niall Ferguson, Laurence Rees, Jeremy Black, Norman Davies and John Morrill. The book, entitled* Historians, *was republished by Palgrave Macmillan in paperback form in 2016.*

What follows is based on my Introduction to the book: an essay (that itself came to be widely reprinted) about the importance of history and historians.

Historians are 'Very Important People' (for reasons I'll come to in a moment). Some of them, anyway. In these essays I have written about some of the best and most important among them. The essays were originally published from October 1998 until October 2005, more or less quarterly, in the pages of *History Today*. From the outset, and in close consultation with *HT's* editor Peter Furtado, I decided to concentrate on historians of proven excellence who were still publishing and whose work had reached a wide audience and raised issues beyond the purely scholarly. In each case, I tried to read everything I could that had been published by the historian concerned and we would then usually have lunch together followed by a lengthy interview which I would record. The essays were reproduced in the order in which they originally appeared (as listed above).

For all the variety of talent represented in the book, there were notable absences. I would like to have included a wider range of expertise (there was little Ancient or Asian history here and not enough North or South American). And there were of course many historians whom I hadn't written about but whose work might well have warranted inclusion. I particularly regretted the absence of two late friends: Raphael Samuel, whom I first met in about 1970, a genial Socrates figure whose immense influence was generated primarily through personal contact and example and only latterly through his published work; and Roy Porter, a scintillating supernova of

STANDING, L-R *Eric Hobsbawm, Rodney Hilton, Lawrence Stone, Keith Thomas.*
SEATED L-R *Christopher Hill, John Elliott, Joan Thirsk.*
Composite painting by Stephen Farthing (National Portrait Gallery)

The journal Past and Present *aimed to give a platform to neo-Marxist historians, including those portrayed above. During my years as a BBC producer, I was able to call upon all these, as well as historians regarded as more 'right-wing', in programmes such as* The Long March of Everyman, History Now and Then *and* Fins de Siècle.

talent, charm and productivity, with whom I had been discussing a possible date shortly before he burned himself out in his mid-fifties.

Most of the historians included in the book were people whose work I was already acquainted with and admired, and many I knew personally: Asa Briggs and Peter Burke were colleagues at Sussex, while several had broadcast for me during my years at the BBC. Some had achieved considerable fame, especially on TV, though it was their work as historians and not their celebrity that I wanted to write about. When I called Simon Schama to discuss our forthcoming meeting, he expressed delight that, for the first time in years, an interviewer wanted to talk about his researches into Dutch and French history rather than his blockbuster TV series about Britain.

One of the historians in the collection remarked to me that over the previous few years I had probably read more books on a wider range of subjects than any other historian he knew. I couldn't quite believe that. But I had certainly been immensely enriched as I worked my way through books about warfare ancient and modern, empires and imperialisms, social and economic history, art and popular culture, food, gifts, witchcraft, plague, banditry, maps, the media, impostors and the very nature of history itself. I spent weeks at a time intellectually immured in medieval England, early modern France and Germany, Tudor and Stuart Britain, revolutionary France and Russia, post-civil war America, Poland, Ireland and Wilhelmine, Weimar and Nazi Germany as well as some of the further reaches of time and place.

On re-reading the resulting essays, they provided an interesting snapshot of history and historians at century's turn. All the major issues in current historiography were there. These historians, indeed, were among the leading figures who helped set the agenda. Thus, social history owed an immeasurable debt to Asa Briggs and Eric Hobsbawm and cultural and women's history to the work of Natalie Zemon Davis. Davis had also led the way in the imaginative reconstruction of the past, and helped pioneer cross-cultural history – an approach that had yielded rich fruit in recent works by David Cannadine and Linda Colley. Some, such as Norman Davies and Jeremy Black, had broadened their purview still further and attempted to incorporate the history of entire continents. Geoffrey Hosking, one of the few historians of Russia to take seriously its religious and regional past, had been vindicated in more recent years with the revival in the former Soviet Union of cultural nationalism and religious observation. Another Russian expert, Orlando Figes, had – like Lisa Jardine – made notable efforts to bring the arts and sciences in from the historiographical peripheries, while Lyndal Roper and Theodore Zeldin (again, like Natalie Davis) had attempted to comprehend the psychology of those they had written about. Peter Burke was a formative influence in our understanding of the 'reception' of culture and its artefacts, while Richard Evans helped lead the fight against excessive postmodernism.

There may be no out-and-out postmodernists among this collection; but if you are interested in 'counterfactual' history, you can read about one of its most persuasive practitioners, Niall Ferguson. Old-fashioned virtues are on display here, too. Is the much-vaunted 'return of narrative history' reflected in the work of these historians? Few can pen a good story better than Schama, while well-researched, well-crafted biographies by Antonia Fraser, David Starkey, Roy Foster and Peter Stansky demonstrated that a long-tested genre was far from exhausted. Some historians had led me, like Watson following Holmes, into the forensic minutiae of specialist investigation; others took a larger view – none more so than Felipe Fernández-Armesto who taught me how to adopt a galactic view of our little global story.

As I encountered my procession of historians, it was illuminating to discover how each, when faced with a large and daunting project or an initially inchoate mass of data, would find a way of drawing upon particular talents and techniques in the struggle to coordinate, shape, pare and share the relevant material. The works they published were as varied as the people themselves, and I found myself reading, and writing about, long books, short books, books that described and books that analysed, books brimming with personality and colour and others stuffed with statistical analysis. Some were chronological, others primarily thematic, some picture-packed, others unillustrated. One historian, like the potter turning his clay this way and that, forever refining it upon the wheel, favoured extended metaphor; another went for the literal. Most were affable and communicative, generously prepared to reveal much about themselves as well as about their work. Thus, I not only learned a lot of history; I also learned about the wide variety of ways in which it could be approached, researched and written.

I was also led to think about the current significance of history and historians. I began by saying that historians were important people. Let me explain why I think this is so.

***

History is everywhere, or so it seemed as we entered our new millennium. On television, Henry VIII and Hitler, Pyramids and Puritans, antique roadshows, costume dramas, *Timewatch* and *Time Team* jostled to fill the airwaves and garner large audiences on a plethora of terrestrial and specialised channels. Visitor numbers to museums, galleries and heritage sites burgeoned while a raft of new historical magazines sprouted. In the bookshops, sales of biographies and war books almost rivalled those on how to enhance your corporate, coital or culinary competence, and the 'qualipop' press mined new gold with daily stories purporting to show how recently discovered documents threw new (often contentious) light upon historical personalities, artefacts and events. Family and local history flourished, while monarchs and emperors, presidents, popes and premiers were pressed to 'apologise' for the actions of their predecessors several generations or even centuries before. The past may be a foreign country; but history, it seemed, was inescapable.

Or was it? Was the succession of sensational press stories new gold or fools' gold? Was the demand for historical apology a serious attempt to come to terms with the past or a form of crude (and often financially fuelled) gesture politics? Did radio and TV programmes, or the opening up of 'Heritage' sites, provide a genuine sense of continuity between past and present or an anaesthetised theme park, fun to experience but nothing to do with us? Our age, many argued, is one that lives in an immediate present, obsessed with the 'new', the fashionable, with little awareness of the ways our living present derived from its continuity with all that preceded it. When Britain marked the great calendrical transition from one millennium to the next, it contrived to do so with a vast domed exhibition that avoided all mention of life in these islands over previous centuries. When the Mayor of London invited suggestions re: the Trafalgar Square statuary, he made a point of displaying his ignorance about – and indifference towards – the statues already there. Interest, it seemed, was focused on the immediate present.

The point was not lost on historians. 'Most young men and women' (wrote a disgruntled Eric Hobsbawm) 'grow up in a sort of permanent present lacking any organic relation to the public past of the times they live in.' And Eric Foner ended his book on the history of American freedom noting that Americans 'have sometimes believed they enjoy the greatest freedom of all – freedom from history,' a chimera, Foner warned, for no people can escape being bound, to some extent, by their past. We live, said David Cannadine (in his 1999 inaugural lecture as Director of the Institute of Historical Research), in 'a society which is increasingly amnesiac and ahistorical'.

So: is an interest in history in the ascendant? Or, *par contra*, do we live in an age singularly bereft of historical awareness? Could both be true? Perhaps there is no mystery and we are simply talking about different groups of people: those who are more interested in history and those who are less so. Evidence from book sales, TV audience and heritage visitor research and the like suggested that people expressing an interest in the past tended to be older, better educated and wealthier than the average. Since the population of Britain and most western societies contained more and more elderly people with disposable time and income than ever before, an overall increase in what we might call the 'consumption' of history would seem to have been almost inevitable. Against that, however, was the fact that it was the younger generation, not the oldies with time and money on their hands, who were most at home with that miraculous modern gateway to local and family history, the computer, while cheap travel enabled even youngsters with limited resources to visit such hitherto remote exotica as Angkor Wat and Machu Picchu. The historical re-enactment societies that sprouted like hydra heads were packed with young enthusiasts keen to learn what it was like living as a Roman or a Roundhead. Yet these were the same youngsters who, in other aspects of their lives, were preoccupied with the transient and the fashionable. While there was a plethora of 'popular' history around, in other words, we also seemed to live in an age in which many who expressed an interest in it nonetheless tended to live their normal lives in a bubble of immediate present and imminent future.

Why, in such a world, would people be so keen to re-visit the past, to consume it, 'experience' it? What can history mean to those who so avidly commodified and consumed it? It seemed the current 'history wave' might have been telling us more about ourselves than it did about the past. What were the messages behind those popular portrayals of the past that people sought, and received, from the ways it was purveyed and consumed? The answers to that question places the purveyors of history – the historians – in an important new light..

***

There is nothing novel in people being interested in earlier times. There was a burst of 'historicism' in the decades following the French Revolutionary wars, for example, when 'Gothic' and neoclassical buildings sprang up across Europe, Victoria and Albert posed for Landseer as medievals and Italian composers placed their latest operas in Tudor or Stuart England. What was new, perhaps, was the sheer scale of modern engagement with the legacy of the past. By the late-1990s, when I began writing these essays about historians, many people were beginning to take note of the emerging history wave, dubbing it 'the new rock and roll' and 'the new gardening' (and even 'the new sex'). Let's not overstate the case. History wasn't any of those things, and has probably never been quite that popular! But there was no doubt: history 'sells', people began to say – not just to a cultured elite but nowadays to a mass market.

An interest in the past can answer many needs. For some, history seemed to provide an imaginative escape from the 'here and now' to the 'there and then': a kind of tourism of the mind. The past was, indeed, a little like a foreign country where they do things differently. Everyone can recognise the pleasure in browsing through the tourist brochures. Similar restorative powers reside in a book or television programme about larger-than-life characters caught up in exciting events in exotic times and places. What better, after a busy day at the office and a debilitating fight with the rush-hour crowds, than settling down to an evening with the Pharaohs, the mistresses of Louis XIV or the epic battles of World War II? The sheer romance and drama of history was part of its attraction.

So was its apparent capacity to provide ballast from the past to vindicate the present. We would enjoy visiting magnificently preserved historic sites and come out feeling good about our 'heritage' or our 'traditions'. To British eyes, a book or TV programme about Elizabeth I, Nelson or Churchill might confirm views about national intrepidity in the face of an invasive continent, much as Americans might find an absorbing account of Jefferson or Lincoln reinforcing their views about the integrity of present-day USA. We all look to the past to help explain, or affirm, aspects of the present. Indeed, one can hardly make sense of the present at all without at least some effort to understand how things came to be the way they are. Every sectarian or nationalist cause has its litany of historical wrongs to be righted: Serbs and Croats, Greeks and Turks, Israelis and Palestinians, Indian Muslims and Hindus, Irish Protestants and Catholics – and all have appealed to history to help boost their cause, justify the present or reinforce the dream of an alternative future.

By the time these essays were published, the political use of the past as a weapon with which to demand a supposedly improved present and future was taking on new forms, in particular the widespread demand that leaders 'apologise' for supposed wrongs in the past. Thus, governments in Australia and North America were being pressed by indigenous and ethnic minorities to apologise for earlier oppression, those in Germany and Japan for their countries' atrocities in World War II, the British for the Irish famine or Amritsar massacre, the Pope for the Crusades, Inquisition and Catholic anti-Semitism.

If history is a favourite refuge for those seeking justification, compensation or vindication, it could also provide a seductive home-away-from-home for those in search of nostalgia. Which of us hasn't succumbed to the golden glow of times faintly but warmly remembered on hearing a song from our childhood or leafing through an old sheaf of newspapers or photo album? Nostalgia has potency beyond personal memory. We may not have been raised in a medieval castle or fought for Cromwell, Bonaparte or Robert E Lee. But anyone with a little historical imagination and a good book can relish the vicarious experience. 'Experience', indeed, became a favoured word of many historical museums and exhibitions which, like 'actuality' television reconstructions of times past, were designed to give the person of today a feel for the texture of life in earlier times.

We cannot literally 'experience' the past, of course. In reality, we are distanced from it, immunised from its deleterious effects, able to savour even its most appalling moments from a position of relative safety. We are similarly distanced, too, from its beauties. Of course, millions might read about the world's most magnificent historic buildings, see them on television and be invited to vote for which dilapidated historic buildings they would most like to 'save'. Huge numbers would visit legions of art-filled palaces and chapels once erected and occupied by the elite and now open to the wider public. You and I might stand where once only monarchs and emperors stood, see paintings and hear music that in former times only they and their entourage would have been able to enjoy.

Yet the way we share these aristocratic glories from the past keeps us firmly at arm's length from the experience of those for whom they were originally created. Many great historic houses and palaces have, in effect, become art museums in which visitors – or television cameras – are led along corridors, past one carefully roped-off bedroom or reception chamber after another, and invited to glance up at a priceless tapestry, an elaborate candelabra, an elegantly-carved *secrétaire* or a superbly painted ceiling before moving on to the next room. Nothing must be touched, no spinet played, no chair or sofa sat upon. The artwork may be magnificent. But it is easy to forget that people used to live here.

Thus, the historical 'experience' becomes anaesthetised, prettified, a degree of clinical safety built into the way we view the past and its denizens. Our predecessors, even the mighty popes and princes we see pictured on palace walls, seem vulnerable to our gaze. We know more and more about them and the times in which they lived as we seek them out, discuss them, argue about them, visit their homes, look at their clothes, read their private letters, gaze on their beds, tables and tombs. But they know nothing of us and our times. History is a one-way traffic. The present can investigate the past, not the other way round. There is perhaps a subtle message of reassurance in all this. The objects of the past, its barbarisms no less than its beauties, are available for our inspection whenever we want, while we ourselves remain safely immured from its dangers. It is almost as though history were a dream, full of colour and drama, from which we know we will wake up, nicely tucked up in our warm modern beds..

***

History has yet more to offer. Many look to it for clarity in a world of confused certainties. How nice, after a day grappling with the complex judgements of daily life, to be able to sit back and relish the 'greatness' of Lincoln or Churchill or the 'evil' of Attila the Hun, Ivan the Terrible, Stalin or Hitler. The past offers clarity in another way too. 'Real life', as you and I experience it, consists of a mass of interconnected experiences, most of them trivial and without clearcut lines of definition between them. But anyone wishing to communicate something of the past must shape and edit his or her material. Thus, there are studies of political, social or cultural history, biographies, books about the Tudors or Stuarts, volumes on a particular decade or century – all of which inevitably omit more than they include. In much the same way, there are places marked off as 'historic sites' – implying that other places aren't. Much history is presented as 'national', even when concerned with periods before the nation state took shape. The fact that the past is packaged in such ways suggests that it had shape, pattern and point, far more than our lives would seem to do while we are living them, and that its conflicts and problems were neatly resolved, usually by colourful and decisive personalities. Unlike the messy real life that we have to live, the past appears to have been composed of discrete lumps that can be safely labelled and categorised. And, unlike those at the time, we know how things worked out later. History allows the comfort of 'closure'.

It offers one other thing, too – currently perhaps the most important. A generation or two back, most people in the West tended to be happy identifying themselves by reference to various more or less immutable institutional criteria. You had a name and address, a nationality, an educational and income level, a job and probably a family and a religion.

But in more recent years, the authority of many social and political institutions came to be questioned. The family was no longer the tightly defined and more or less universally accepted unit of society it had once been. Similarly, there was by the early 2000s a sharp erosion of respect for political elites, the judiciary, the church, the academy, the medical profession and the police. When people come to have doubts about the integrity of such formerly defining institutions, their own self-definition comes under scrutiny, a tendency further stimulated by the growing ease with which people could move from one job, partner, home or part of the world to another. If I am no longer sure I see myself primarily in terms of my nationality, domicile, work or political, church or family affiliation – who am I?

People sought new forms of identity: in ethnic origin, for example, or sexual orientation or religious commitment. New identities are fragile and take time to substantiate. They do not grow on trees, to be plucked with every passing desire. But they can be enriched if nourished by ancient roots so that many people found themselves turning to the past for guidance, reassurance and validation. This was probably in part what lay behind the growing popularity of historical re-enactment and the boom in family and local history. You could detect it in countless small bookshops, too, where, alongside works on the Pyramids, doomed duchesses and the triumphs and tragedies of World War II, space came to be devoted to old maps, do-it-yourself genealogy guides, 'then-and-now' photographic albums, new histories of Wales and Scotland or of Irish or Arabic nationalism, and biographies of hitherto underappreciated women or members of ethnic minorities. Down the flag pole of popular history came the banners of such former heroes as Richard the Lionheart, Columbus, Raleigh, Drake or Clive, to be replaced by newly iconic figures as varied as Saladin, William Wallace, Olaudah Equiano, Mary Seacole or Roger Casement. Historians of art gave new prominence to the homosexuality of Michelangelo and Leonardo da Vinci, music historians to the black creators of jazz or the work of hitherto obscure composers like the medieval nun Hildegard of Bingen or the 'Black Mozart' of 18th-century France, Joseph Boulogne, the Chevalier de Saint-George. The lesson was clear: for anyone seeking intellectual ballast for new forms of identity, an excellent place to look was – the past.

In sum, history was coming to provide many messages to those who turned to it for succour. It could provide opportunities for escape, blame, resentment, consolation, vindication, nostalgia. For some it might provide a welcome gateway into unparalleled aesthetic fulfilment, or an opportunity to enjoy the frisson of safely viewed horror. It could feed an appetite for 'experience', reinforce pride in heritage and tradition and proffer a degree of reassurance and reaffirmation regarding the closure of the past and the nature of our own identity in the present and future. It could also fuel serious – sometimes explosive – social and political aspirations.

These are heavy burdens to bear. They are not born by the real past, of course, but by a marketable commodity created in our own time that we call 'History'. It is important to make this distinction. The 'past' is always there. It is what happened. And even if nobody ever wrote about it – or even knew about it – the past would still be there. What happened in the past did happen. But what happened in 'history' is another matter altogether. History is not what happened; it is what was subsequently said or written or exhibited or broadcast about what happened. And every age, it has often and rightly been pointed out, has to recreate its own history, its own version of the unchanging past. My book *Historians* was not about the past. It was about some of the highly talented people in our own time who had tried to transmit to those in the present something of what life was like in the past. Historians are the conduits between past and present, the alchemists who conjure up lost eras. And since, as we have seen, people look to the past for all kinds of potent messages, those who conduct them there are, as I have said, Very Important People.

***

I sometimes think that historians are like the high priests of modern society. History, after all, has acquired many of the qualities of a religion. It provides ancient justifications for present-day actions and beliefs and recounts colourful tales of larger-than-life characters whose doings and misdoings provide examples and warnings to those living long afterwards. It adds legitimacy and pedigree to nations and would-be nations and to the new, less institutional forms of identity many seem to seek. And it bestows dignity upon time-honoured practices and places which become sanctified as 'heritage'; history, like religion, has what amount to its sacred relics. And as in any religion, adherents delve into the past as prologue to the future. Some indulge in what virtually amounts to ancestor worship. In this sense, it is perhaps not altogether fanciful to regard historians as today's priests, mediating between our present anxieties and the ancestor gods looking down on us from an elevated past. Priests are important figures in all the religions they serve. As priests in the new quasi-religion of history, in which the Past is used and abused in the service of the Present and Future, historians play an absolutely crucial role.

There are of course good priests and bad priests, good and bad historians. The historians I wrote about in this volume were among the best, though I can think of several who might be faintly surprised, and amused, to hear me refer to them as anything so elevated as high priests. Honest, workaday scribes, I suspect they'd respond, with a twinkle. And, it is true, no historian in this anthology would claim to have created (as perhaps Ranke, Marx, Braudel or Toynbee aspired to do) an all-embracing, systemic interpretation of the past capable, at least in principle, of encompassing the whole of human history. Ambitions nowadays are more limited. The growing demands of academic life haven't helped, with their built-in insecurities and the pressure to publish. One by-product, wrote David Cannadine, is that too many historians adopt the perspective of the 'truffle-hunter' and too few that of the 'parachutist'. More and more historians these days, it sometimes seems, know more and more about less and less.

It is true that I had no grand system-builders in this volume. But I included some pretty intrepid parachutists. They had been helped in their ambition, I would suspect, by a number of relatively recent developments, each of which had offered the imaginative and enquiring historian the opportunity of a more panoramic view of the past. The first was the opening up of new material from a huge and growing range of sources. For example, since the fall of Communism, historians such as Ian Kershaw, Geoffrey Hosking, Orlando Figes and Norman Davies had been able to benefit from the new availability of archive sources in Russia and Eastern Europe that would have been the envy of older colleagues.

But it was not just the amount of material that had expanded. Not so long before, the respectable historian had relied almost entirely on written documentation, those sacrosanct 'primary sources' kept in great libraries and other formal collections. Many more recent historians were much more adventurous and learned to incorporate sources and methodologies from other disciplines into their work. In *Theatres of Memory*, Raphael Samuel wrote of 'an expanding historical culture, in which the work of inquiry and retrieval is being progressively extended into all kinds of spheres that would have been thought unworthy of notice in the past'. He himself gave as an example the analysis of biota above gravesites that gave indications of diet. Several of the historians in my collection (e.g. Peter Burke, Natalie Davis, Lyndal Roper) were clearly benefiting from the insights of cultural anthropology and ethnography, while Christopher Dyer acknowledged his debt to archaeology and to local history. Oral history was represented here, too; Laurence Rees's television programmes and books relied extensively on the lengthy interviews he had conducted with people who were active participants in the wars he was able to document. Niall Ferguson, capable of the most rigorous, statistically based economic history, also revealed (as did Schama, Brewer and Davis) the signs of the novelist manqué while Antonia Fraser had clearly walked through the palaces and battlegrounds she described so evocatively. John Keegan's battlefields were strewn not only with bodies but also with a rich harvest of literary references while Lisa Jardine enriched her historical writings with more than a laywoman's understanding of science and art. Natalie Davis went even further, drawing on film, for example, a self-evidently fictionalised recreation of the past, and on what she frankly acknowledged as her own historical imagination.

Most of the historians included in the volume were as much concerned with context as content (Asa Briggs placed 'contextuality' at the heart of the educational revolution he spearheaded at Sussex). When Peter Burke wrote about the Renaissance or Louis XIV, he would ask what these meant to ordinary people at the time and subsequently. He was also one of several historians able to strengthen his analysis by comparative reference to other cultures. Thus, Eric Foner enriched his account of the emancipation of the American slaves and the Reconstruction era with illuminating parallels from European and Caribbean history. Whether Jeremy Black was writing about domestic politics, diplomatic history or international warfare, he was always at pains to emphasise the links between them.

Finally, of course, historians, like everyone else, were beginning to get used to the unprecedented opportunities – and hazards – offered by the revolution in information technology. It is still early days, and none of us can be sure what kinds of sources and methods might be available in years to come. But for well over a decade, most of the historians I interviewed had been routinely using computers to facilitate forms of work in a way that would have been unimaginable to previous generations of scholars. Nor was this just a question of Googling up some historical figure to check birth or death dates, printing off a learned article, or working out complex statistical correlations. John Morrill's Royal Historical Society bibliography on the History of Britain and Ireland, containing nearly a quarter of a million cross-indexed, digitised items, would have been unthinkable before the arrival of the microchip.

So the historians represented in my anthology (or most of them) were men and women inspired by a wide and catholic view of the past and of the sources and methodologies by which it could be captured. They were also good writers. I can honestly say that there was not a single historian here whose work it was not a pleasure to read. That is no empty compliment, as seasoned readers of academic history will attest. Even when tackling the (to me) most unfamiliar or abstruse topics – John Keegan on ancient or medieval warfare, or Fernández-Armesto on the Maya Renaissance – the sheer élan of their scholarship and literary ability carried me through. There is of course no single way of writing history and these historians didn't by any means all write the same way. Where Hobsbawm or Roy Foster tend to be coolly analytical, even a little patrician in their approach, Jardine and Black preferred straightforward narrative interspersed with lengthy quotations from the sources, while my telly dons – notably Starkey, Schama and Ferguson – had the rare facility of marrying painstaking historical scholarship with seductively accessible prose. Many had written about historical subjects with strong contemporary resonances. Some, indeed, had probably played a part in setting the contemporary agenda. Antonia Fraser's biographies of Mary Stuart and Cromwell appeared just as feminism, and then concerns about the monarchy, were approaching a first high tide. Important works by Linda Colley and Natalie Davis helped give a strong impetus to current concerns about individual and national identity and the importance of cross-cultural understanding, while Richard Evans provided reassuring intellectual ballast against some of the more tendentious relativism that shook the historical establishment a few years earlier. The environmental history assayed by Schama and the bold globalism of Fernández-Armesto, too, undoubtedly helped set agendas others subsequently pursued.

Good priests help their flock to learn from the past in the hope that they might make better use of the present and future, and we might construe a good historian as doing much the same. But, quite apart from whether the historian should be concerned with drawing lessons, there is one mighty difference between the two. The priest is at liberty to embroider the past and use it as myth, parable or allegory whereas whatever inferences the historian might derive from the past must normally be based on demonstrable, verifiable fact. This is both a limitation and a liberation. It is a limitation because it restricts the historian's room for inspirational manoeuvre. No serious historian nowadays would feel at liberty to embroider the story of Charlemagne, Henry VIII or George Washington in order to fashion a morally uplifting myth. These days, scholars routinely subject what they discover about the past to rigorous intellectual scrutiny.

But it is precisely this professional discipline that provides the good historian with a degree of intellectual leverage unavailable to the priest. The priest, usually preaching to the converted, will hold views unlikely to sway those inclined to be sceptical. The conclusions of the good historian are harder to resist. As I worked my way through the *oeuvre* of the historians represented in this volume, I did not always find myself accepting the analysis and conclusions of each and every book I read. But at the same time I found myself, again and again, pressed by a powerful and persuasive mind to reconsider some of my own prejudices, predispositions and arguments.

History is not a religion, of course, its relics are not worshipped and historians are not priests. But a lot of people these days take history extremely seriously and, as I have suggested, its widespread use and abuse can have momentous consequences. Those who purvey the past to the present – a quasi-priesthood, perhaps – therefore perform a highly sensitive function and bear a profound responsibility. Very Important People, indeed.

Is Biography 'History'?

Daniel asks whether historical biography can be considered a serious contribution to history and assesses the latest trends in the field.
History Today, 11 November 2014.

Once upon a time historical biographies were written by men and were mostly about ('Great') men: from Plutarch and Suetonius on the grandees of the ancient world, to Vasari on the artists of Renaissance Italy, Boswell on Johnson, Aubrey's *Brief Lives*, Carlyle on Frederick the Great, Morley on Gladstone, Trevelyan on Garibaldi and Churchill on Marlborough. Many still are. I think of Ian Kershaw's authoritative life of Hitler or Simon Sebag Montefiore's Stalin, for example, or Jonathan Steinberg's Bismarck and several recent (or imminent) books about Napoleon and various US presidents (not to mention the many biographies of leading cultural figures by Michael Holroyd, Richard Holmes, AN Wilson, Peter Ackroyd and others). No doubt the trend was boosted by the recent centenary of the First World War and the appearance of new studies of men associated with it: Guy Cuthbertson's Wilfred Owen or the third and final volume of John Röhl's biography of Kaiser Wilhelm.

Nevertheless, it seems that a growing number of historical biographies are being written by women. Some, such as Lucy Riall's exploration of Garibaldi or Lindsey Hughes on Peter the Great, have focused on political figures, as do Antonia Fraser's lives of British monarchs. More commonly the spotlight has been falling on prominent personalities from the literary and cultural worlds: Claire Tomalin's biographies of the actress Mrs Jordan and of Dickens and Hardy, Hilary Spurling on Matisse, Hermione Lee's lives of Edith Wharton and Virginia Woolf or Miranda Seymour's exploration of the worlds of Henry James and of Robert Graves and the recent biographies of Nikolaus Pevsner by Susie Harries and of Gabriele d'Annunzio by Lucy Hughes-Hallett. Similarly, a large, evidently insatiable public appetite for lives of the *grandes dames* of history has been fed (and led) by the work of such writers as Stella Tillyard and Amanda Foreman.

As more biographies come to be written by (and often about) women, this chimes with much else that has changed across our culture in recent decades. Back in the 1960s and 1970s the historiographical frontier swung away from the traditional study of kings and conquerors to incorporate the story of 'ordinary' people. The new 'history from the bottom up', while revolutionary and welcome, had little time for biographies of individual achievers of the past (especially those in the 'high' arts). Things moved on, with social history augmented by the emergence of 'cultural' history, in which historians learned much from anthropology and brought to the fore such issues as ritual, gender and ethnicity. In 1963, EP Thompson said that he hoped to rescue the poor stockinger, the Luddite cropper and the handloom weaver from the condescension of posterity, and subsequent scholarship attempted to do the same for those previously marginalised by mainstream historiography on account of their race or sex (or sexuality). Thus, studies began to appear of such hitherto relatively obscure figures as Felix Mendelssohn's sister Fanny or the Chevalier de Saint-George while, at the same time, the intimate personal lives of famous figures from the past, traditionally ring-fenced as sensitive territory, emerged as a *sine qua non* of modern biography.

***

Can biography ever be a serious contribution to history? A reservation sometimes voiced in the academic community is that, by focusing on the life of an individual, the writer can hardly embrace the wider historical picture. This is a dilemma of which every good biographer is acutely aware. Antonia Fraser tells how, when writing the life of Marie Antoinette, she was impishly tempted to circumvent the whole problem by inserting a sentence to the effect that, at this time, 'the French Revolution happened'! She didn't, of course, and not the least of the literary-cum-historical skills adduced by Fraser and other leading biographers is their capacity to slip almost imperceptibly between the micro and macro, allowing each to reinforce the other. Lawrence Goldman, the outgoing editor of the *Oxford Dictionary of National Biography* (and subsequent Director of the University of London's Institute of Historical Research) put it well: the aim of the ODNB, he said, was to enable the reader not only to learn about a life from the past but also to understand that person's place in the history of their age.

Is there a danger that biographers develop an emotional relationship with the subject of their research in a way that a *bona fide* historian should not do? Many men have no doubt found themselves drawn to write about admired (or detested) political or military leaders, just as a modern-minded woman might well choose to research the life of a somewhat parallel figure from earlier times. One biographer recounts how she was reduced to tears when encountering a diary written long ago by the subject of her research;

others have come close to despair (like the narrator of Henry James's *The Aspern Papers*) on discovering that a body of all-important documents – a collection of love letters, perhaps – was deliberately destroyed precisely in order to keep things from the prying eyes of posterity. But maybe all good historians experience a degree of emotional identification with what they write about; certainly, studies of the past are the poorer when clothed in such a way as to distance the reader from the 'feel' of the subject matter. In biography, as in all history writing, the result can only be enhanced if built upon emotion recollected in careful, critical tranquillity.

Perhaps history and biography have been drawn closer by the emergence of 'meta-biography', a form of reception history examining a sequence of biographies of the same subject. A good introduction to the changing attitudes towards women, creativity, sex, landscape and much else – from early Victorian times to the present – is provided by Lucasta Miller's study of the many portrayals of the Brontë sisters. But, as Miller's book reminds us, Elizabeth Gaskell's ground-breaking life of Charlotte Brontë dates back to 1857. Maybe the trend I identified earlier, of women writing biographies of female cultural and literary figures, is not as new as I had imagined.

'IFS' of History

Could the past have been different?

Based on the Introduction to my book *If I Had Been... Ten Historical Fantasies* (Robson Books, 1979).

In 1976, when working at the BBC, I invited three historians to imagine they were each an important historical figure faced with what proved to be a pivotal decision. Each would write a script in the first person and tell us how, in the genuine circumstances of the time, he might have opted for an alternative decision – and to end with a brief outline of what the consequences might have been if he had done so. Owen Dudley Edwards opted for Gladstone and how, with his 'mission to pacify Ireland', he might have been able to do so when he became Prime Minister again in 1880. Harry Shukman, focusing on 1917, considered how Kerensky, who headed the Russian government between the fall of the Tsar and the advent of Lenin, might have been able to prevent the Bolshevik Revolution, while Philip Windsor moved on to 1968 and, identifying himself as Alexander Dubček, told us how he might have been able to prevent the Russians from invading Czechoslovakia.

In due course, I expanded the cast and the subject matter and produced an anthology of ten essays that were published in 1979 by Robson Books. Jeremy Robson is my second cousin, and we called the book If I Had Been... *Much of what follows is built from my original Introduction to the book.*

How different would my world have been if Winston Churchill had been killed when he was knocked down by a car in New York in December 1931 or if Giuseppe Zangara had succeeded in his attempt to assassinate President-elect Franklin D Roosevelt just over a year later? Suppose Hitler or Stalin had died in their twenties or that Harry Truman had not ordered the dropping of atomic bombs on Hiroshima and Nagasaki?

Speculating about who and what 'makes history' has long been an attractive intellectual pursuit. Back in Victorian times, Thomas Carlyle famously wrote that:

> Universal History, the history of what man has accomplished in this world, is at bottom the History of the Great Men who have worked here... the practical realisation and embodiment of Thoughts that dwelt in the Great Men sent into the world.

From that day to this, many historians (biographers such as Andrew Roberts, for example) have focused on the importance of individual leaders in the making of history. Others have emphasised how what we call 'history' has primarily occurred in response to broader economic and social developments. To Carlyle's contemporary, Karl Marx, it was ultimately a question of economics and of which section (or class) of society controlled the means of production: from the power of the church and aristocracy to that of the emerging bourgeoisie as industrialisation took hold and, ultimately, the working-class proletariat. Or, as historians like EP Thompson, Raphael Samuel and their contemporaries emphasised during the 1960s, a shift from 'top-down history' to what came to be dubbed 'history from the bottom up'.

But if there have been many different views about what ultimately makes for historical change, could events in the past actually have been different? I was not the first to speculate about the 'ifs' of history. In 1931, the journalist JC Squire published a fascinating collection of essays entitled *If It Had Happened Otherwise*. Winston Churchill contributed a piece imagining that the US Confederate army had won the Battle of Gettysburg in 1863 and, in due course, the Civil War, while Philip Guedalla imagined the Moors of southern Spain defeating the Catholic armies descending from the north. One essay speculated about subsequent American history if Lincoln had not been assassinated, while Trevelyan tried to imagine the repercussions if Napoleon had won the Battle of Waterloo.

Nor was I the last: some years after my book appeared, distinguished historians such as Niall Ferguson and Richard J Evans picked up the fundamental issues in what was increasingly coming to be dubbed 'counterfactual history'.

Looking back, I can see how speculating about the 'ifs' of history has proved of continuing interest. It's something we all do at times, if only as part of casual conversation. 'If I were you' we say to a friend, I'd have done this or that instead. Or, looking back further, 'I wish I'd been in his (or her) shoes'. As often as not speculations like these are not so much the 'ifs' of history as its whims; there are no rules as to the degree of 'iffiness' permitted and the results can be as wildly fanciful as the mood dictates.

But could the past really have been different? What causes historical change? Let's go further back in time. Would – could – Wellington have fought the Battle of Waterloo and defeated Napoleon if the Prussians under von Blücher had not agreed to help him? Are you sure Spain would have become united and Catholic in the later 1400s if Ferdinand and Isabella had not married? And what if Guy Fawkes had not been discovered and the British parliament been blown up in 1605?

The further back we look, the more deeply embedded any particular event tends to appear within what we understand as its fixed causal context. How nonsensical it would be, at this distance of time, to imagine that Caesar had not crossed the Rubicon or that William of Normandy might had not launched – and carried through with success – his invasion of England in 1066. Or that (to take another Spanish example) Elizabethan England had been defeated and conquered by the Armada launched by Philip II in 1588. This, surely, is the stuff of the novelist, if anyone. But not that of the serious, intellectual historian!

***

This issue has been vigorously debated over the centuries and is a sub-section of the eternal debate between those who incline towards a deterministic view of the world and the advocates of free will. In a way, we are all to varying degrees drawn to both. Like all really interesting debates, that between determinism and free will is inconclusive. One reason for this is that there is a conflict between the way our intelligence interprets the world and the way in which our senses transmit experience to us. Our intelligence tells us that there are no effects without causes, and that if anything appears to have occurred as a result of chance or accident this is a function of our ignorance of its prior causes. Imagine asserting that lightning or a sunset were capable of no physical or meteorological explanation, or that a war or a drop in the birth-rate 'just happened'. Such views would be greeted with scepticism for we assume that such phenomena do have causes even if we do not happen to know precisely what these were, and we would be disturbed if told authoritatively that this or that occurrence were, by its very nature rather than by reason of our ignorance, without causal explanation. And once we are aware of these prior causes, the event itself, we tend to think, could not but have occurred when, where and how it did.

Yet our senses tend to transmit a somewhat different world, one full of genuine alternatives which can be freely resolved in any number of possible ways. 'Shall I go for a walk, or stay at home and watch television?' we ask, confident that we are faced with a genuine choice and are at liberty to make a decision either way. Or 'shall I appoint Smith or Jones to this post?'

Thus, the way we *sense* the world, as opposed to the way we commonly *think* about it, suggests that events did not necessarily have to turn out in precisely the way that they did. How different would the world have been if Mark Twain had decided not to publish *Huckleberry Finn* or Einstein the Special or General Theory of Relativity?

***

The determinism vs freewill debate is likely to remain inconclusive for another reason – namely, that we often adopt different methods of perceiving the *past* and the *present*. We tend to regard the past as having been a series of inter-related developments all taking their place along a vast chain of causation. And, as we have seen, the further in the past they occurred, the more embedded they appear to be within that causal chain.

By contrast, the present or recent past does not seem quite like that. As we look around us we see a world full of options to be taken, choices to be made, contingencies that may or may not arise. What actually transpires may sometimes occur in what looks like a response to rational considerations while other developments may appear to happen almost as a result of caprice. Historians, notoriously, while often claiming arrogantly to be able to explain the causes of everything that occurred in the past, are often useless when it comes to predicting the future. Which historian of the USSR and Communist Central Europe, for example, anticipated accurately the imminent reunification of Germany and the collapse of the entire Soviet system in 1991? And in the here and now I sense that I am free to appoint Smith or Jones to this post or to stay at home and watch television if I like or go out for a walk. But once decisions have been made and acted upon, whether political or personal, it is usually not hard to look back and pinpoint the causes of even recent decisions and perhaps show that that, under the circumstances, these were the ones that were bound to have been reached.

What am I saying? That the further back in time something happened the more inevitable it appears to have been? We historians look not just for the facts about the past but for explanations. For causes and effects. Those among us with adequate expertise can explain with confidence much about when and why the Roman empire developed and collapsed. Or about what led to the Crusades, the Renaissance, the Reformation or industrialisation. And what were the longer-term repercussions of developments such as these. Or the life and times and activities of individuals such as Leonardo da Vinci, Louis XIV or Hitler. Might Benjamin Franklin have inadvertently been able to prevent the warfare that led to American independence, for example, or indeed Gladstone the 'Irish problem' or Kerensky the Bolshevik Revolution?

All these questions are, on the face of it at least, worth a degree of investigation. But that is because we know something of the subsequent context. But can you or I genuinely understand an event, place or personality in the past as if we have no knowledge of what in fact came later? And can we, as historians, cast off our own lives and times, our own personal strengths and weaknesses, and place ourselves fully into the physical and mental livery of a religious, political or military leader of long ago? Or of a cheerful young man leaving home to fight in the Crusades or of Napoleon or a young farmgirl dreaming that one day she might be admitted to a Convent?

***

As mentioned earlier (p. 39), it is important to distinguish between 'history' and the 'past'. The past is always there. It is what happened. And even if nobody ever wrote about it – or even knew about it – the past would still be there. But 'history' is a different matter altogether. Historians are the conduits between past and present, the alchemists who conjure up lost eras, often looking to the past for currently applicable messages. Those who try with integrity to investigate the causes and effects of what happened long ago, and perhaps speculate on whether some things might have developed differently, must therefore be respected.

Or maybe not. Are you saying that Queen Boudica may not have had spikes on her wagon wheels or that King Alfred may not have burned the cakes (or that Marie Antoinette may or may not have said of hungry people 'Let them eat cake')? How can you be sure? The factual answer, after all, lies in the unchangeable past. Not in history.

History and the BBC

Wireless is More

From *The Long March of Everyman* to *Fins de Siècle*.
BBC History Magazine, August 2002.

When I joined the BBC in 1967 after four years as a Lecturer at the new University of Sussex, I was encouraged to turn my hand to production of scripted talks (mainly for what was still the Third Programme). 'Dons talking to dons,' scoffed the critics. But it seemed to me there was value in inviting an intelligent speaker to share with a non-expert audience the historical background to (for example) the 1968 overthrow of the regime in Czechoslovakia or, a few years later, of the Allende regime in Chile. Often, talks were commissioned with no 'hook' other than that the speaker was a good communicator and had something to say: EH Carr on the early history of the Soviet Union, for example, or Isaiah Berlin on Romanticism.

There were other kinds of history programme, too: interviews, imaginary conversations and lots of historical drama. But dramatised history was beginning to sound a little dated as yet another intrepid crew cried 'Aye aye!' to the orders of Columbus or Nelson, or the Light Brigade sallied forth once more to the accompaniment of coconut shells. Moreover, broadcasting needed to catch up with important shifts in the intellectual world. EP Thompson and others were painting a broader picture of the past, including in their canvas not only the principal actors but also those who were primarily acted upon, the hitherto mute voices of the women and children, the poor labourers, the sick, the indigent, the elderly, the illiterate.

Some historians were also beginning to record the reminiscences of elderly people as they looked back across the events of their own lifetimes. A controversial departure, 'oral history' was dismissed by some as adding little to the sum of human knowledge – or perhaps too much! I remember visiting the so-called oral history archive at an American university only to discover that they had proudly transcribed their recordings and destroyed the tapes. 'It's so much faster to work from a text than from a recording,' explained the librarian.

Two BBC colleagues were especially sensitive to these shifts and tried to reflect them in their programmes: Charles Parker, creator of the *Radio Ballads*, and Michael Mason who masterminded *The Long March of Everyman*. They could not have been more different. Charles wore a permanent air of studied resentment – the scars, I presumed, of endless battles to hymn the working classes against what he saw as recalcitrant BBC management. Michael, equally committed to a radical view of society, was a romantic optimist, always inclined to believe that patient explanation would ultimately win the heart and mind of the most sceptical interlocutor. Charles's *Ballads* were exquisitely crafted radiophonic poems, while Michael's masterpieces (*The Bayeux Tapestry, Rus, Plain Tales from the Raj, The British Seafarer*) were on a more epic scale. Michael was Shakespeare, Verdi and Tolstoy where Charles was Flaubert, Baudelaire, Gorki.

The two came together in Michael Mason's *The Long March of Everyman*, a series of twenty-six 45-five-minute programmes covering 'themes and variations in the history of the people in Britain', first broadcast on Radio Four from November 1971. I worked with Michael throughout the project and produced half the programmes.

The Long March covered British history from Roman times to the present, and called upon the services of many of the country's leading historians, including Asa Briggs, Theo Barker and Peter Mathias, revisionists such as Gwyn Williams and George Rudé and young turks like Raphael Samuel. As far as possible, we aimed to tell the story through the words and voices of 'the people': archive recordings for more recent periods, but also authentic documents – letters, diaries, official pronouncements, court proceedings, gravestone inscriptions, graffiti, popular rhymes, lyrics or jokes – each spoken by somebody who was today's nearest equivalent. This is where Charles Parker came in. His job was to criss-cross the country, tape recorder in hand, as head of a team that recorded some 800 historical documents for us in voices and accents that corresponded as far as possible to those of the people originally responsible for them.

These tapes were intercut with popular and 'art' music, sound effects, literary excerpts (read by actors) and the voices of our historians, the final ingredients mixed in the BBC's Radiophonic Workshop at Maida Vale. Certain sounds and documents were repeated, in the spirit of a Wagnerian *leitmotif*, within or between programmes to make a thematic point; the disciplined, 'rectilinear' beat created for the Roman legions on the march, for example, found echoes in later programmes as Britain's rigid road network or factory system was established. The intention throughout was to find links, parallels, connections, to concentrate on 'synthesis' rather than 'analysis' – to create what Michael called 'total audio', a series of through-composed sound symphonies that would attempt to evoke the world of our ancestors.

The Long March was innovative in three important ways: in its attempt to view the past primarily from the point of view of ordinary people rather than the elites who mostly filled the radio programmes (and history books) at the time; in the decision to cross chronology with theme and to emphasise the connections linking historical experience rather than the analysis of its separate elements; and in the free-flowing, unnarrated radiophonic style of production adopted. All this provoked considerable debate. We had doubtless tempted providence by saying we hoped the series would 'give back to the British people a sense of their roots', while the crosscutting of chronology and theme (not to mention the Wagnerian comparison) was bound to cause offence to purists. Some felt the programmes needed a narrator so that listeners could know who was talking, where a document had come from, and whether we were still in the 16th century or had jumped to the 18th.

Perhaps. But we stood by our aim: to present history, for once, as essentially a seamless web of experience unmediated by extrinsic signposting. Here, we were helped by the introduction a few years earlier of magnetic tape which was already enabling producers to aim at far higher standards of recording and editing. Looking back, some claim to see today's 'soundbite' culture as having been preceded – heralded – by the Goons, Monty Python and the telly commercial with their rapid edits, dissolves, striking juxtapositions and highly economic foreshortenings of sound, speech and meaning. I would be sorry to think that *The Long March* contributed to a diminution of the nation's attention span. But as an exploration of the possibilities of radio montage, I believe it covered new ground. Perhaps that is why, on sampling the programmes once again, I find them less 'dated' than I had anticipated.

***

Thirty years have passed since *The Long March of Everyman*. Much that was radical and revisionist then is accepted truism today. The concepts of ethnic, women's or 'people's' history, or of featuring regional and local experience, are by now in danger of sounding like a fading litany of political correctness, while the recording of 'oral history' is part of many a schoolchild's homework kit. The broadcasting environment, too, has changed, becoming more streamlined, more concerned with packaging, cost-effectiveness, strands, slots and streams. 'Why these programmes – and why now?' ask the commissioners, as producers seek a 'hook' of contemporary relevance. *History Now and Then* was the title I gave a series in which Roy Porter invited participants to consider ways in which our present perspectives colour our views of the past and vice versa.

Something of this spirit lay behind a 6-part series of historical features I produced in the mid-1990s entitled *Fins de Siècle*. We certainly had a 'hook': the run-up to the end of the century and millennium, and the growing sense that we were approaching some kind of historical turning point. The idea was to capture this *fin-de-siècle* mood by turning the spotlight on previous ends of centuries in British history. As with *The Long March*, I used the full range of sounds available to radio to try and evoke something of the experience of life in earlier periods via carefully structured, unnarrated montage. The series included interviews with some forty leading historians, including such veterans of the *Long March* as Theo Barker and Asa Briggs. Asa's collaboration and advice was invaluable throughout the project, and it was with him that, in due course, I went on to edit a book arising from the series.

When the time came to broadcast the programmes, I decided to do so 'backwards', starting with the 1890s, followed a week later with the 1790s and so on until we reached the final programme, that on the 1390s. More listeners would tune in, I thought, if we began with the death of Queen Victoria rather than the ousting of Richard II. Moreover, I have long felt there was virtue in telling history in this 'neo-Whig' fashion: pointing to something familiar and then, in effect, saying that if you want to know how things came to be like this, read on (or tune in next week). After a further thirty years, I came up with an essay outlining this back-to-front approach to the past (see p. 93). Maybe, one day, I'll even write a book in this fashion…

BBC Centenary

This essay was drafted in 2021 with the approach of the centenary of the creation of the BBC. Versions of the essay were subsequently published in a variety of journals, and it was also used as the basis for a number of different lectures.

The BBC has always meant a great deal to me. Born in the week of *Kristallnacht* in November 1938, my earliest memories are of wartime London. My father, an anti-aircraft gunner, was away most of the time on the Kent coast. Every now and then he would come home on leave and, the next morning back in his army uniform, would smile at my mother and little me and tell me to 'look after Mummy while I'm away', at which I would salute and, trying to look as grown up as I could, promise to do my best. While he was away, Mummy and I would listen to 'the BBC' and I'd imitate the news broadcasts as I lay in bed at night ('The Russian tanks are approaching the river so-and-so...'). As the war neared its end, I asked her in all innocence whether, once it was concluded, the 'news' would cease. After all, there would be nothing to report. I listened to Churchill's broadcasts by her side and remember celebrating the news of Hitler's death. A few weeks later, I danced joyously around the street bonfire on what I learned to call 'VE Night'.

Daddy came home and, by now, I was going to school. My priorities, I knew, were learning to read and write (and to 'add up' and 'take away'). But that didn't stop me listening to the wireless. On the contrary, while my parents and their friends would laugh over the previous night's *ITMA* I became an addict of *Dick Barton: Special Agent* (any time you want me to sing what I learned to call the 'signature tune' just ask!). Later it was *Much Binding in the Marsh, Workers' Playtime* and *Up the Pole*. Programmes such as these (and celebrity broadcasters like Arthur Askey, Tommy Trinder, Charlie Chester and Ted Ray) might regularly reach 12 million people or more. I mostly listened to the BBC Home Service (later Radio 4) but also gradually became aware of the newly launched Light and Third Programmes and, by the later 1940s and early 1950s, BBC television. One way and another 'the BBC' became an all-important presence in my life, and in that of everyone I knew.

***

The 'British Broadcasting Company' was created in 1922 and financed by a royalty on the sale of wireless receiving sets. John Reith, a tall, religious thirty-three-year-old Scottish engineer, was appointed the new company's General Manager, his staff consisting at first of just four people. In 1923, with by now more like thirty employees, the BBC moved to Savoy Hill on the north bank of the Thames between Waterloo and Hungerford Bridges.

Savoy Hill, off the Strand in central London, was opened for medical use in 1889. It became the home of the Institute of Electrical Engineers, which offered accommodation to the British Broadcasting Company in 1923. Early radio contributors in Savoy Hill included HG Wells and George Bernard Shaw who were offered whisky and soda as they relaxed in the atmosphere of a gentlemen's club. Here, radio drama flourished while weather forecasts and Big Ben chimes were introduced.

The first edition of *The Radio Times* appeared in September 1923 and from February 1924 the BBC broadcast six electronically generated 'pips' to mark the precise start of every hour and indicate the Greenwich Time Signal. To this day, the BBC aims to follow the Reithian directive to 'inform, educate and entertain'.

***

In May 1926, Britain underwent the highly controversial 'General Strike'. This temporarily interrupted newspaper production, and the BBC suddenly became the primary source of news. This placed the BBC in a delicate position: on the one hand Reith was acutely aware that if the BBC were seen to step out of line politically it might simply be commandeered as a mouthpiece of the government, but on the other he was anxious to maintain public trust by appearing to be acting independently.

The Baldwin government was divided on how to handle the BBC, but in the end trusted Reith, granting the BBC sufficient leeway to pursue the government's objectives largely in a manner of its own choosing. On balance, the BBC did well out of the crisis which helped cement a national audience for its broadcasting. This in turn led to the establishment by Royal Charter of the new, non-commercial 'British Broadcasting Corporation' in 1927 (and a couple of years later the BBC established *The Listener*: a weekly magazine that reproduced the texts of important broadcast talks while previewing and promoting the good things to come). Reith – newly knighted – was appointed the BBC's first Director-General and the new corporation adopted a coat of arms containing the motto 'Nation shall speak peace unto Nation'.

***

Broadcasting developed exponentially: two studios quickly became nine, and by the later 1920s it was becoming clear that the BBC was rapidly outgrowing the cramped but cosy confines of Savoy Hill. It was decided that a purpose-built headquarters was required. A plot of land on Portland Place was acquired in early 1928, next to the church, All Souls in Langham Place and the concert venue Queen's Hall, both of which would prove useful in presenting programmes. By late 1931 Savoy Hill was gradually abandoned as the new art-deco style building was becoming ready to receive the first staff members. Over the course of several weekends in spring 1932 the BBC gradually moved to its new site, its first purpose-built centre, and officially transferred to Broadcasting House in May 1932. A new era had begun.

Soon the BBC was able to develop an additional form of broadcasting: what people learned to call 'television'. The idea of visual broadcasting had been pioneered by another talented Scotsman, John Logie Baird who, in September 1929, transmitted his first experimental television broadcast from his studios near Covent Garden. Next time you are walking along the north side of Long Acre, look up as you approach the turnoff to Slingsby Place and you may just catch a glimpse of the faded memorial plaque.

Baird continued to develop his new invention and in November 1936 the world's first public television transmissions were broadcast from Alexandra Palace. 'Ally Pally' was never owned by the BBC, but in 1935 the Corporation leased the eastern part of the building from which the first public television transmissions were made.

***

In December 1932, King George V became the first British monarch to broadcast on radio, his Christmas message heard simultaneously by millions. This historic broadcast enabled the King to introduce the new BBC Empire Service (forerunner of today's World Service) which, the King said, was intended for 'men and women, so cut off by the snow, the desert, or the sea, that only voices out of the air can reach them'.

Four years later, in 1936, the BBC hosted another royal-related programme: the abdication broadcast by Edward VIII. Reith introduced

ABOVE LEFT *King George V broadcasts Christmas message.* (Alamy)

ABOVE RIGHT *Abdication broadcast by Edward VIII.*

LEFT *September 3, 1939: Neville Chamberlain: 'This country is at War with Germany'.*

(BBC Archives)

the ex-King (as 'Prince Edward'), before standing aside to allow Edward to take the chair. Doing so, Edward accidentally knocked the table leg with his foot, which was picked up by the microphone. Some headlines interpreted that as Reith 'slamming the door' in disgust before Edward began broadcasting!

Above all, much of the nation tuned in at 11.15am on 3 September 1939 when Prime Minister Neville Chamberlain announced over the wireless that 'this country is at war with Germany'.

***

During the run-up to war, well over 50,000 people, mostly of Jewish origin, had managed to migrate to Britain from Nazi Central Europe. As with every wave of migration, they had not all been made welcome and, indeed, many were arrested soon after the outbreak of war and interned on the Isle of Man and elsewhere as (technically at least) 'enemy aliens'. In due course, all were released, and most did their best to contribute whatever they could to help their new, beleaguered 'homeland'. And, in many cases, to the BBC.

All branches of broadcasting attracted refugee talent, but none more so than the BBC's German Service. This originated not as a response to the war but as part of Britain's desperate attempts to prevent it. But from the day war broke out, the BBC German Service came to be overtly aimed at the people of Central Europe, intended to undermine any hopes they might hold and to convince them that there was no future for Nazism. With the onset of war and the subsequent Blitz, the BBC moved many of its departments out of London to Bristol and other provincial centres. One improbable location was a mansion called Wood Norton near Evesham in Worcestershire. Here, amid the groves and orchards of rural England, the BBC set up a quasi-secret department whose members spent eight-hour shifts monitoring Axis broadcasts in a variety of languages and dictating summaries for a 'BBC Digest' that was sent to government departments.

The BBC Monitoring Service came to include a number of highly cultured refugees from Central Europe – people like Martin Esslin (later BBC Radio's Head of Drama), the art historian Ernst Gombrich and the future publisher George Weidenfeld – many of whom, while still technically 'enemy aliens' in some cases, were deemed to be doing work vital to the war effort and therefore exempt from internment. Using their languages, they helped keep the British authorities up to date with speeches by Hitler, Mussolini and their henchmen which, recorded in London, were sent to Wood Norton for translation and analysis.

Inevitably, perhaps, officialdom at first regarded this exotic platoon of beret-and-borscht boffins with some ambivalence. As did the local families with whom they were billeted, most of whom had never encountered a foreigner before, let alone a forceful Austro-German intellectual. Gombrich, working late night shifts, had to endure the disapproval of his host for the apparently disreputable habit of returning home at 2 or 3 am and sleeping on until ten in the morning.

In 1943 the Monitoring Service moved to Caversham Park near Reading (where it remained until 2018). Listening to foreign broadcasts for eight hours at a time was hugely important but – almost all the time – perilously tedious. Gombrich, deprived of his books and art works, spent some of his spare time penning whatever he could remember of the history of art (for a book later destined to become the most famous ever published on the subject). One night in April 1945 he heard the German radio play a movement from a Bruckner symphony written to commemorate the death of Wagner. Gombrich listened intently. Shortly afterwards, a solemn announcement came over the airwaves that 'Our Führer has fallen in the struggle against Bolshevism' and it was Gombrich who immediately arranged for the news of Hitler's death to be forwarded to Churchill.

***

Once the war was over, the changes wrought to and within the BBC were spectacular. I choose that adjective carefully since the most important in many ways was the re-introduction of television in 1946. A ground-breaking children's television service was inaugurated that autumn, one of its earliest successes focusing on *Muffin the Mule*, a loveable puppet whose antics were accompanied on the piano by Annette Mills. In 1948, the first regular news service appeared on TV (*BBC Newsreel*), introduced by John Snagge. Scarcely more than 100,000 British households owned a television set at this time, but in summer 1948 BBC TV broadcast over 68 hours of the London-based Olympic Games and, a year later, began to transmit regular weather forecasts. On radio, meanwhile, the BBC initiated such long-term successes as *Woman's Hour* (1946) and *The Archers* (1950), both of them running to this day.

In 1946, the BBC's Director-General, William Haley, reorganised the radio networks introducing the new 'Home' and 'Light' Services and a cultural network called the 'Third Programme'. The Home Service included most of the BBC's talk and discussion programmes and news presentations as well as educational and children's broadcasts while the Light Programme, aiming at a larger audience, focused on popular music and drama and was the home of *Woman's Hour*. The most innovative network, the Third Programme, while appealing to a relatively small, educated audience, was very much in the Reithian tradition and devoted its airtime to 'serious' music, drama, talk and culturally oriented discussion.

It was on the Home Service that the BBC's debt to its inspirational founder was perhaps most memorably created: the annual 'Reith Lectures' presented by someone regarded as among the most widely respected intellectuals of the day. Inaugurated in 1948, the first series of Reith Lectures was given by the philosopher Bertrand Russell and, within a few years, he was followed by the physicist Robert Oppenheimer on the

Early Reith lecturers: Bertrand Russell (1948) and Nikolaus Pevsner.
(BBC Archives)

understanding of science and the German émigré art historians Nikolaus Pevsner on the Englishness of English Art and Edgar Wind on why, and how, great art is often produced in turbulent circumstances.

In many ways the 1950s were the decade of television. In 1952, King George VI died, and he was succeeded by his elder daughter whose Coronation as Queen Elizabeth II took place on 2 June 1953. This spectacular and historic event was the first coronation to be shown live on television and the first major world event to be broadcast on tv internationally. It was shown by the BBC in black-and-white (and filmed in colour) and, during the run-up, sales of TV sets soared. As did audiences to BBC television.

By the end of the decade, the BBC had moved into what was the first purpose-built television production centre in the world, a building complex in White City in West London that became the headquarters of BBC TV for over half a century. 1958 saw the launch of what was to become the world's longest-running children's TV show, *Blue Peter*, broadcast from the BBC's Television Centre until the Centre's imminent closure in 2011.

The 1960s and 1970s were an era like no other: for the BBC and for Britain more generally. A period of optimistic, well-financed cultural expansion that saw the creation of seven new universities, the appointment of Jennie Lee as Britain's first Arts Minister and the renewal of the Arts

Council Charter. The era of 'Swinging London', of the Beatles, Carnaby Street, Biba and Mary Quant, of David Bailey, Jean Shrimpton, Twiggy, Julie Christie and the young David Hockney. Colours and textures were in. So was the pill. And the jet plane. Britain may (as Dean Acheson put it in 1962) have lost an Empire and not yet found a role. But for younger people what was supposedly important was the here and now, and their heroes and models were the 'beautiful people' who set the styles of a generation brought up after the war was safely won and reaching adulthood when the Empire was safely lost.

Much of this was reflected in the world of broadcasting. BBC television's rival, the commercially based ITV, had been launched in 1955, but the BBC retaliated in 1960 by renaming its television service 'BBC TV' and with the creation in 1964 of a second channel, BBC 2, the widely publicised home for more ambitious programming.

In 1965 David Attenborough was appointed Controller of BBC 2 and in 1967 the Vienna-born Stephen Hearst became Head of Television Arts and Features. Among the projects commissioned under the Attenborough regime were two outstanding thirteen-part series: Kenneth Clark's *Civilisation*, a vivid and personalised history of Western art and culture, which appeared in 1969 and, four years later, a somewhat complementary, science-based history of the evolution of mankind, *The Ascent of Man*, presented by Jacob Bronowski.

Throughout these years the BBC was quick to adopt and adapt all the latest technology. Videotape, for example, was a recent innovation when Sydney Newman, the BBC's head of drama (and son of a Russian-Jewish immigrant to Canada) proposed a new science fiction series. This became *Doctor Who* which, launched in 1963, went on to prove one of the BBC's most successful projects. The similarly popular *Forsyte Saga*, a twenty-six-episode adaptation of the Galsworthy novels which revolutionised costume drama, was launched in 1967 – the year in which BBC 2 became the first TV channel in Europe to broadcast regularly in colour. Meanwhile, as early as 1962 the BBC began to relay pictures that it received via the communications satellite Telstar from the USA, a phenomenon that, by the end of the decade, British viewers came to take for granted.

In radio, similarly, the arrival and enthronement of magnetic tape enabled producers to aim at far higher standards of recording and editing than had ever been possible before. Charles Parker's *Radio Ballads* and Michael Mason's *Long March of Everyman* would have been impossible before tape. Both radio and television benefited from the BBC's 'Radiophonic Workshop' in Maida Vale where a multiplicity of signature tunes, themes and sound effects came to be concocted, increasingly making use of the latest electronic synthesisers.

***

I joined the BBC in 1967. I had done a history degree at Cambridge and postgraduate work in the USA during the Kennedy years and thence to the new University of Sussex where, at twenty-four, I was appointed a lecturer in Politics and American Studies. My boss was the historian Asa (later Lord) Briggs. Asa was already at work on what was to become a five-volume history of broadcasting in the UK. At Sussex, in addition to my academic duties and obligations, I found myself writing articles for various magazines, presenting lectures to outside organisations and being interviewed about the latest developments in American politics.

One day in 1967, I received a phone call from Lord Archie Gordon (who later succeeded his elder brother as Marquess of Aberdeen and Temair). Archie was Head of BBC Radio Talks and Documentaries. He told me they intended to offer a six-month attachment to someone with a knowledge of American politics during the run-up to the following year's US elections. Might I be interested?

I had a word with Asa about the offer. 'Go ahead, Daniel,' he said. 'I think you'll enjoy it. See how things work out and if you want to come back to Sussex just give me a ring.' I called Lord Archie and said yes, I'd be delighted to accept his kind offer. It was initially for six months, over the course of winter 1967–68. I stayed on for nearly thirty years. My last big project for the BBC was the six-part series produced in the 1990s, with Asa, about ends of centuries going back through them all as far back as the 1390s which together, as mentioned above, we turned into a book.

Nobody in the BBC gave me anything so vulgar as a brief, remit or job description when I arrived, but my senior colleagues in Radio 3 and Radio 4 made it clear that they would like me to help enrich the airwaves by calling upon my contacts and supposed expertise not only in matters American but in history, politics and culture more generally. When I joined, the Third Programme (or Radio 3) still included in its schedules something like fourteen hours of speech programming per week.

The Controller of Radio 3 at the time was PH Newby, a quiet, thoughtful man whose offers meetings, held every Thursday morning, were the most civilised I ever attended. Howard Newby spent his weekends writing engaging novels and was recipient of the first Booker Prize while, around the table, were highly cultured fellow producers such as the poet George MacBeth, the film critic Philip French and (by now close to retirement) such legendary feature producers of an earlier era as Douglas Cleverdon and Geoffrey Bridson.

I quickly learned that a twenty-minute talk would involve commissioning someone, probably an academic historian or critic, to write and read some 2,700 words ('no abstract nouns or passive verbs') on a topic of broad general interest. The result would conveniently fill a concert interval. Before long I produced my first radio documentary; it was about Martin Luther King, who was assassinated in April 1968 in Tennessee, the state in which I had undertaken civil rights work four years earlier. Shortly afterwards, I was asked if I would like to visit the USA, armed with the latest BBC tape recorder, in order to produce and present a major documentary as the nation gradually approached its next elections. I had not been to the USA since 1964; but this year, 1968, looked set to be every bit as dramatic.

In the wake of King's murder, a series of riots occurred in many parts of the country with black citizens angrily venting their wrath against white racism. On university campuses, meanwhile, across the USA and much of western Europe, successive waves of student protest immobilised hitherto supposedly respectable homes of learning. In New York that spring, I visited the campus of Columbia University and found it to all intents and purposes closed. A witty student placard declared: 'If You Are Lost, You Have Come To The Right Place!' Later, I watched as a huge anti-Vietnam demo marched through mid-town Manhattan, led by a banner proclaiming: 'LBJ: Pull Out – Like Your Father Should Have Done!' Soon afterwards, Lyndon Johnson pulled out of the presidential race. Who would replace him as the Democratic front runner?

From New York, I went on to Washington DC and the tour took me across via Minneapolis to Winnipeg in Canada, thence to Seattle, down the West Coast to Los Angeles and San Diego. In LA, I watched Robert Kennedy as he campaigned for the Democratic presidential nomination. Six days later, he too was murdered.

Everywhere I went across America that spring and early summer, I recorded interviews, impressions and the bustle and noise of a great but troubled nation. Back in London that autumn, I edited all the material

I had recorded, and produced and presented a substantial radio portrait of America as it limped its way towards November's presidential election. I called the programme 'Grave New World'.

***

By now, many of the former refugees from Nazism had settled successfully into new jobs: as scientists and historians, artists, architects and film makers, as musicians, writers and publishers. Many became well known as broadcasters, while others found themselves working full-time for the BBC in editorial and managerial roles. In January 1972, the Vienna-born Stephen Hearst (born Hirshtritt), Head of Television Arts and Features under David Attenborough, came over to radio as Controller of Radio 3, beating his fellow émigré Martin Esslin to the job.

Esslin, head of Radio Drama since 1963, was born in Budapest and educated in Vienna before coming to Britain as a refugee from the Nazis. He was multi-lingual, prodigiously well-read with a widespread reputation as a rigorous critic with brilliant books to his credit on Brecht and what he called the 'Theatre of the Absurd' – a category which encompassed the work of not only Brecht but also playwrights such as Eugene Ionesco and Samuel Beckett. Esslin felt it was his job to introduce the work of writers such as these over the BBC airwaves and also to help promote the work of new young talent such as that of Harold Pinter.

Radio 3 meetings soon became lively affairs. I have vivid memories of meetings when sparks would fly between Stephen Hearst, Esslin and their fellow émigré the assertive and witty musicologist Hans Keller, all of whom seemed far more knowledgeable and articulate about current trends in British cultural life than the rest of us around the table.

Also present was Leonie Cohn, an outstanding radio producer with the rare ability to make art, architecture and the built environment 'visible' over the airwaves. Born to a cultured, assimilated Jewish family in Königsberg (now Kaliningrad) in what was then East Prussia, she was lucky enough to migrate to Britain under the sponsorship of the art critic Herbert Read through whom she became acquainted with many of the refugee artists and architects who lived at the time in and around Hampstead. During the war, Leonie had worked as a translator in the BBC's German Service under Hugh Greene (brother of novelist Graham Greene and BBC Director-General in the 1960s) who became Controller of Broadcasting in the British zone of occupation in north-west Germany. Here, his deputy

A montage of emigrés at the BBC.
CLOCKWISE, FROM TOP LEFT *The Amadeus Quartet (by Milein Cosman),*
Leonie Cohn, Ernst Gombrich (by R.B. Kitaj), Hans Keller (by Milein Cosman),
Stephen Hearst, Martin Esslin, John Tusa.

was Paul Findlay, whom Leonie married. Paul later became Head of BBC
TV Administration and then Director of Administration at the London
Festival Ballet. In retirement the couple continued to enjoy their home
in Lawn Road (Belsize Park) a few paces from the famous Wells Coates
Isokon flats.

***

Hearst became a forceful, proactive Controller of the nation's premier
cultural network. If he was not familiar with a name or a topic that came
up in discussion he would ask; if he knew but disapproved he could
crush. The tension between Hearst and Keller was palpable. When Keller
proposed a Radio 3 series on psychiatry, a subject that to him was all-
embracing, Hearst, who knew a thing or two about the subject (his wife
was a psychotherapist), was scathing. Keller, always game for a scrap, went
away to regroup and returned to the next meeting even more belligerently
confident of his case. Hearst, aroused, was even more vehement in his veto.

All were very good company up close. Early on during my time at the

BBC I was planning to make a programme with Rosemary Brown, the musical 'medium' who claimed to be in direct touch with the spirits of long-dead composers such as Beethoven, Chopin, Liszt and Brahms who would speak to her directly and dictate new compositions which she would dutifully write down. Was Mrs Brown a fraud? A hoaxer? Was she really a thoroughly trained musician trying to conceal her highly sophisticated skills under a cloak of mystery? Or was she genuinely gifted with some kind of extrasensory perception (ESP) denied to the rest of us? One way or another, Mrs Brown and her work were beginning to create quite a furore in musical circles. Before I visited her, I had a word with Hans Keller. We had a good laugh and he suggested I get her to ask Mozart (who lies in an unknown, unmarked grave in Vienna's St Marx cemetery) precisely where he is buried. Not surprisingly perhaps, Mozart did not appear to Mrs B! As for Stephen, I remember one day, seeing me in a coffee queue, he strolled over and, after a few words of gentle flattery, invited me to come up with whatever interesting ideas I might have that could possibly develop into potential programmes.

Nowhere was the impact of the émigrés greater than in the music – live and on recordings (and in discussions) – that the BBC chose to broadcast: the Amadeus Quartet, for example (three of whose members were refugees), or conductors such as Otto Klemperer, Rudolf Schwarz, Georg Solti and Walter Goehr. Alexander ('Sandy') Goehr, the talented son of Walter (b. 1932), recalled that it was at the BBC that his father felt most at home, and Sandy himself was invited to join BBC staff as a young producer by Music Controller William Glock before going on to become a celebrated composer, professor of music at Cambridge and, in 1987, the BBC Reith Lecturer.

The overall impact of the émigrés on BBC history cannot be overestimated, not only in radio but also in television. And, in some instances, the links between the two. Many people in radio felt that what especially characterised the creative genius of Stephen Hearst was the vision he had brought with him from his years in TV.

Something of the same was true of John Tusa. Born in Czechoslovakia in 1936, Tusa moved to England as a child shortly before the Nazi occupation of his homeland, later joining the BBC as a leading presenter of TV news programmes. And in 1986 he became managing director of the BBC 'World Service' in Bush House. Originally known as the 'BBC Empire Service', created by Reith in 1932, this expanded to become the

'Overseas Service' (or the 'External Services') as war approached, by now funded not by the license fee but by a direct grant from the Foreign Office.

In 1941 it moved to Bush House in Kingsway in central London where it remained for over seventy years. Tusa, a hugely versatile and creative leader, went on after his years at Bush House to become managing director of the recently inaugurated Barbican Arts Centre.

Bush House was full of talented people from around the world, many of them émigrés from Central Europe. You may remember the name of the brilliantly witty Hungarian refugee George Mikes. He used to say that my fellow Hungarians think my name is now George 'MIKES' while the British think I should properly be called 'MIKESH'!

Mikes worked for the BBC's Hungarian Service from 1939 onwards, interrupted only by his internment as an enemy alien on the Isle of Man in 1940. He broadcast to Hungary for the BBC throughout much of World War II, became a British citizen in 1946, and in 1956 went back to Hungary to cover the Hungarian Revolution for BBC TV.

***

As we look back over the history of the BBC as a whole, is it possible to sum up the legacy of that particular group of immigrants? All migrations bring 'culture' with them, as much of British history testifies; consider the 400-year Roman occupation, the Angles and Saxons, the Normans, the Huguenots, the Irish following the Great Famine, Jews escaping Russian pogroms in the later 19th century and many another migration. And the 'Hitler Emigrés' who worked with or for the BBC? It is arguable that they helped impose a stricter sense of professionalism upon a very British organisation that, hitherto, had largely relied upon a sense of moral idealism. In the same way that Gombrich ran the Warburg Institute or Solti (or Claus Moser) the Royal Opera, for example, people like Stephen Hearst or John Tusa undoubtedly helped professionalise the branches of the BBC that they ran.

In addition, the presence of the émigrés helped cosmopolitanise the still somewhat insular (or imperial) culture of the BBC, acting as an all-important bridge between British cultural life and that of resurgent continental Europe. One only has to think of Pevsner helping to introduce the ideas of Gropius and the Bauhaus to a generation raised on Tudorbethan revival and the Garden City, or Esslin bringing the work of Central European playwrights, as well as Pinter, to British audiences. Or Hans

Keller as a leading advocate of the work of both Benjamin Britten and Schoenberg. Weidenfeld strove to bring a truly international perspective to his publishing list, telling me 'I always saw myself as somebody who bridges and who straddles worlds. Someone at home everywhere – though not, perhaps, completely rooted anywhere!'

***

The presence in the BBC of the 'Hitler Emigrés' lasted from roughly the late 1930s through until the 1980s, by which time most had resigned, retired or in many cases died. Looking back, this was something of a golden age in the history of the BBC. If I as a producer wanted to call upon Isaiah Berlin or Eric Hobsbawm to participate in a discussion programme, or to visit Germany to interview Wagner's daughter-in-law or Antarctica with the climate scientists, I had but to ask, and my civilised and courteous managers would doubtless comply.

By the later 1980s, things became harder as, like many times before and since, governments tended to become critical of an editorially independent, publicly funded institution committed to a supposedly 'balanced' presentation of complex issues, accusing it of bias in one direction or another. Think back to the General Strike of 1926, the Suez invasion of 1956 or the Falklands War. Or forwards to the problems of our own times when the BBC is having to try and retain its traditional role as an essentially British-based flagship of cultural communication alongside a rapidly growing worldwide digital revolution. What room is there for traditional Reithian principles in a digital system capable of bringing whatever kind of 'news' you want to anyone who seeks it?

Today, more and more people, rather than watch or listen 'live' to BBC shows on radio or television, turn to watch Netflix, Amazon Prime or BBC iPlayer at a time of their own choosing or to catch up on 'BBC Sounds' with any number of available radio programmes or podcasts.

As the BBC approaches its centenary, some worry about its very existence in the years to come, and we historians, supposedly brilliant at explaining the past, are notoriously bad at predicting the future! But, as I look back over the BBC's first hundred years, I find myself full of admiration for a unique institution that has struggled successfully throughout its existence to 'inform, educate and entertain' and (in another Reithian phrase, beloved by many of the 'Hitler Emigrés' as well as by myself) to 'educate by stealth'. Long may it continue to do so.

History and the Institute of Historical Research (IHR)

History Now and Then

This was a title I first used for a series of BBC Radio 4 discussion programmes I produced, chaired by Roy Porter, starting in 1994. Twenty years later, I adopted the title for a series of six public seminars held at the Institute of Historical Research (IHR), University of London, aimed at examining ways in which we use (and abuse) the past. The project ran at the IHR over the course of academic year 2015/16.

I decided to begin the series by re-examining a fundamental issue first raised in my introduction to Historians, *the anthology of essays I had published some years before. 'History' had never been more popular, I suggested. Yet many people seemed to live in a bubble of the immediate present. Did this matter – and if so, why? This article was published by the* BBC History Magazine *in January 2016.*

I've loved history since childhood. Brought up during the war, I remember my mother pointing out the overhead fighter squadrons as they flew out in the morning and then, in the evening, watching them return, often with a poignant gap or two in their formation. And the noise – and then the ominous silence followed by a distant explosion – of the 'flying bombs' that we listened to together in our makeshift shelter. From my grandparents and others, I gradually learned about the previous world war, also against 'the Germans', and how there must never be another one. And later, as a schoolboy, something about earlier times: from Disraeli and Gladstone back to the Tudors and Stuarts and beyond, and went on to do a history degree.

I still love history, and hold a Senior Research Fellowship at London University's Institute of Historical Research. One of the things I am currently doing at the IHR (2015/16) is chairing a series of public seminars in which some of our top historians are debating the ways in which people use – and abuse – what they understand to have happened in 'history'. The series kicked off with what remained something of a paradox. On the one hand there was clearly a huge market for what you might call 'popular' history. Yet, at the same time, many people also seemed to lack any real sense of the continuity between past and present: how what happens today is the product of all that has preceded it. Could both be true – and, if so, did it matter?

***

'History' in its various guises is more popular nowadays than ever: in schools and universities, on film, TV and the internet, in sales of historical biographies, visitor numbers to heritage sites, family history, re-enactment societies and the like. In Britain, millions watch costume dramas such as *Downton Abbey* or *Wolf Hall* while books and TV programmes have abounded on historical anniversaries (Magna Carta, Agincourt, Waterloo, World War I). Or consider the huge popular interest aroused in 2012 by the rediscovery and subsequent reinterment of the bones of King Richard III. There were parallels elsewhere too; in the USA, for example, where the 150th anniversary of the end of the Civil War and the death of Abraham Lincoln were marked by a flurry of new books and tv programmes.

Yet we also live in a culture that can be markedly lacking in historical awareness. Press and politicians like to alarm us by reporting polls revealing that (for example) only one British teenager in six knows that the Duke of Wellington led the British army in the Battle of Waterloo and only one in ten can name a 19th-century British Prime Minister. Or that 33 per cent of respondents in a US poll did not know when the Declaration of Independence was adopted and 80 per cent had no idea who was president during World War I.

It's not just a question of being ignorant of the 'facts'. More profoundly, important current issues are frequently discussed with little regard for the backstory: migration policy, for example, or continued (or discontinued) British membership or the EU, Russian involvement in Ukraine or continuing war and violence in the Middle East. When people do turn to a version of history or a pivotal personality or event in the past when addressing contemporary concerns it is often highly selective history that is sought and cited: an invocation of the past to help bolster present-day attitudes. Think of the way one foreign 'hate' figure after another has been lazily compared with Hitler, for example, or how advocates of overseas military intervention have routinely invoked questionable analogies with 1939.

***

For all this, popular interest in the past remains high. One manifestation of this is the widespread appeal of 'Heritage' (see chapter 3, above). There have of course always been those, in Britain and elsewhere, concerned to conserve or renovate valued remains from the past. This was the day job of Prosper Mérimée (better known as the author of *Carmen*) and of his protégé Viollet-le-Duc in Paris from the 1830s and 1840s, while our own National Trust dates back to 1895. But our reverence for Heritage (with a capital 'H') has become more widespread than ever in recent decades, perhaps alongside a growing sense that much of our historic fabric was in danger of being lost.

As we saw earlier, the idea of Heritage had its critics. What exactly should be conserved and what scrapped? Why this building but not that? Isn't it, in some sense, false to history to restore a derelict building back to its 'original' state? Uppark, a magnificent 17th-century country house in Sussex, was devastated by fire in 1989 but superbly restored and, in 1995, reopened to the public. And who can deny the magnificence of Dresden's *Frauenkirche*, painstakingly rebuilt (partly with British help) exactly as it was when destroyed by Allied bombing in February 1945? Yet I wonder whether, had St Paul's Cathedral been badly hit during the war (which it nearly was), we would subsequently have erected a replica of Wren's masterpiece on the old site; more likely, I suspect, something 'modern' like Liverpool's Catholic Cathedral or Spence's Coventry. And one can understand the argument (see below, p. 87) that, in the interests of 'authenticity', the great tower in Pisa should be engineered back to its intended perpendicular position – or allowed to fall – rather than remain permanently, artificially, propped up at an angle akin to the one it assumed some time after its original construction.

Then why renovate Uppark, the *Frauenkirche* or the Pisa tower while continuing to clear away surviving industrial-era slums or factories? To its critics, 'Heritage' can be something of a sentimental, rearguard movement in danger of overvaluing the aristocratic and clerical past, a symptom of our anxious quest for a shared national identity, perhaps, that too often prioritises the 'beautiful' over the merely 'historic'. Yet how can we hope to learn from the past without making the effort to preserve and conserve those valued products of it that have survived? All told, the idea of 'Heritage' remains a topic capable of arousing powerful passions.

***

So does the relationship between history and myth, another of the themes discussed in the IHR Seminar series. What do you know – and how, and from what sources – about 'Boadicea' and her knife-endowed chariot, King Alfred and the cakes or Drake playing bowls before defeating the Spanish Armada? Or about the Trojan Wars, or of Joan of Arc trouncing the English (if you are French), George Washington and the cherry tree (if you are American) or the Emperor Barbarossa (if German)? Who were the 'heroes' and 'villains' of history? Many widely repeated historical myths concern the origins, creators and subsequent continuity of nation states. As a child growing up in London, I proudly repeated that 'we won the war' and how we'd had a continuous monarchy and never been successfully invaded for something approaching a thousand years. True? At best true-ish, as Jonathan Miller might have said. But the very repetition of certain mythologies, from those of Homer or Virgil, via the 'cake' anecdotes associated with Alfred the Great or Marie Antoinette to the preternaturally unsmiling Queen Victoria, remind us of the historical resonance such stories can acquire.

Any self-respecting historian would of course avoid repeating myths about the past as though they were 'true'. Then why does no work of historical research ever seem to be definitive, the final word on the subject (the theme of this month's IHR Seminar)? Is there even such a thing as historical 'reality'? Perhaps we all, despite protestations to the contrary, see the past through the shifting perspectives of the present with each generation seemingly constrained to reinterpret and even (dare I say it?) re-mythologise the past. Often, the myths and distortions of the past are essentially political. Thus, the Japanese in recent years have been rewriting their school history books (particularly the sections about World War II), and they're doing something of the same in Ukraine and Poland as they attempt to distance themselves from Russia. Did the British Empire help educate millions around the world into the benefits of democracy or was it primarily a form of ruthless (and racist) commercial exploitation? How do you regard – and label – the mass murder of Armenian Turks a century ago, or the evacuation of Arabs from Palestine in 1947/8? Did Lincoln fight the Civil War in order to free the slaves or just to prevent his nation from falling apart? This coming Easter (2016) marks the centenary of the Dublin uprising, and next year (2017) that of the Soviet Revolution: plenty of scope here, I would surmise, for new bouts of historical rewriting!

***

How far can art provide us with genuine insights about the past (the focus of our IHR Seminar next February)? I first came to know something about Henry V and Richard III and other historical figures from Shakespeare. His narratives about the Plantagenets and Tudors certainly misrepresented some of the facts, and we might say the same of the picture of a battle on a Greek vase, a painting or statue of Louis XIV, Schiller's (or Verdi's) portrayal of Philip II of Spain or Rodin's *Burghers of Calais*. But perhaps artworks, however much they may mythologise the past, can nonetheless help provide a pathway towards our understanding of it. As authentic products of their own time and place they surely tell us something of how people in a previous era regarded those of a still earlier period, thus providing data like any other for the historian to use.

With the recent rediscovery and reinterment of the remains of Richard III, I had another look at the 1955 Olivier film of the Shakespeare play. The fact that the Bard was no historian is acknowledged in the opening titles where an imitation late-Medieval manuscript informs viewer that, while the play may not be a work of historical scholarship, it is none the worse for that:

> The history of the world, like letters without poetry, flowers without perfume, or thought without imagination, would be a dry matter indeed without its legends, and many of these, though scorned by proof a hundred times, seem worth preserving for their own familiar sakes.

So is academic history a 'dry matter' in danger of being like flowers without perfume, thought without imagination, if devoid of myth and legend? Let's hope not. In any case, I sense that nowadays we have come to expect more exacting standards of historical accuracy from creative artists than anyone would have asked of Shakespeare; works such as Hilary Mantel's Tudor novels (or the TV version of *Wolf Hall*) are liable to arouse academic criticism if found to be in any way historically misleading. Yet at the same time, while few would seriously claim to have learned authentic Scottish history from Mel Gibson's *Braveheart*, for example, the film proved as inspirational to some emerging Scottish nationalists as an early Verdi opera might have done for those yearning for Italian statehood.

***

One way and another, what we loosely call 'history' is evidently massively popular. But what does it mean to all those who so avidly consume it, use it and abuse it? History means many things to many people. But its focus has moved on since I first learned all about kings and generals and political leaders to an emphasis on economic and social history, then to cultural history, a burst of post-modernism from some historians and, more recently, a much heralded 'return to narrative'.

For some, especially amongst older history lovers perhaps, the past can no doubt provide a heart-warming element of nostalgia or of consolation, while others might find themselves experiencing a sense of shared pride or vindication. Some doubtless seek affirmations of personal identity as they sift through the past; think of the popularity of national and family history and, increasingly, of histories touching on once-sensitive aspects of gender and ethnicity. And which of us has not relished learning more about a much-loved hero of earlier times or a much-reviled villain?

What new historiographical 'turn' should we be anticipating in the years to come? Already, many are probably more inclined to turn to the internet or iPlayer than to lengthy books; museums and heritage centres flourish as bookshops and publishers appear to falter. As the digital era takes increasing hold, how will people seek their historical fix?

'History' is a blanket term for all that has preceded – and can therefore help to throw light on – everything in the present. Nothing comes of nothing (as King Lear almost said), and one cannot understand the world of today without knowing what led things to be the way they are. Let's hope that, in what is said to be an increasingly 'present-oriented' age, debate about the present and future will be properly buttressed by an informed awareness of all that has preceded it. I am reminded yet again of those wise words of Marc Bloch: 'Misunderstanding of the present is the inevitable consequence of ignorance of the past.'

History Now and Then (continued)
IHR Seminar Series 2016/17

The 2015/16 seminar series History Now and Then *proved highly successful and the Director of the IHR, Lawrence Goldman, invited me to set up and chair a further series for the following academic year.*

This essay is taken from a blog written in August 2016 to help promote the second series of seminars (2016/17). It first appeared under the heading Talking Humanities *on the website of London University's 'School of Advanced Study' (SAS) of which the Institute of Historical Research was, and remains, an integral part.*

This series of public seminars at the IHR took off back in 2015 from an extraordinary (and potentially dangerous) paradox. On the one hand, 'history' seemed to be more popular than ever: in schools and universities, on film, TV and the internet, in sales of historical biographies, visitor numbers to heritage sites, the growth of family history, re-enactment societies and the like.

Yet we also seemed to be living in an aggressively here-and-now culture in which many people appeared to lack any real understanding of how the present was linked to all that preceded it. Thus, major current issues were frequently discussed with little sense of their longer-term historical roots: migration policy, for example, or continued British membership of the EU or Russian involvement in Ukraine. As Jo Guldi and David Armitage argued in their *History Manifesto* (published in 2014), it was vital to understand the past if we were to have any chance of planning sensibly for the future.

This was the thinking that led to the series of six public seminars, entitled *History Now and Then*, held at the IHR over the course of 2015/16. The project attracted large audiences who came to hear panels of top historians discussing such issues as the widespread popular appeal of historical 'Heritage', the relationship between art and history, the ways aspects of the past become mythologized and much else. As the series progressed, month by month from October to March, it became increasingly obvious that 'history' was a topic capable of raising widespread interest within and beyond the walls of academe. But what did 'history' mean to those who so avidly consumed it? Nostalgia to some perhaps (especially among older aficionados). And perhaps it also offered elements of consolation, affirmation, vindication. And for some, a sense of identity: think of the popularity of family history, for example, and of histories touching on gender, ethnicity or nationhood. Any debate about the past could also arouse powerful passions.

One way or another, the whole subject – the ways we regard (and sometimes disregard) the past – clearly 'hit the spot' with a wide and varied audience, and it was decided to run a second series during the following academic year, 2016/17.

***

This new series is, if anything, even more adventurous in its reach than the first. Panellists include many of our best-known historians and the series begins with the issues raised by the controversy over the Rhodes statue at Oriel College, Oxford. Should memorials to figures of whom we might now disapprove be removed, or is this false to history? What about the creation of prominent new memorials to people from the past whom we have only now come to admire (Mary Seacole, for example, whose recently erected statue stands at St Thomas' Hospital, directly across the Thames from the Houses of Parliament)? Is it appropriate for people today to apologise for supposed wrongs committed by their ancestors in the distant past? More generally, how far should history be rewritten in accordance with current values?

The second seminar focuses on the nature and causes of historical change. Why does so much history tend to concentrate on great discontinuities in the past, and how far have major changes been brought about by individual leaders? From there, we move on to examine the proper political, geographical and temporal focus of history. Many historians choose to concentrate on the nation state, though some have preferred to focus on the locality – or maybe the wider world. And should 'history' have a short, precisely defined temporal focus, or a longer *durée*? A month later (Seminar 4), the spotlight falls on the question of how far history can be said to repeat itself and, more generally, what kind of 'lessons' (if any) we can learn from the past. What about the 'ifs' of history? Could the past have been different if, for example, Wellington had lost the Battle of Waterloo or there had been no Hitler? In the fifth seminar, we examine the historical role of religion. Has religion, with its sometimes charismatic leaders and powerful ideals, provided a fundamental motivating force in history – in the Crusades, for example, or the Thirty Years' War or British Civil Wars? Or has it primarily reflected deeper socioeconomic trends and priorities?

In the sixth and final seminar, we will attempt to look at 'the future of the past' as we ask our panellists to travel forwards through time and imagine themselves looking back, half a century hence, on those of us here and now. What will future historians consider we have over-emphasised or under-emphasised as they examine the first decade or two of the new millennium and come to judge the ways you and I currently try to look back at earlier times? What impact will new digital technologies have on how the past is regarded? More generally, what new historiographical 'turn' should we be anticipating? Maybe the IHR could re-run this series of seminars a decade or two hence so we can all find out!

IHR Website

A Promised Land by Barack Obama

Volume 1 of the former US President's Memoir.

Reviews in History, February 2021.

'We are the Moses generation.' Dr Otis Moss, veteran of the civil rights movement, friend of Martin Luther King and former adviser to Jimmy Carter was addressing reassuring words to the latest aspirant for the presidency, the young Barack Obama. 'We marched, we sat in, we went to jail … We got us out of Egypt, you could say.' But, added the Rev Moss, we could only travel so far. 'You, Barack, are part of the Joshua generation ... ultimately it will be up to you, with God's help, to build on what we've done, and lead our people and this country out of the wilderness' (p. 122). In *A Promised Land* (Penguin Random House, 2020), Obama describes in intimate and often touching detail his attempts to lead the American people, Joshua-like, into the great national homeland it had always aspired to become, the very embodiment of life, liberty, and the pursuit of happiness.

Obama was elected US President for two four-year terms, from 2008–2016, handing over courteously to Donald Trump on the latter's inauguration day, 20 January 2017. Shortly afterwards, drained after eight years at the helm – and all the more so by 'the unexpected results of an election in which someone diametrically opposed to everything we stood for had been chosen as my successor' (p. xiii) – Obama settled down to work on this, the first of what is intended to be a two-volume memoir. It is a detailed account of Obama's political life, from his early decision to run for local office (and then the US Senate) in Illinois, through to his campaigning for the US presidency and his first two-and-a-half years in the White House. The present volume concludes after the execution of Osama bin Laden in May 2011. There is clearly a long way to go in Volume 2, on which Obama is presumably working right now, his former Vice President Joe Biden having taken over the top spot from Trump.

As in his previous books, Obama is a highly engaging writer. In 1995, when in his mid-thirties (and considering running for a seat in the Illinois Senate), Obama published a basic autobiography, or at least a memoir of his youth, which he entitled *Dreams from My Father: A Story of Race and Inheritance*. Born in 1961 in Honolulu (two years after Hawaii had achieved US statehood), Barack never really knew his Kenyan-born father, as his parents divorced when he was a small child. But his highly independent-minded American mother, Ann Dunham (originally from Kansas) had a profound and beneficial impact on the lad. After her divorce, Ann – 'forever the architect of her own destiny' (p. 26) – married a young man from Indonesia and, when Barack was six, the family moved to Jakarta. At age ten Barack was back in Hawaii, where he attended high school, then went to live for the first time in mainland America, where he enrolled at Occidental College in Los Angeles for a couple of years, going on to Columbia University in New York, where he majored in political science. Barack's next move was to Chicago, where he undertook community work on Chicago's South Side (and made an emotionally-charged visit to Kenya to visit some of his relatives on his father's side). Then, from Chicago to Harvard Law School, where he was the first black person to be president of the *Harvard Law Review*, after which he returned to Chicago, where in 1992 he married Michelle Robinson with whom he went on to have two daughters, Malia and Sasha. Obama became a civil rights attorney and an academic, teaching constitutional law at the University of Chicago Law School while also, in 1997, becoming a Democratic member of the Illinois Senate, commuting back and forth to the state capital, Springfield.

Ambitious for further advancement, Obama ran unsuccessfully for the US Congress in 2000, while retaining both his academic and state senatorial posts until 2004 when, having been the hugely impressive keynote speaker at the Democratic National Convention, he went on to be elected a member of the US Senate. In his DNC speech, Obama stressed the importance of having 'the audacity to hope', a phrase that had first caught his attention from a sermon he had heard in church, and which led to the title of his next book, *The Audacity of Hope*. Published in October 2006, this contained a series of essays about Senator Obama's political views and values, his all-embracing and ultimately optimistic attitudes towards race, religious faith and family, the US Constitution, and the wider world. *The Audacity of Hope* proved an instant bestseller and, in early February 2007, Obama announced his candidacy for the US Presidency. In the elections of November 2008, Obama won the presidency and the Democrats won a majority of seats in both Houses of Congress.

A Promised Land is richly infused with details of Obama's personal background. Barack's 'mom', for example, is a frequent presence, especially in the earlier sections of the new book. When she is diagnosed with uterine cancer, Barack invites her to come and live with, or near, his home in Chicago. But Mom says no: she's happy to stay where she is in Hawaii under the eye of her ageing mother 'Toot' and Barack's half-sister Maya. Maya keeps in touch with Barack, reporting on their mother's gradual decline. But when she calls to tell him that Mother has died, his sadness is intensified by a sense of shame that he was not there at her bedside. Again and again, such as when Obama is struggling to get his healthcare programme passed by Congress, he thinks back to his 'mom' and, praying and hoping he won't let her down on a project he knows she would have approved of, weeps a little. As for 'Toot' (short for Tutu, or Grandma in Hawaiian), she lived on until late 2008 and, just a few days before the all-important presidential election, Obama made a thirty-six-hour trip to Hawaii to say goodbye to her. Toot died shortly afterwards and at his final campaign rally Barack spoke about his granny: how she had grown up during the Depression and worked on an assembly line while 'Gramps' was away during the war. 'She was one of those quiet heroes that we have all across America,' he told his audience (p. 199). 'And in this crowd,' he continued, 'there are a lot of quiet heroes like that' – parents and grandparents, he said, who, working hard all their lives, have the satisfaction of seeing that their children, grandchildren, and maybe their great-grandchildren live a better life than they did. 'That's what America is about,' Obama concluded. 'That's what we're fighting for.' Next day, he was elected President.

A Promised Land contains substantial sections on the Obama administration's efforts to confront and reverse the financial crisis that broke out in 2008. The housing market was in nosedive when he became President, while US troops continued to be heavily involved in the ongoing wars in Iraq and Afghanistan. Meanwhile, Obama had promised voters that, once in power, he would create a healthcare policy from which all could benefit and also, in time, effect an American-led global agreement whereby to tackle and solve the problem of climate change. To all these projects Obama gives detailed attention, much of it devoted not only to the complex issues involved but also to the often crude partisanship of his opponents in what he senses is becoming an increasingly divided and destructive political world. Under these circumstances, how far can he, as

President, fulfil all the promises and expectations with which he had come to power? When he heard he had won the Nobel Peace Prize in October 2009, his initial reaction was one of somewhat embarrassed surprise. With the ongoing conflict in Afghanistan, he knew he might soon find himself pressed to commit more soldiers to war rather than to usher in the new era of peace for which he yearned, and for which he was being rewarded.

In the course of a highly absorbing, almost novelistic, but arguably overlong book, we are introduced to a large and varied cast. Some are well-known public figures such as Hillary (Clinton), Nancy (Pelosi), Joe (Vice-President Biden), Mitch (McConnell) and Ted (Kennedy). In addition, we encounter advisers like David Axelrod ('Axe') and Jon Favreau ('Favs') and a host of other aides, friends and political colleagues, and adversaries, all of whom we gradually get to know by their first names and nicknames. Typically, when introducing someone new, Obama tells us not only the public role the person performs but also something about the personality concerned, what he or she looks like, how they act and are regarded. Rahm Emanuel, Obama's first Chief of Staff for example, the 'enfant terrible of the Clinton administration', was '(s)hort, trim, darkly handsome, hugely ambitious and manically driven. Rahm was smarter than most of his colleagues in Congress and not known for hiding it' (p. 209). Carol Browner, Obama's 'climate czar', was '(t)all and willowy, with an endearing mix of nervous energy and can-do enthusiasm' (p. 490) while Senator Lindsey Graham was '(s)hort in stature, with a puggish face and a gentle southern drawl that in an instant could flip from warming to menacing' (p. 505). Obama, while fundamentally opposed to almost everything his predecessor George W Bush had stood for, found Bush and his wife personally kind and courteous when they showed the Obamas over the White House prior to the presidential handover. 'I promised myself that when the time came, I would treat my successor that same way' Obama writes (p. 207).

Throughout the book, Obama links the public and the personal. Whether it's his mom or his granny, Michelle or the girls, or the professional friends and colleagues with whom he becomes close (or opposes), the writing is packed with character and personality – his own not least. He is forever wondering about his motivation and his capabilities, especially when considering running for office. From the outset Michelle was sceptical, discouraging even, asking her highly sensitive husband why he would want to undertake the risks involved in any political campaign. In order to achieve what, she'd ask, adding sardonically that he must imagine he's got some magic beans in his pocket and that he'd climb up the resulting beanstalk, kill the giant in the sky and bring down a goose that will lay golden eggs (p. 45). She was equally sceptical when they discussed the possibility of Barack running for the presidency. Late one night, soon after he had announced his candidacy, Barack found his brain in overdrive and his nerves jangled. Michelle, the 'early bird' in the family, was asleep beside him and Barack crept downstairs and poured himself a drink. 'My deepest fear,' he began to feel, 'came from the realization that I could win' (pp. 74–5).

Once in office, Obama's highly trained intelligence was no doubt a bonus. He clearly understood all the documents that arrived on his desk, insisting he was thoroughly briefed regarding every issue, staff meeting, Congressional bill, or foreign trip coming up in the diary. Unlike many US Presidents before (and since!) Obama liked to draft, often by pen, the basic text of all the major speeches he was due to deliver. He had always read very widely, from Tocqueville, Whitman and Thoreau to Russian novels, the works of Toni Morrison and John le Carré, and histories of the US Civil War, the Victorian era, and the fall of the Roman Empire. At a meeting with Prime Minister Maliki of Iraq, Obama had discussed basic ideas of democracy, including how far to accommodate the needs and views of opponents. Afterwards he notes in passing that Maliki clearly hadn't read the *Federalist Paper* No. 10, one of the great founding documents in American history, in which James Madison, contemplating the potential US Constitution, had considered the political implications – and dangers – of a democracy in which all decisions arose simply from the fact of everyone having a vote.

But perhaps Obama's intellectuality was also, in some ways, a disadvantage. Describing himself as a 'flawed, often uncertain person' (p. 196), he admits that, when asked a question, he would often offer 'circuitous and ponderous answers, my mind instinctively breaking up every issue into a pile of components and subcomponents ... If every argument had two sides, I usually came up with four!' (p. 83). When on the campaign trail, Axe told him repeatedly that questions on TV shows were not there to be answered. 'Isn't that the point?' Obama would reply. 'No Barack, that is *not* the point,' said the assertive but ever-amiable Axe, explaining that, half the time, the moderator's job was to trip you up and Obama's was to say a few words to make it seem he had answered the question and then move on to what he really wanted to talk about (pp. 88–9).

In some ways, *A Promised Land* reads like a latter-day *War and Peace*. As with Tolstoy (whose work Obama mentions during a description of his first official visit to Russia), historical references and legacies abound. He reminds us how the West Wing of the White House was constructed during the presidency of Teddy Roosevelt, and we read in some detail of Franklin D Roosevelt and the New Deal. When Obama is sworn in as President, the Bible he uses is the one used by Abraham Lincoln at his inauguration, and he relishes the desk in the Oval office that was presented to the United States in 1880 by Queen Victoria, ornately carved from the hull of a British ship that an American whaling crew helped salvage after a seaborne catastrophe. Like Tolstoy, Obama employs a wide and varied vocabulary, his text frequently enriched and embellished with metaphor, dialogue, and, when appropriate, relatively unusual words such as tamp, lede and passel (as well as others you will doubtless know but which I would not wish to use in an essay addressed to a respectable IHR readership!). Sometimes Obama fails to remind us clearly of exactly what or whom or when he is writing about, and the text can be annoyingly lacking in precise dates. The reader must also get used to a host of initials and references, not always explained to the uninitiated. Some, such as the FBI, the CIA, ASEAN and the GOP, you will doubtless already be familiar with, as you will possibly be with the DREAM Act, START, AARP and TARP. But remember that what came to be called 'Obamacare' was the Affordable Care Act (ACA), and be prepared to familiarise yourself with COIN (Counter Insurgency), SWAT (the Special Weapons and Tactics unit detailed to protect the President) and the PDB, the President's Daily Brief, the top-secret intelligence package delivered to the President each morning (which Michelle called Barack's 'Death, Destruction and Horrible Things' book). But don't give up; one of the book's many strengths is a lengthy and minutely detailed index. And it is also richly and beautifully illustrated with photos, public and private, including a lovely snap of Obama walking along a corridor of the White House with his beloved little dog 'Bo'.

The more immersed I became in the minutiae of this memoir, the more I wondered whether Barack Obama was, perhaps, too intelligent, too well-read, too aware of all sides to all arguments to be able to cut through the sometimes crude politics of an increasingly divided, impatient America, to be able to lead it as he had had the audacity to hope. Highly equipped with the ability both to campaign and to govern, he would cry out confidently to his admirers during the run-up to becoming President, 'Yes, we can!'. But sadly, as his new book makes clear, he sometimes couldn't. From his earliest years in the White House, Obama evidently confronted widespread and fundamental antipathy towards, for example, his idea of pump-priming a failing economy, Keynes style; closing Guantanamo; establishing a nationwide system of healthcare; or setting up a global agreement to reduce the dangers of climate change. This was not the American way, his opponents would argue. As some of the more antagonistic cried out, Obama was essentially an alien to the American Dream, as the USA became increasingly divided between a traditional 'left' and an increasingly vociferous and angry 'right'. He was foreign-born (a lie promoted by Donald Trump), black-skinned, and trying to impose centrist, socialistic rule upon a nation governed since its foundation by a federal system subject to regular state and national elections. Somehow, Obama maintained his dignity, his intelligent affability, and his political dream. And, as his first two years in the White House stretched eventually to eight, his achievements, though less than he had hoped, were nonetheless impressive. If many of the fundamental aims and ambitions of the Joshua generation remained and remain unfulfilled, I greatly look forward to reading about Obama's further advances towards the promised land when he has completed Volume 2.

IHR BLOGS, 2022/23

Below are a series of four essays, all raising and illustrating provocative issues about how we regard and memorialise what we think of as 'history'. The first three blogs were issued monthly on the IHR Website: in May, June and July 2022.

1. Leaning Tower of Pisa

(May 2022)

We all seek what we think of as 'historical authenticity'. In which case, shouldn't the famous Tower of Pisa be restored to its original perpendicular form? Or allowed to collapse with the passage of time? The one thing that isn't historically authentic, surely, is to use modern technology to retain its (otherwise temporary) leaning position.

Italy is crammed with historic works of art in need of restoration. Like the figures on a rotating weathervane, one great building or gallery pops out for all to see just as another goes into hiding for a while. In the 1990s, as tourists in the Vatican's Sistine Chapel marvelled at the renewed brightness of Michelangelo's ceiling, visitors to Pisa were in for a letdown. The Leaning Tower, which all came to see and perhaps had hoped to climb, was out of bounds, encased in scaffolding – with copious explanations about how here, in the *Piazza dei Miracoli*, the latest miracles of modern science would finally freeze the tower's historic tilt. The issue was not so much the restoration of a fading or eroding work of art dating from long ago. If the proposed solutions here in Pisa were new, the problem was not.

The origins of the tower go back to the 12th century, when Pisa's city fathers decided to celebrate the power and spiritual authority of their state with the erection of a superb marble cathedral and baptistery, topped off by a great campanile or bell tower. An adjacent cemetery, the marble-encased *Camposanto*, would complete the project. Here would be a sanctified spot of incomparable beauty where all the rites of passage – baptism, marriage, death, and burial – would be guaranteed appropriate care, each heralded by the pealing of bells from Pisa's great campanile.

Things didn't quite work out that way. The cathedral, baptistery, and subsequently the *Camposanto* were completed as planned. But not the cylindrical tower. Soon after it began to take shape, it started to tilt. Those responsible for its construction came to realise not only that the alluvial terrain on which it and the adjacent buildings rested was soft and unstable,

Leaning Tower of Pisa in the 1890s. *Tower of Pisa: kicking it over and holding it up.*

but that that the great, hollow weight of the emerging tower rendered it particularly prone to buckling and possible collapse. Work was repeatedly suspended as successive generations of engineers tried to work out whether it was possible to stabilise their precarious structure; indeed, whether the bell-tower would be viable at all. For well over a century, it had no belfry (and therefore no function) and altogether it took nearly 200 years before the entire building was completed. By now, the late 14th century, Pisa had suffered a succession of military, political, and economic downturns, rendering it far from the proud and powerful city state its great *Piazza* had originally been intended to celebrate. Thus, the great campanile, conceived in an era of triumph, was finally born into one of acute anxiety. The painful but precise symbolism of Pisa's increasingly tilting tower was not lost on people at the time.

From that day to this, the big question has been how to render the Leaning Tower as safe and stable as possible. Of course, if safety were the only concern, the best thing to have done at various stages in Pisa's history would have been to demolish the tower, or perhaps to rope off the entire area and leave the tower to collapse in its own good time – thus becoming an authentic historic ruin, not unlike much of the Roman Forum. Another kind of historical authenticity might have been achieved if efforts had been made to re-straighten the tower, thereby rendering it as close as possible to the perpendicular structure originally planned. Some have argued that the tower should simply be anchored more deeply, encased and corseted, or held in position by a series of stakes, guy ropes and wires in a state of permanently enclosed suspense. Suggestions have ranged from the highly practical to the unimaginably bizarre. The only ones to have been seriously entertained have been those aimed at maintaining and stabilising the historic tower, as it is and where it is,* tilt and all, so that future generations could continue to experience a remarkable inheritance from the past. But how?

The issue was never simply one of engineering; security concerns jostled with religious, aesthetic and financial considerations. And, all the while, the intertwining of myth and history added a patina of inviolability to Pisa's flawed masterpiece. Pisans grew to love their leaning tower, its all too evident disablement providing an integral part of its attraction – not only for Pisans, indeed, but to visitors from across Europe and the wider world. Like the Pyramids or the Sphinx, the tower attracted an accretion of legends as an old boat gathers barnacles. From its earliest years, its tilt was popularly attributed to various malign forces: a nefarious builder wreaking revenge on the city fathers for his poor wages, or one or other of Pisa's traditional enemies – the Genoese, Florentines or Saracens. Perhaps it was God's punishment against the Pisans for their vanity and presumption, just as he had punished the builders of the Tower of Babel. Or, *par contra*, maybe the fact that the tower didn't actually fall was a sign of divine grace and beneficence. The mythmaking did not stop there. Galileo is said to have climbed the tower in around 1590 with two cannon balls (or stones) of different weights and dropped them simultaneously in order to prove his point that the velocity of a falling object is unrelated to its mass.

Over the next couple of centuries, as travel opportunities expanded, word of Pisa's freakish tower spread among young men embarking upon the Grand Tour. To Shelley and his friends (including Byron and Leigh Hunt) Pisa came to be something of a headquarters, the city – especially its stooping tower – endowed with rich, romantic associations normally reserved for the ruined residues of ancient Greece and Rome. By the later 19th century, the Tower of Pisa was firmly on the international tourist trail,

---

* When Venice's historic opera house, La Fenice, was burned down in 1996, all agreed it should be rebuilt 'com'era, dov'era': as it was, where it was.

a Mecca for lovers of art and history – and a favoured last stop for lovers of a different kind: the rejected, scorned, and star-crossed, set on suicide.

Throughout much of its history, few seem to have believed the tower would actually fall. It had, after all, survived since early Renaissance times and, for long periods, its angle of tilt had scarcely shifted. Then, in 1902, a spectacular event forced everyone to think again: the venerable campanile of St Mark's, Venice, developed a fissure and collapsed. One of the most famous landmarks in Italy, revered by generations of visitors, was no more (it was later reconstructed a safe distance from the church). If this could happen in Venice, where the fallen building had been sound and upright, but merely old, something similar could surely occur in Pisa. More commissions were set up, a whole string of them by Mussolini in the 1920s and early 1930s. Measurements were taken, wind speeds monitored, earth drained, holes drilled, cement injected, ballast added, soil extracted and counterweights installed on the side opposite the lean – and still the Tower tilted, permanently and self-evidently close to catastrophe.

Soon, the tower faced a novel risk. As Allied forces pressed their way up the Italian peninsula in 1944, some historic treasures were inevitably damaged or destroyed. At Montecassino, where German troops were believed to be holed up, the Allies decided there was no alternative but to bombard the great Benedictine monastery. The Pisan *Piazza dei Miracoli* was soon faced with the possibility of a similar fate. In the event, the Tower was reprieved (though the *Camposanto* and the priceless art works it contained were firebombed, while much of the town south of the Arno was severely damaged).

After the war, Pisa's tower soon regained its status as one of the most familiar buildings in the world, comparable in fame and instant recognisability to the Pyramids, the Taj Mahal and the Eiffel Tower. Then, in 1989 in Pavia, north of Pisa, a late medieval bell tower suddenly collapsed, killing four bystanders. The shockwaves emanating from Pavia were felt most intensely in Pisa and, in January 1990, the Leaning Tower was closed to the public and a new commission appointed. Many Pisans, denied their city's most marketable product, watched with understandable cynicism as the latest experts tackled the city's oldest problem. Their cynicism grew when, in 1995, the tower suddenly lurched even closer to collapse, partly in response (it seemed) to the alleviative measures being taken. A year later the commission was dismissed. But a year after that, in 1997, an earthquake wrought huge destruction to another of Italy's most revered locations, Assisi. Hastily, the Pisa commission was reconvened. The Leaning Tower of Pisa simply had to be saved – and quickly.

A new chapter was added to the 800-year-old story when, in 2001, eleven years after the tower was closed and after the expenditure of $25 million, it was finally pronounced safe and reopened the public. Once again, tourists thronged to Pisa and were permitted to ascend the 290-odd stairs of the tilting tower – in parties of no more than thirty at a time. The restoration work apparently pulled the tower's inclination back from the brink of collapse by forty-four centimetres, but it didn't feel like it as visitors climbed their way gingerly up the ancient spiral staircase. It was not unlike climbing up from deck to deck aboard a ship in rough seas – except that the Pisa tower offered no railings or ropes to hold onto. This was not a walk for the weary, the faint of heart, or those prone to vertigo. Atop the belfry, for those who had managed this giddy summit, was a lookout post that protruded some four-and-a-half feet beyond the base of the tower: a crazy crow's nest caught severely off-centre in a storm-tossed yet frozen ocean. From here, if your stomach could take it, was a wonderful view of the cathedral and the surrounding city and countryside. A few moments of calm and you were off again on the similarly vertiginous descent – probably having to move aside to make way for another party on their way up. Nowhere else did the idea of walking 'in the footsteps of history' resonate quite so meaningfully.

Why have people flocked to the Leaning Tower of Pisa? The city is replete with history. It contains a famous university, is the birthplace of Galileo, and houses many historic and religious buildings, among them a church along the banks of the Arno whose treasures include a reliquary supposedly containing a thorn from the True Cross. The handsome *Piazza dei Cavalieri* boasts a palace that was richly embellished by Vasari in the 16th century for the Medici family and turned by Napoleon into a university college in the early 19th. But it is to the *Piazza dei Miracoli* that every visitor has turned, a monumental testimony to an earlier, rich, confident age. Most visitors enter the superb cathedral and baptistery, savouring the work of Nicola and Giovanni Pisano, and the adjacent museums packed with artistic and historic treasures. But above all, of course, they come to the Leaning Tower. The tower, as we have seen, brings together an unusually wide range of concerns: historical, spiritual, aesthetic, financial, political, and scientific.

Deeper psychological imperatives seem to be involved, too. Risk and danger clearly have their enticements. Just as part of the attraction of bungee jumping or whitewater rafting or watching a bullfight, a Formula One race or high-wire act is the unspoken awareness that the worst might occur but probably won't, the irresistible point about the Leaning Tower of Pisa is the thought that it (or you) might just possibly fall. Nobody would bother about the white-knuckle rides at fairgrounds if all sense of danger were removed. In much the same way, Pisa's tower would lose its special appeal if straightened. Italy is full of medieval and Renaissance towers you can climb. But none is as famous as Pisa's, for there is something deeply unnerving about a tower that is leaning so precariously, an unnerving yet ultimately reassuring sense of natural law successfully defied.

What Pisa offers is a kind of freak show. This is what people come to see, to be photographed against, to climb. This is the image the souvenir stalls sell in their superabundance: Leaning Tower books, aprons and ashtrays, tilting coffee mugs and postcards. But look a little closer and another souvenir, just this side of decency, keeps recurring: little models of naked women embracing phallic-looking leaning towers. It would seem that, for some, in addition to its many other enticements, Pisa's celebrated erection does more than merely tilt or lean.

2. **Telling History Backwards**

(June 2022)

In the second of my IHR blogs examining provocative issues about how we regard and memorialise what we think of as 'history', I suggested that instead of starting at the beginning of the story and going forwards we might start in the present and unravel the story backwards.

Why do history books begin at the beginning and end at the end? Not all of them, of course. Some historians combine straightforward chronology with theme, while others feature the life and times of a particular community or group of people. Others, like screenwriters or playwrights, incorporate flashbacks (or flashforwards) into an otherwise chronological narrative. But few serious historians dispense entirely with chronology. The sequential passage of time gives us a sense of our own place in the wider scheme of things, anchoring us firmly in the otherwise unnavigable waters of past, present, and future. If we lose our sense of time, whether through dreams, drugs, or dementia, we become helplessly disoriented.

I would like to suggest, however, at least as an experiment, that we stand traditional views of chronology on their head so that, instead of starting at the beginning of the story and going forwards, we start at the end and unravel the story backwards (as in the 2002 film *Irreversible*, or Pinter's *Betrayal* or Martin Amis's experimental novel *Time's Arrow*). This, after all, corresponds in some ways to how we situate ourselves in history. If I reflect on current events, whether in my own life or in the wider public sphere, I can develop a more informed view about how things got to be the way they are by looking backwards rather than focusing on where they might be leading. Looking ahead means guesswork, but looking back can be clarifying. And this was presumably just as true for our predecessors as they tried to make sense of their own lives. If, therefore, we want to know what it was like living in earlier times, we should perhaps turn around and face not 'what came next' but 'what came before'. Think of those vast family trees that have become popular. These are essentially of two kinds. Some start with an individual – a famous king or emperor, say – and show the multiplication of his progeny, and then of theirs, moving forwards through the centuries. Others begin at the end, with an individual (you or me perhaps), and show an efflorescence of ancestors above and before us.

I see no reason why history should not be written in either of these ways. And since it is less often done, let's consider the case for starting in the present, then fanning out backwards into the past. Right now, I'm at home in my office on a warm spring evening typing this article on my computer before emailing it off to the IHR. This innocent little sentence contains a good half-dozen themes, any of which might mark the end point of a rich historical inquiry. Take that computer: what it does, where it comes from, how it was assembled and marketed. How long have I had it, and what came before it? Do you remember 'electronic' typewriters, and before them ordinary old Olivettis and Xerox copiers or, earlier still, carbon paper, fountain pens, bottles of Stephens ink and blotting paper? Or quills? What did our parents and grandparents write with – and on – when they were young? How were their messages delivered, and responded to? And *their* parents? In no time, you find yourself deep into the historical development of mass literacy.

And who am I that am writing this article? The short-order House-that-Jack-built answer is that I am the author of a number of books and that I worked as a BBC producer for many years. I was recruited into BBC Radio in the late 1960s when they sought someone who knew American history and politics, subjects I was teaching at the University of Sussex at the time, having studied them as a post-graduate student at Cornell during the Kennedy years.

When I first crossed the Atlantic in the summer of '61, I travelled by ship, with all my valuables locked away in a trunk. My parents waved me goodbye at Southampton docks. I was off to America, a romantic and optimistic New World led by a handsome and intelligent young man who wrote books, had been a war hero and had a glamorous wife and family. There was an energising impatience to the Kennedy entourage as the President, succeeding the aged Eisenhower, talked of a 'New Frontier' and of 'getting this country moving again.' Eisenhower was revered for his war record, but widely regarded (at least among young political scientists at Ivy League universities) as a lacklustre leader in peacetime. Yet it was during his administration that the US Supreme Court outlawed 'separate but equal' education for black and white children in the South – an historical landmark.

Not just education, but housing and health care, too, separated the races in the states of the Old Confederacy. At bus stations there were separate waiting rooms and drinking fountains. 'Negroes' routinely sat at the back of the bus, a convention famously challenged when the young Martin Luther King organised a bus boycott in Montgomery, Alabama,

Daniel presenting a lecture in 2004.

Daniel at the typewriter, circa 1965.   *Daniel the soldier, 1944.*

after a black woman, Rosa Parks, courageously sat at the front, causing outrage among local whites. When I first travelled through the South, these conventions still prevailed, widely accepted on both sides of the racial divide. But they were palpably weakening. Blacks, having recently fought and died in a world war against fascism and racism, returned to question traditional hometown conventions. During the war, blacks had served in the US Army in about the proportion (roughly 9 per cent) that their numbers warranted. Almost a third of them were northerners whose families had come up from the southern states to escape the 'Jim Crow' laws, and had settled in New York, Boston, Philadelphia, Detroit and Chicago, a migration that helped nurture the jazz boom and the Harlem Renaissance of the inter-war years.

Many of these new northerners encountered severe economic conditions and *de facto* racism. But things were arguably even harder in the South during the Great Depression – not just for 'Negro' families, but for whites too. Many landed estates and farms were reduced to dust by drought and over-farming. John Steinbeck, in *The Grapes of Wrath*, paints a poignant picture of a family of 'Okies' who, reduced to penury with their home foreclosed, pack all they have on a van and move west to California, the 'Golden State'. The Joad family, and thousands like them, depended for finance on banks that, far from extending their loans, were suddenly calling them in. Northern finance had let down southern agriculture precipitately – or so it seemed to embittered dust bowl farmers like the Joads. Of course, the bankers themselves were in desperate straits. Yet many Southern farmers and plantation owners regarded their fate as a product of Yankee vindictiveness – a tradition that old-timers traced back to the period of 'Reconstruction' when twenty years of selfish Northern triumphalism rubbed the nose of defeated Dixie in the dust. 'Wouldn't have happened if Abe Lincoln had lived,' they believed, a judgement many historians endorsed.

So, in brief, we've sketched a history here that begins with me lecturing in recent times and ends (arbitrarily) with events precipitated by the Confederate surrender at Appomattox in 1865 – an example of a single historical thread that might emerge with a story told backwards rather than forwards. The actual subject matter, of course, is something the historian decides; it isn't dictated by the methodology. From the same starting point, I could as well have moved backwards to my own birth in London on November 4, 1938 – a few days before *Kristallnacht*, when the Nazis burned and destroyed Jewish synagogues, shops, and private premises throughout Germany. My parents were Jewish, and I've long wondered how my mother must have felt reading of these horrors with a new-born Jewish infant in her arms. She was twenty-three. People married and reproduced younger in those days, one interesting thread for backward pursuit. And while my father and mother and three of my grandparents were born in England, their families had roots in the *shtetls* of Tsarist Russia and Eastern Europe…

You get the drift. Any of the themes I've touched on above could be expanded – with the necessary research – into a serious historical study: of the development of mass literacy, of transport, broadcasting, British or American academic life, Anglo-Jewry, Nazism, American race relations, Tsarist Russia, British immigration policy. And I haven't even mentioned where I live, with whom, the kinds of homes I have lived in or the changes in my diet, clothing, or speech styles over the years. Start anywhere, and you can tell an illuminating story working backwards from effects to causes

***

To be sure, telling history backwards is not free of problems. Just as conventional histories can be tedious, recounting one damn thing after another, so an unimaginative history moving backwards is equally dull if every 'Z' leads to 'Y', then inexorably to 'X'. There are further hazards. A few lines back I suggested working backwards from effects to causes. That notion is a minefield. Conventional historians often seem to confuse sequence with cause. Thus we read that Henry VIII's infatuation with Ann Boleyn 'led to' the Reformation, while the excesses of the French *ancien régime* 'foreshadowed' the French Revolution. 'Foreshadowing' and 'leading to' are not the same as 'causing'. For the historian telling the story backwards, the problem of apparent causality is acute: not everything is a direct result of the item that chronologically preceded it. And where does one end a history told backwards? With Adam and Eve?

But if there are problems with 'counter-chronological' history, there are also benefits. Especially, perhaps, for teachers. Rather than plunge bewildered students into the origins of the American Constitution or the *arcanae* of Victorian politics, I'd ask mine what they'd had for breakfast, what they were wearing, how they'd travelled to the classroom, etc. – and then push the questioning back, factor by factor, until we got into details of earlier industrial, economic, social, and political history. I did the same in the BBC in the late 1990s. When producing my Radio 4 series about previous 'ends of centuries' (see above, p. 55), I decided to broadcast the programmes backwards, starting with the 1890s, followed a week later with the 1790s and so on until we reached the final programme, that on the 1390s. More listeners would tune in, I thought, if we began with Queen Victoria rather than Richard II. 'If you want to know how things came to be like that,' each week's closing announcement said in effect, 'tune in next time!'.

This approach to the past ties in with the current interest in genealogy and family trees. Try drafting your own family history backwards (as in the TV series *Who Do You Think You Are?*), starting with yourself as the initial focus. The text will gradually become augmented by material garnered from interviews with parents and older relatives, until individual memory merges with an ever-widening back-history.

Or consider the 'micro' studies of particular people or communities in which historians have attempted to approach their data purely in its own terms. Thus, Le Roy Ladurie described life in a medieval Provençal town, Natalie Zemon Davis a returning French soldier who proved to be an impostor, Carlo Ginzburg a miller in a small Friuli town and Robert Darnton a bunch of French apprentices massacring local cats. Each of these historians, like an anthropologist, drew wider lessons and implications from otherwise unremarkable data. None claimed that the story they told led to anything of subsequent historical significance. To the traditional historian telling a conventionally chronological history of France or Italy, therefore, *Montaillou*, *Martin Guerre*, or *The Great Cat Massacre* would be of little account. But if history were told backwards, such stories might emerge more prominently. And it is important that they should. For they help 'situate' the specific and apparently inconsequential – that is to say, most of life! – as part of legitimate historical discourse.

In an age when people are said to live in a permanent present, telling history backwards can help to hook those not otherwise inclined to think about the continuities between past and present. As a device, it allows the historian, and the reader, to start with the familiar before moving on (backwards) to the less familiar and the general. By telling history 'backwards', therefore, we may find we can reinstate more of the specific and apparently inconsequential from the past. If so, we will greatly enrich our understanding of the present – surely, one of the fundamental goals of the study of history.

3. **Should we concrete over 'dark tourist' monuments?**

(July 2022)

Is there a danger that a powerful historical memorial (and place of pilgrimage) like Auschwitz might, with time, morph into a monument to a distant, forgotten past and, eventually, become just another historical museum?

I was born in London the year before the war broke out, and learned as a child that I was living through 'history'. My father helped put out the fires as the city was 'blitzkrieged' and he was later an anti-aircraft gunner on the coast. My mother took me into the garden to watch our chaps flying out on their bombing missions and then, in the evening, returning with a sad gap or two in their formations. I sat next to her as she listened to the news on the wireless, rejoiced when we heard of the death of Hitler, and danced around the street bonfire on what I learned to call 'VE Night'. As Churchill growled his uplifting messages over 'the BBC', everyone knew that history was being made.

History, or what we regard as 'history', keeps shifting with the passage of time, reinterpreted through the perspectives of the ever-changing present.

Tourists entering Auschwitz.

Thus, the Japanese have been rewriting school history books (particularly the sections about the Second World War), and I recall being told that they were doing something of the same in Ukraine and Poland as they attempted to distance themselves from Russia. Did the British Empire help educate millions around the world into the benefits of democracy or was it, as many have increasingly insisted, primarily a form of ruthless (and racist) commercial exploitation? How do you currently regard – and label – the mass murder of Armenian Turks over a century ago? In Israel, intellectual life has been much exercised in recent years over new interpretations of the evacuation (expulsion?) of Arabs from Palestine in 1947/8.

If these examples are contentious, consider the questions raised by a site such as Auschwitz and nearby Birkenau. Auschwitz is a monument, a museum and a memorial, as well as being a 'site of historical interest'. As a museum, it has to cater for large visitor numbers and this means providing such mundane facilities as car and coach parks, conference rooms, cafeterias, toilets, and retail outlets.

Many come to Auschwitz in a spirit of pilgrimage, perhaps to mourn the loss of parents or grandparents and to seek out information about their fate. But the neat streets and buildings they see on entering the camp, and the carefully displayed and labelled exhibits, can create an almost sanitised view of what once went on here. Buildings and barbed wire have, after all, required periodic renovation after exposure to decades of freezing Polish winters and, to that extent, are no longer 'original'. Some visitors do not at first realise that the mass murder occurred not here but a couple of kilometres away at Birkenau: a huge, empty, often windswept open-air site now containing little more than a few huts and a railway line – in its sheer bleakness all the more appalling to anyone with an ounce of imagination. All this raises profound questions about the relationship between present and past. Is there an element of conflict between the maintenance of Auschwitz-Birkenau as monument, a museum and a memorial? And is there (as some have suggested) a touch of almost ghoulish voyeurism in the growing popularity of what has come to be known as 'dark tourism'?

***

Some forty-odd years ago (in 1979) I was visiting Munich for the BBC and set off one morning for the nearby suburb of Dachau, site of one of the earliest Nazi concentration camps and by then a museum and memorial. While I was there a group of young German soldiers arrived for an educational visit and, after an initial briefing, they were invited to ask questions and express their views. 'I understand the importance of retaining the memory of the dreadful things the Nazis did,' said one earnest young man in his late teens. 'But the result is that we, who had nothing to do with the crimes they committed, continue to be labelled by the outside world almost as though we did.' He had a point, everybody agreed. But wasn't it right that places like Dachau (not to mention a mass murder camp like Auschwitz) should be preserved? Well, yes of course, someone else said. But why are we so selective about what we do and don't choose to memorialise from Germany's Nazi past? 'Here in Munich we have made a museum out of Dachau. But there is no plaque marking the Beer Hall where Hitler staged his notorious 1923 putsch.' Not, he hastened to add, to celebrate it; merely to mark it as a location of historical significance. Fair enough, piped up another young soldier. 'But if there *were* a plaque outside the Beer Hall – or the house in which Hitler lived when in Munich – the danger is that the neo-Nazis might leave flowers at these places and turn them into political shrines.' The debate, much of which I recorded, was vigorous, and I found it moving to see and hear the honest integrity with which this younger generation of Germans struggled to come to terms with the barbarous legacy of their recent predecessors.

I didn't leave Dachau to return to my hotel in Munich until well into the afternoon. I suddenly realised how hungry and thirsty I was, having had nothing to eat or drink since early morning. Somehow, the minor and temporary discomfort I felt seemed deeply appropriate. As I thought back over the day I had just experienced, I decided not to break my fast until dinner time that evening.

***

I have often wondered, looking back, whether there might there be a case, if only out of deference to the dead, for leaving the site of a Nazi concentration camp to disappear with the passage of time. Or even to build over it, perhaps creating a memorial park in the hope of creating a better world hereafter? I don't pretend to have easy answers to disturbing questions such as these. And I have been shaken to the core when contemplating them during visits to Auschwitz over the years, deeply conscious that the war and Holocaust occurred during my own lifetime, not so long ago. I pray that Auschwitz never becomes just another stop on the tourist trail.

But time is passing. When I began work some twenty-five years ago on my study of the cultural impact of the 'Hitler Emigrés', many of the most famous of them – the refugee writers, musicians, architects, film-makers, historians, publishers and the rest – were still alive and prepared to let me record lengthy interviews with them (many now in the sound archives of the Imperial War Museum).

Today, most of those I interviewed have passed on as the entire story moves out of 'memory' and gradually becomes 'history'. Most scholars studying the war nowadays have no personal memory of it; rather, it is coming to be regarded as a subject requiring cool and balanced research, like the study of, say, the Napoleonic Wars.

This is right and proper and not to be demeaned. I would not argue that everyone has to become a highly sophisticated quasi-professional historian. But a proper awareness of the passage of history is surely among the more important skills any responsible person should strive to acquire.

What new historiographical 'turn' should we be anticipating in the years to come? Already, many are probably more inclined to turn to the internet or iPlayer than to lengthy books; museums and heritage centres flourish as bookshops and publishers appear to falter. As the digital era takes increasing hold, how will people seek their historical fix?

4. Is it the Job of the Historian to Judge the Past?

(September 2023)

In August 2023 the IHR asked Senior Research Fellows if they would say something about what they had been reading over the summer break. I had been reviewing (among other things) a new book by Julian Jackson about Philippe Pétain: the French military leader widely known as the victor of the Battle of Verdun in World War I – and the man who collaborated with the Nazis in World War II as ruler of Vichy. Was Pétain a good guy or a bad guy? More profoundly, is it the job of the historian to judge the past?

Was Philippe Pétain a good guy or a bad guy? Pétain led the French Army to victory against the Germans in the Battle of Verdun in 1916, a decisive turning point in the First World War.

After the war the nation's heroic Maréchal, by then into his sixties and having seen up-close the suffering that warfare can impose, was determined to do all he could for the rest of his life to avoid, or at least minimise, any further such barbarity.

The Second World War broke out a generation later and in May 1940 German armies invaded France. In June, Pétain became head of the French government and signed an armistice with the occupying enemy. Northern France would be under the control of the Third Reich while much of the south, to be based in the spa town of Vichy, would nominally remain in French hands. The two regimes, it was agreed, would collaborate under what would be essentially German terms. In October, Hitler and Pétain met and were photographed shaking hands.

Julian Jackson, British born and Cambridge educated, is a leading historian of 20th-century France, much of his work focusing on the wars and depressions by which France was afflicted and the lives of pivotal figures such as Charles de Gaulle. And now Pétain. The new book is not a formal biography. Rather, a thoroughly researched and vividly narrated attempt to understand and assess a man alternately among the most admired and most abhorred in modern French history. And to do this, Jackson invites us to sit in on the trial, starting on 23 July 1945, at which the frail and elderly Maréchal was accused of treason.

Pétain was found guilty and sentenced to death. However, General de Gaulle, President of the Provisional French government, agreed to commute the sentence to life imprisonment and Pétain was incarcerated on the Île d'Yeu, a small island off the Brittany coast, where he died in

Pétain shaking hands with Hitler. (Alamy)

Pétain on trial. (Alamy)

1951, aged 95. Before the trial Pétain had proclaimed that, if no longer able to be his nation's sword, he sought to be its shield.

Was Pétain a true shield of the French people, a morally committed leader determined to do all he could to limit the suffering of his beloved compatriots? Was he wrong to sign an armistice with the Nazi invaders who, many believed at the time, would be the inevitable victors of the current war? Might his decision to collaborate with the enemy, if regarded by some as illegal, have at least been understood as 'legitimate' given the circumstances of the time?

To some degree Pétain had stood up to the Nazis, as Jackson reminds us. In May 1942 Pétain rejected the Nazi demand that Jews living under the Vichy regime wear a yellow star, and the following year, when the Germans ordered the denaturalization of all Jews in the 'Unoccupied Zone', Pétain refrained, knowing that this could lead to their mass arrest and deportation.

Might Pétain have been able to oppose the Nazis more effectively if only he had been a more forceful political leader? Might the fate of French Jews have been worse if Pétain had not collaborated with Nazis? At one point, Jackson touches on these 'what ifs', the kind of counterfactual issues some historians like to consider (see above, pp. 47 et seq). But more than that, the Pétain story raises fundamental questions about whether, how and to what extent we can, or even should, feel we can judge the past at all.

Consider not only Pétain but earlier controversial figures, similarly loved and hated, such as Oliver Cromwell, Jefferson Davis or Roger Casement. Can the British (or French) Empire, or the Catholic Church over the course of its history, be labelled as 'good' or 'bad'? What about historical artworks? Should a novel, once revered as 'great' but now regarded as 'racist' or 'sexist' (e.g. Mark Twain's *Huckleberry Finn*), be censored? Should we eschew the works of Handel since, after all, much of his income was derived from investments in the slave trade? What about paintings by that murderer Caravaggio or a molester of young girls like Gaugin, or the Nazi-commissioned films of Leni Riefenstahl or sculptures of Arno Breker? Was Lenin a leader who genuinely wished, if necessary through violent means, to bring to the people a more egalitarian, post-Revolutionary set of values? Or what of Abraham Lincoln, who helped retain the unity of his country and free the USA of slavery as a by-product of a four-year civil war that cost some two million lives? Should he, like Gorbachev, have reluctantly acknowledged the division of the country over which he ruled and gone into dignified retirement?

Then there was Winston Churchill, a recurrent figure in the Jackson book whose wartime Prime Ministership of Britain overlapped almost exactly with the period from Pétain's takeover as leader of the Vichy regime until his trial in July 1945. Churchill was a major figure in my

Image courtesy of the Churchill Archives Centre, Churchill College, Cambridge.

childhood. I was born the year before the outbreak of World War II and grew up knowing that 'we' won the war and that Churchill had in all probability saved my life. In 1959, while a student at Cambridge, I went to see Churchill, then nearly 85, deliver one of his last public speeches. By now a bent and somewhat flabby old man, he had come to Cambridge to dedicate the ground on which Churchill College was to be built.

When the ceremony was over, Churchill's car drove slowly past me. For a fleeting moment, those once fierce eyes looked out benignly into mine, and into those of a young German girl who was accompanying me. She and I waved back, and fancied that we had been present at possibly the final page in one of the most remarkable chapters of British history.

Later, I learned in some detail about how the younger Churchill had been a ruthless white racist, the very embodiment of an old-fashioned British imperialism which I, with my growing aspiration towards a cross-cultural internationalism, found utterly abhorrent.

***

Let me return to France, and that greatest, and most controversial of Pétain's predecessors, Napoleon. Was Napoleon primarily a ruthlessly ambitious, egomaniacal conqueror? Or an energetic advocate of higher education, a would-be conciliator with Jews across Europe and the instigator of a properly functioning banking system and a civilised, accessible legal code? When Pétain shook hands with Hitler in 1940 there were echoes of the 1807 Tilsit agreement between Napoleon and Tsar Alexander I which ended hostilities between the two emperors. In the context of 1940, says Jackson, 'Hitler was Napoleon and Pétain was Alexander'. And in 1840, precisely a century earlier, Napoleon's remains were returned from the island of Saint Helena to France and ceremoniously placed in the Hôtel des Invalides in Paris.

The story of Pétain and his historical assessment, too, didn't end with his death. On the contrary, the disputes and debates about his legacy have continued (like that of Churchill) from that day to this. Soon after the passing of their beloved Maréchal, supporters of Pétain argued passionately, but in vain, that his body should be transferred to the Ossuary of Douamont, a memorial to the soldiers who had died at Verdun. Rather as Napoleon's remains had been transferred to the Invalides. And in our own time, Pétain has been proclaimed a heroic patriot yet again, especially by many among the French far-right such as Éric Zemmour, a prominent (Jewish-born) candidate for the Presidency in 2022. But when in November 2018, to mark the centenary of the end of World War I, President Macron said it was legitimate to pay tribute to Marshal Pétain who had helped lead the French army to victory, he raised a storm of protest, especially on the left. While acknowledging Pétain's subsequent collaboration with the Nazis, Macron added wisely: 'I pardon nothing, but I erase nothing of our history'.

I wonder how we will be judged by future historians. What might be pardoned and what erased? You and I may realise that many people and places of the past, once celebrated by historians, were often racist and sexist in ways we would find intolerable. Something of this has been rectified by recent scholarship so we can now perhaps look back on earlier times with a more balanced view. But how will our intellectual successors look back upon our own failures and inadequacies? Not just the possibility of increasing warfare between enemy states and regimes, but our evident incapacity to confront and resolve the imminent climate crisis that could possibly threaten the entire future of humanity? Let's hope that, like all good historians, those in the future (if there are any!) won't simply judge us. Rather, that they might try to understand the era in which we are living, the attitudes and actions of our times and how these might have contributed to the potential non-viability of humanity on this overpopulated, overheating little planet of ours.

Britain, Germany, War and the World

Prussia 1701: A European Affair

A new exhibition in Berlin.

History Today, May 2000.

If you drive in to Berlin from the former Tegel airport in the north-west of the city, keep an eye on your right for the blue-domed, gold-topped Charlottenburg Palace, the finest Baroque building in town. It wasn't in town when, originally no more than a charming villa, it was constructed three hundred years ago. On the contrary, the palace was built as a summer residence for Sophie Charlotte of Hanover, the young wife of the Elector of Brandenburg – near enough to Berlin that she could attend the capital when required, yet a pleasantly rustic location on a lazy bend on the River Spree. Today, the district is one of the wealthiest in Berlin.

Some see Schloss Charlottenburg, with its extravagantly beautiful rooms hung with portraits of bewigged royals and generals, and its extensive Orangery, as Germany's equivalent of London's Kensington Palace. The links between the Schloss Charlottenburg and London are certainly close: Sophie Charlotte's brother became George I of England, and in 1888 this was where Vicky, Queen Victoria's daughter, grieved over the decline and premature death of her husband 'Fritz' with their son – who thereby became Kaiser.

This month, a major exhibition opens in the Orangery at the Charlottenburg Palace to commemorate the 300th anniversary of 'Prussia'. I have to word that carefully. There isn't a Prussian state today; its final vestiges were formally abolished by the Allied Control Commission in 1947. All that happened in 1701 was that Frederick III, Elector of Brandenburg, husband of Sophie Charlotte, had himself crowned Frederick I, King in Prussia, in far-off Königsberg (today's Kaliningrad, now a Russian enclave between Poland and Lithuania, but then an important city and in 1525–1618 the capital of ducal Prussia). But the repercussions of this symbolic act in a remote capital were to lead to the international prominence of Berlin and to the eventual establishment, under Prussia, of the German state.

Frederick, heir of the Hollenzollerns, inherited Brandenburg from his father, the 'Great Elector', who had built Brandenburg into a powerful, efficiently ruled state. To be an 'Elector' – one of the seven grandees to choose the Holy Roman Emperor – gave you great status. But if you wanted real power in an era of emergent Realpolitik, you needed a crown. Frederick, presiding over one of the leading Protestant territories to emerge from the Thirty Years' War, could hardly ask the Pope to bestow kingship upon him. Hence his venture eastwards, beyond the domains of the Holy Roman Empire, though with the agreement of the Emperor, to the territory of Poland-Prussia (later designated East Prussia).

The man who had departed Berlin as the Elector Frederick III thus returned as King Frederick I. Immediately, he began to behave like a king. His model – every monarch's model – was Louis XIV of France. Thus, the new monarch engaged some of the finest and most expensive architects and artists to embellish his capital with buildings appropriate to his new status (including the great Stadtschloss by Andreas Schlüter, finally pulled down after the Second World War). This was when he began to expand the summer house into a mini-Versailles. Wings were added at right angles to enclose a grand new ceremonial courtyard, while the original villa was greatly extended on both sides, one of which was to contain the great Orangery. The extensions would afford the visitor spectacular views of the grounds – which were magnificently landscaped by a pupil of Louis XIV's great gardener Le Nôtre, with all the fountains and avenues typical of Baroque gardens. In the midst of these changes, Sophie Charlotte unexpectedly died; it was then that the palace was named after her. Today, the tall, gilded dome of the Charlottenburg Palace, reproduced after its destruction in the Second World War, is one of the great landmarks of Berlin.

This summer's exhibition in the Orangery of the Charlottenburg Palace – 'Prussia 1701: A European Affair' – is the central feature in a wide range of celebratory activities sponsored by the city of Berlin and the Land of Brandenburg to mark the anniversary of King Frederick's coronation. The word 'Prussia' may be popularly associated with a kind of crude militarism. But this exhibition shows there was a great deal more to Prussia than that.

Visitors are welcomed by a video (with commentary in both German and English) explaining the basic facts about the 1701 coronation and placing this apparently local event into its wider European context. They then pass through the exquisite chapel, with its carved and gilded altar table by the Englishman Charles King. The chapel is dominated by a portrait by Antoine Pesne of Frederick I.

Frederick's own childhood and upbringing are told in the exhibition via an impressive array of authentic objects and artefacts. These are counterpointed with the larger story, from the Thirty Years' War through to Frederick's attempts, once he was king, to gain international recognition as an ally of his relative, William of Orange (England's William III), in the wars against France's Louis XIV.

The coronation itself, represented by an array of insignia and official portraiture, is displayed in conjunction with an evocation of old Königsberg, a comparison with other coronations at the time, and a portrayal of King Frederick's triumphant return to Berlin. It was from this moment that Berlin rapidly began its ascent as a major European capital.

Frederick's enthusiastic (some thought extravagant) expansion of Berlin is fully represented in the exhibition. The Schloss itself, after the death of Sophie Charlotte and the naming of the palace after her, underwent further expansion: the Orangery dates from these years, as does the great domed tower.

Frederick died in 1713, to be succeeded by his son, Frederick William I, 'the soldier king'. Frederick William was a ruthless military disciplinarian best remembered for the 'giants' he employed as palace guards. Perhaps his most important contribution to history was that he fathered Frederick II – the flute-playing Frederick 'the Great' who befriended (and alienated) Voltaire. Frederick was also a voracious military conqueror who outdid his grandfather in the grandeur with which he bedecked his capital. If Frederick I's Charlottenburg Palace was a jewel of Baroque architecture, Frederick the Great's estate at Sanssouci in nearby Potsdam – a vast park which includes Frederick's ornate private palace as well as the vastly imposing Neues Palais – almost vies with Versailles itself in extent and grandeur.

The exhibition at Schloss Charlottenburg – the centrepiece of 'Prussia 1701' – is an attempt to place Prussian history into its wider historical context. In an introduction to the Prussian Yearbook issued to accompany the various events and celebrations, the Governing Mayor of Berlin, Eberhard Diepgen, reminds us that 'the Prussian virtues, like the Prussian reforms, are among the best things the country has produced'. We should not think only of the period starting with Kaiser Wilhelm, he says, but go back much earlier and seek out the 'productive traditions within our history'. As examples of those historic Prussian virtues, Diepgen goes on to write 'of Prussian modesty, service to the state, of discipline and economy'. An exercise in historical revisionism? Perhaps. But doesn't every exhibition do a bit of that?

World War II: Forty Years On: Is the War 'just history'?
The Listener, 30 August 1979.

Shortly before the 40th anniversary of the outbreak of World War II, I found myself, as producer of BBC Radio 4's forthcoming series Forty Years On, *travelling across Europe and asking what the war meant to the younger generation who had no personal memories of it.*

Hitler inflicted intensive bombing on the USA in World War II; but the Germans, having defeated France (and burned Paris), couldn't occupy Vichy because it was a stronghold of the Resistance. These are just two of the breathtaking adolescent revisions of the historical record that came my way while I was recording interviews in the schools and colleges of Europe.

Howlers about history can be amusing – witness the popularity of *1066 and All That*. But is World War II really 'history', something to be consigned to the textbooks, like Napoleon, Bismarck or Henry VIII? Or do we still – even those with no personal memories of the war – live in its inescapable shadow?

Most of the young people I spoke to were initially inclined to distance themselves from the War. They were born some twenty years after it ended, and it was not their parents who fought but their grandparents. To them, the war was 'just history', they would tell me firmly, something which they learn about from their parents and television and school but which does not impinge directly upon them personally.

But the more this question was discussed, the more inadequate the initial response proved to be. World War II may, by now, be 'just history'; but everything else I heard from my young friends convinced me that it was history with a difference.

For one thing, most of the youngsters I met (the howler-merchants apart) simply knew so much more about the Second World War than I, at their age, had known about the First. I met British children who could name, and even identify, every British or German warplane, young Yugoslavs who were steeped in the Partisan tradition, German boys and girls from whom no details of the horrors of Nazism had been spared, French children who were surprisingly *au fait* with Pétain and Vichy, and even young Swedes who, despite their country's wartime neutrality, were well acquainted with the main issues, combatants, and events.

This sort of knowledge was far from universal, of course, but the general standard was impressive. Furthermore, many youngsters also showed a lively interest in the War and seemed keen to discuss it further. I had expected that my request for interviews would sometimes be dismissed with a sniffy 'Why are you old-timers always going on and on about the war?' But to my surprise (and allowing for the fact that most people like to oblige when invited to perform for the media), I scarcely ever encountered this attitude. On the contrary, young people in all the places I visited would question me closely about my project and then, after ritually denying that they could contribute much, chatter away at length.

Why should World War II continue to have such a hold on the imagination of young Europeans forty years on from its commencement? Different countries offer different clues. In Britain, the war has never been off the agenda. Any nation likes to recall and enshrine into mythology its finest hour, particularly if most of its hours have been somewhat less worthy of celebration. Youngsters brought up today on a news diet of tawdry political rows or industrial disputes are understandably stirred by the larger heroics of Churchill and Montgomery, the excitement of Dunkirk and Normandy, the global struggle of good against evil.

I met children in many parts of the country who were eagerly doing school projects on 'the Home Front' or 'the Battle of Britain' and whose principal resource was elderly relatives and friends who would scurry about in store-cupboards and attics turning up dusty old newspaper clippings, pieces of shrapnel, medals, gasmasks and the like. 'The last great moment of British glory' was how one teacher described the war to me, an epoch that could hardly fail to touch the imagination of a younger generation to whom anything resembling British glory was personally unknown. But – and this was a theme reiterated again and again by the youngsters themselves – it is important not to be bowled over by the national mythology. To many, Churchill was a hero with feet of clay, while the Allied bombing of Dresden was often equated with the German bombing of London.

In France, by contrast, the war was not a glorious episode (though the Resistance was). For years, the story of defeat, occupation and collaboration was a dark secret not easily discussed; and even now the air occasionally resounded with accusation and counter-accusation, journalistic exposé and alleged political cover-up. Did Françoise Giroud really have the Resistance Medal she claimed? Should *L'Express* have published an interview with the notorious French Nazi Darquier de Pellepoix? Why had French television to this day not screened Marcel Ophuls's controversial film *Le Chagrin et la Pitié*? French boys and girls were not untouched by official mythology and tended to exaggerate the role of the Resistance and underrate the extent of French collaboration with the Nazis but, by and large, those I met were better informed than their parents or teachers had thought. Above all, they were adamant that the time had come to learn the unvarnished truth.

In each country the details were different but the pattern was the same. In Sweden I met young people who, while accepting the inevitability, and even the virtue, of wartime neutrality (and the relatively small impact of the war on Swedish history), were nevertheless keen to know whether their much-vaunted neutrality was genuinely even-handed. In Yugoslavia, as the Partisan generation lived out its years and its aged leader assumed the role of national icon, children more than seventy years younger than Tito were beginning to wonder if the story of the wartime origins of their socialist revolution was as simple as they have been told. They didn't deny the heroism of the Partisans or the evil of the Nazis, but some questioned (for instance) whether all the 'good' Yugoslavs were necessarily working-class Communist Partisans and all bourgeois Yugoslavs collaborators and quislings. A recent feature film, *Occupation in 26 Pictures*, suggested that the class lines were by no means as clear-cut as the national mythology had maintained.

In all these countries the war was a more or less romanticised episode which could, according to taste, be celebrated, studied, or disregarded. In Germany, however, the war remained a heavy cloud from whose oppressive shadow it was impossible to escape: a central fact on which one had to take a position. German children, like those elsewhere, would assure me at first that, to their generation, the war was 'just history'. But there, more than anywhere else, I was constantly reminded of its continuing presence.

'All over Germany', I would remark, as innocently as I knew how, 'there are commemorative plaques – Holbein was born here, Hans Sachs lived there; so shouldn't the appropriate walls of, say, Munich bear a 'Hitler's Putsch' or a 'Site of the Munich Agreement' sign? Not, I would add hastily, to glorify Hitler but simply out of historical interest. This sort of suggestion invariably produced heated debate. 'You're right', someone would say, 'we should by now be able to accept the facts of the Third Reich'. 'But if we did have such a plaque', another would pipe up, 'there'd be flowers there the next morning'. 'True' a third would add, 'but there are neo-fascist nuts everywhere and that is no reason for us to repress all legitimate mention of a major era of our past'. Some pretty nifty intellectual footwork would often follow: while the Third Reich was, by now, 'just history', it was, nevertheless, too early to permit its landmark events to be publicly commemorated.

This understandable confusion was one indication that the Hitler period loomed more heavily over today's young Germans than they liked to acknowledge. Another surfaced during the discussion I witnessed (and recorded) when a number of young German soldiers visited Dachau on an educational visit (see above, pp. 100–101). 'Isn't there a danger', one young man asked, that by perpetuating the memory of what the Nazis did here we are also perpetuating anti-German feeling in the wider world and forever taking on our own shoulders the guilt for what our forebears did?' – a viewpoint that (like the advocacy of a statute of limitations for war crimes) elicited an angry 'Why are you defending the Nazis?' retort from a number of colleagues. Young Germans may want the war to go away and be 'just history', but the time for such hopes to be fulfilled had not yet arrived.

Two further indications: a young journalist I met in Berlin said he was always relieved when, on trips abroad, people took him for a Swede or a Dutchman, 'because when they know I'm German I know exactly what goes on in their heads'. And another, in Munich this time, agreed when I asked him if it was harder for him, as a young German, to write critically of Israel than it was for a French or British colleague. 'We can and do say some pretty harsh things about (Israeli Prime Minister) Begin from time to time,' he told me, 'but it would be difficult for any reputable West German newspaper to question the Jewish right to Israel or to espouse too wholeheartedly the Palestinian cause'.

Thus, to young people in all the countries I visited – though for different reasons in each – World War II was still a living presence, a major episode of the recent past of which those born too late to have personal memories were nonetheless acutely conscious. Indeed, as the fact itself receded further into the past, youthful interest in it appeared, if anything, to be on the increase. In recent years, I was told, the number of school parties visiting the Dachau Memorial had risen dramatically – a trend reflected in various ways everywhere I went. Why should this have been so?

***

For one thing, Western Europe had been blessedly free from major conflagration since 1945 so that no subsequent horror had come to edge World War II away from the centre of folk memory. To Vietnamese or Nigerians or Nicaraguans, 'the war' no doubt referred to more recent events. But not to Europeans, to whom the distant events and personalities of World War Two were generally acquiring the status not of memory but of myth. Furthermore, the scale of the destruction and barbarity unleashed by the Second World War was unlike any other. More soldiers might have been killed in the First World War, and the trenches of Flanders possibly represented the nadir of organised warfare. But the systematic application of assembly-line techniques to highly mechanised death factories in the conscious pursuit of genocide had never occurred before or since and appeared to be taking on, with the perspective of time, an increasingly awesome place in history.

A further reason why interest in the war appeared to be not merely maintained but growing (particularly in the one country with, on the face of it, the greatest incentive to think about other things) was implied in the formula repeated everywhere I went that 'it must never happen again'. Nobody seriously thought it was about to happen again, but there were neo-fascist movements everywhere and in some places they had been growing, or at least becoming more vociferous, in recent years. In each country I met young people who, alarmed at these movements, felt that the lessons of the war had to be relearned.

Perhaps the most commonly advanced reason, though this is surely as much symptom as cause, was the role of the mass media and, in particular, the enormous effect of the TV miniseries *Holocaust*. This Hollywood-style soap opera, for all the banality of some of its scripting, was 'more successful than a thousand books' (in the rueful words of the books editor of the *Süddeutsche Zeitung*) in both feeding and stimulating serious interest in the war among young people in Germany and elsewhere. *Holocaust* did not create the popular appetite for World War II films; all television planners know they can attract a large audience by scheduling a rollicking goodies vs baddies war project. But *Holocaust* attempted something which most feature films do not: it concentrated on the darkest side of the war, the Nazi barbarism, rather than on the more easily portrayed heroism and suffering of the battlefield. Furthermore, like *The Diary of Anne Frank*, its impact was greatly enhanced by its personal approach. 'I was far more moved by the plight of the Weiss family,' said one Berlin girl to me, 'than I had ever been by all the statistics of death and destruction that I had learned before' while a young Bavarian boy told me that, paradoxically, it took the fictional treatment of the war in *Holocaust* to convince him of the literal truth of the most unpalatable facts.

Holocaust came just at the right time. A decade earlier, the war period was too close and the wounds it had inflicted were still too tender. A twenty-four-year-old German schoolteacher told me, after sitting in on my discussions with members of her class, that her pupils knew far more about the war than she had done at their age. At that time, she said, looking back nearly half a lifetime, the war was scarcely mentioned in school, at home, or in the mass media, for the generation by which she had been raised was still scarred by its own sense of guilt. Today's young parents and educators represented the first generation of Germans with no personal memories of the war, no embarrassments when faced with the innocent yet deadly question, 'What did you do in the war?' For them, the war must be an open book, a topic of supreme importance the whole truth of which had been denied them in their own youth but which must be made available to the next generation.

Wherever I went, I met young people who showed a lively and serious interest in the war – or, at least, in the war as understood in their particular country. As I travelled in Britain, France, Sweden, Germany and Yugoslavia, I learned much about heroic backs-to-the-wall battles, the trials of occupation and resistance, the virtues of neutrality, the barbarism of Nazism, and the glorious victory of the revolutionary people. But while these national viewpoints may distort the focus they seldom violate the facts. And in any case, they are rarely accepted by the younger generation without a pinch of healthy scepticism.

'Just history'? Perhaps. But an era of the past that each generation must insist on learning about for itself. This combination of serious interest in the war and a somewhat cautious regard for the various national mythologies into which it was being packaged seemed to me to give grounds for optimism. For if, to paraphrase Santayana, those who do not know their history are condemned to relive it, the young Europeans I met appear reasonably well set to avoid the more catastrophic follies of their grandparents' generation.

Dresden

What do you do if your city has been destroyed?
Rebuild the past - or move with the times?

Drafted in February 2004 for potential adaptation in a variety of lectures and publications.

Next time you go to Dresden, stand on the southwest corner of the old market square and look diagonally across. There, beyond the concrete-and-glass modernity of Walter Ulbricht's *Kulturpalast*, is the towering, domed *Frauenkirche*, once the foremost Protestant church in Europe and now resurrected sixty years after being reduced to rubble by Allied bombing. Here, in sharp juxtaposition, are two radically opposing answers to a question that civic authorities around the world have had to confront: what do you do if your city has been destroyed – by earthquake, flood, fire or bombardment? Move with the times? Or rebuild the past? London faced it after 1666, San Francisco after 1906. And Dresden faced it after aerial destruction rained from the skies in 1945.

***

The celebrated Baroque centre of Dresden was planned and built in the early 1700s under the leadership of Augustus the Strong, the Prince Elector of Saxony. Like many others at the time, Augustus hoped to emulate something of the glory of Louis XIV. Dresden was no Versailles. But it is to the era of Augustus that we owe the magnificent cluster of dark-hued sandstone churches and palaces that the world was to admire for the next two centuries. Much of the Zwinger, originally an ornamental open-air ballroom and now one of the world's great art museums, dates back to the initiative of Augustus the Strong. It was Augustus, too, who initiated the porcelain works in nearby Meissen.

Early in his reign, Augustus acquired the crown of Poland, a move that prompted this most pragmatic of men to convert to Catholicism. Alarmed but evidently not intimidated at this turn of events, the predominantly Lutheran citizenry of Dresden began to erect the towering Protestant 'Frauenkirche' (Church of Our Lady), a move that, in turn, prompted the building after Augustus's death of a Catholic court church, or 'Hofkirche'. By the middle of the 18th century, visitors approaching Dresden from the north bank of the Elbe would pass a golden equestrian statue of Augustus, cross the Augustus Bridge – and behold a skyline dominated by these two great churches: the Protestant *Frauenkirche* to the left, crowned by its great bell-shaped dome which locals dubbed the 'stone bell', and the Catholic *Hofkirche*, just ahead, with its delicate tower above balustrades bedecked with statuary. 'Florence on the Elbe', people called the city.

A century later, visitors would also remark on the magnificent opera house by the city's great architect Gottfried Semper. They would take note, too, of the additional gallery completing the Zwinger courtyard designed by Semper and, perhaps, of another Semper building, the lofty synagogue at the far end of the waterfront walkway known as Brühl's Terrace. For two hundred years, from the mid-18th-century paintings of Belotto (the nephew of Canaletto) to the bustling 20th-century photographs of Richard Strauss and the conductor Fritz Busch on their way to or from the opera, the imagery of Dresden suggested a city of high culture.

A conservative city, but no more prone to Nazism than elsewhere in Germany, Dresden was singled out for bombardment by Allied air strikes on the night of 13–14 February 1945. Much of Baroque Dresden was destroyed, and, with it, the lives and homes of many thousands of people who lived there. The art works in the Zwinger had been removed for safety. But the building itself, like the *Hofkirche* and the *Semperoper*, was a shell, ceilings and statuary in a state of charred collapse with little but outer walls left to show what once stood so proud. The *Frauenkirche*, dominating Dresden's picturesque *Neumarkt*, at first seemed to withstand the concentrated bombing even as much of the housing around it succumbed. But a day after the Allied bombing, as the immense heat to which the stones had been subjected began to cool, the stones of the *Frauenkirche* gave way and – like the Twin Towers in New York – simply collapsed, its mighty stones reduced to a derelict pile of ruins.

Thus it remained throughout the forty years of communism. The rigidly ideological East German regime was prepared to finance the provision of workers' housing projects and social amenities, to erect a Culture Palace for the edification of the people and to find funds for the restoration of such high-prestige temples of culture (and earners of hard currency) as the *Zwinger* and the *Semperoper*. But they wouldn't authorise the rebuilding of an old church. At first, they planned to clear the area to construct a new 'Socialist City'. But the project was abandoned and the pile of rubble in Dresden's *Neumarkt* finally declared a permanent memorial to the destruction of Dresden, a visible symbol (like the Kaiser Wilhelm Church in Berlin) of the evil wrought by war. The site became overgrown and was pastured for a while by a small flock of sheep. Wild roses and other flowers began to appear, a tacit protest, perhaps, against an unpopular, atheistic regime. A sense of permanence pervaded the new stillness of the once-bustling square. Tourists came to survey the sad but tranquil ruin.

Then, against everybody's expectations, came the tumultuous events of 1989–90: the Berlin wall came down, Communist rule was dismantled throughout Europe and the two Germanies were united. Everywhere, the sense of joyous liberation was tangible. Much that was thought lost returned. Churches, long regarded as little more than the bleak refuge of the elderly and impotent, found large, devout congregations and people in Dresden began to talk again about what had hitherto been but a dream: the rebuilding of the *Frauenkirche*.

In 1993, the rubble began to be cleared, the damaged old stones cleaned and classified. I remember visiting Dresden and seeing gigantic shelves of sleeping monoliths, each carefully sorted and labelled, awaiting the day when, like the bones of Ezekiel, they would rise up once more. Scaffolding was set up around the site as men in hard hats brought in cranes and heavy machinery. Visitors were ushered into a spacious crypt, given a talk, shown a film – and, as in a church service, asked to dig into their pockets on their way out as they made way for the next sitting. More than half the vast cost of this ecclesiastical resurrection was raised by voluntary action, most prominently by the UK-based Dresden Trust, and by 2004 the great Orb and Cross were re-erected to crown the completed and once again reopened church.

Today, the 'stone bell' again dominates the great Baroque skyline and the talk now is of the restoration of the entire *Neumarkt* area, including surrounding streets of 18th-century houses whose sites and surviving foundations are being actively investigated. Meanwhile, several of Dresden's old palaces are being or have been restored. Against the odds – including economic recession and the disastrous floods of 2002 – the resurrection of the most historic part of pre-1945 Dresden is all but complete. A city destroyed in one ferocious night has determinedly put the clock back.

***

Well, not quite. For even the old historic centre contains at least one incontestably modern building. The new Dresden synagogue sits on the site of its predecessor. The old synagogue, a noble house of worship designed by Semper to combine traditional Oriental and Jewish themes, was dedicated in 1838 and opened shortly afterwards. A century later,

Dresden Frauenkirche.

this building, like so many synagogues in Germany, was put to the torch by Nazi sympathisers on *Kristallnacht*, the night of 9 November 1938. For the next sixty years, Dresden contained no synagogue. Then, with the demise of Communism and the subsequent flood of people Westwards, many Russian and Ukrainian Jews came to Germany, some of them to post-Communist Dresden. Soon, the leaders of Dresden's renascent Jewish community, perhaps inspired by the example of the *Frauenkirche*, began to talk of the need once more for a synagogue.

One option would have been to rebuild the great edifice of Gottfried Semper; if Semper's opera house could rise again, why not his synagogue? But the *Semperoper*, gutted in 1945, was reconstructed forty years later with the aid of meticulous records reinforced by clear memories. By the time there was talk of a new Dresden synagogue, memories (and records) of Semper's original were sparse and unreliable. In any case, the Semper synagogue would have been too large for what was still a small community. Also, it was felt that, nowadays, a synagogue should be as much a social and cultural centre as a house of worship. So the leaders of the Jewish community, with the governments of the city of Dresden and the state of Saxony, agreed to commission a new complex that would be consistent with both the traditional needs of Judaism and the taste and style of the 21st century. Public funds were augmented by voluntary contributions – not least, through fund-raising events held, in the new spirit of cooperation, in the crypt of the *Frauenkirche*. On 9 November 1998, on the land that had once held the Semper synagogue and sixty years to the day since its destruction, the first cut of the spade was made. Three years later, the new Dresden synagogue was inaugurated: a pair of asymmetrical but complementary golden-yellow boxes built of sandstone-coloured bricks. One of the two cubes is the synagogue itself, the other a community and educational centre. They are separated by a courtyard, symbolically empty but shaded by trees, marking in glass splinters the outline of the Semper synagogue. The only object retrieved from the old building – a golden Star of David bravely saved and hidden by one of the firefighters – takes pride of place above the entrance to the new.

Few cities have faced in so extreme a form as Dresden the fundamental question of how to build – literally – upon the ruins of the past. With the completion of the ultra-modernist synagogue, and now of the resuscitated *Frauenkirche*, Dresden can look forward with confidence to the celebration of its 800th anniversary in 2006.

The Bauhaus Group: Six Masters of Modernism

Nicholas Fox Weber (Yale University Press, 2011).

Literary Review, March 2015.

The Bauhaus Group focuses on the lives of six 'Masters of Modernism' who, we are told, 'were geniuses for all time' and who 'created and lived out a dream that was never equaled before or since'. Nicholas Fox Weber, long-time director of the Josef and Anni Albers Foundation, is nothing if not an enthusiast for his subject. The six geniuses were the architects Walter Gropius and Ludwig Mies van der Rohe (the first and last directors of the Bauhaus), the painters Paul Klee and Wassily Kandinsky and the Alberses. *En passant*, we also encounter other important figures for whom the author has less regard. Colour plates illustrate some of the artworks and the book also contains black-and-white reproductions and – most striking – informal snapshots of (and often by) the leading figures.

The Bauhaus, a German college of art, architecture, industrial design and engineering, was virtually coeval with the Weimar Republic, lasting from 1919 until its disbandment in 1933. The vision that inspired Gropius and his colleagues was to link art and technology. Why not design chairs and light fittings (indeed, entire housing estates) that, while strictly functional, were also pleasing to the eye and affordable by ordinary working-class people? The school was intended to be, in effect, a community of like-minded artist-craftsmen financed in part by its own industrial mass-production of high-quality goods. The teachers, or 'Masters', would live on site in homes specifically designed in the Bauhaus spirit.

It was initially based in Weimar, but local political pressures made its presence there increasingly uncongenial and in 1925 Gropius moved the Bauhaus to the less attractive but more welcoming town of Dessau where he himself designed its main buildings. In 1928, Gropius resigned to devote more time to his private practice and he was succeeded as director by the overtly (and controversially) left-wing Hannes Meyer. Meyer was ousted a couple of years later and the final director, Mies van der Rohe, led the school to Berlin where in 1933 the advent of Nazi rule made it no longer viable. After its demise, several of its luminaries found refuge in the USA (in some cases after a brief sojourn in Britain). Here, Bauhaus ideas flourished and post-war America became the home of Modernism: in the architectural departments at Harvard, Yale and Chicago universities, at North Carolina's Black Mountain College, in the rapidly expanding metropolis of Los Angeles and elsewhere. But Bauhaus ideals were evident across the world – for example in the flat-roofed, white cube buildings that sprang up across Tel Aviv. In Britain, an ambitious young designer named Terence Conran set out in the 1950s, inspired by Bauhaus ideals.

The Bauhaus remains famous, partly because of what it achieved, but also because of the enduring fame of some of its 'Masters', including those on whom this book focuses. Gropius, sexually predatory and insatiable, also managed to retain strict self-discipline in professional matters, Weber tells us. The Swiss-born Klee, inhibited and taciturn, found a degree of inner calm by canalising his inner neuroses into art and, in particular, seeking parallels between the processes of nature and those of artistic creation. Weber is probably at his best when describing and deconstructing a painting such as Klee's *Dance of the Red Skirts* of 1924 or *Fish Magic* created the following year (both reproduced in colour). But the art critic soon gives way to the gossip columnist as we read of Klee's propensity to sit quietly at a party or a dance, observing the proceedings and sucking quietly on his pipe, while his Russian friend Kandinsky, a man of more aristocratic mien, loved to party. Both men adored music. Klee's violin case was always open, though his passion for Mozart may seem at odds with his reputation as an aesthetic modernist; Kandinsky sought profound, quasi-spiritual links between sight and sound and 'considered music the ultimate art form'.

Mies van der Rohe (like Josef Albers) came from a working-class background, but rose to the top of his profession through a combination of tenacity, architectural vision and sheer force of personality. Inventing an aristocratic-sounding twist to his name, Mies resented the upper-crust celebrity of Gropius, whose architecture he thought inferior to his own. Much of the Mies chapter is devoted to non-Bauhaus projects, but illuminating evidence about his Bauhaus years comes from the transcript of an autobiographical talk he gave to a student group after the war and from conversations Weber had with Mies's on-again-off-again friend and admirer the American architect Philip Johnson.

Then there are the Alberses. Both came to the Bauhaus originally as students, though Josef was a professor by the time Anni arrived. In 1933, the couple emigrated to the USA where both lived to extreme old age. Weber tells of his first meeting with them when a post-graduate student at Yale in 1970, and of the many conversations he had with them over the years; their friendship clearly provided the inspiration for this book and provides much of its human texture. The elderly Josef, we read, did not dwell much on the old days, preferring to hold forth about the present, pouring bemused scorn upon the pretentiousness of modern artists (such as Robert Motherwell, claiming his work will bring him 'Eternity'), for example, or dismissing all museum directors as *'SCHWEIN!'*. But Weber's especial confidante and source is Anni who died in her mid-nineties. It was 'Anni's description of the key players at the Bauhaus,' he writes affectionately, that 'made me see life in Weimar and Dessau as if I had lived there.'

The strength and weakness of this book is that it is clearly a labour of love. The text is lengthy and its treatment uneven: Klee (whom Anni revered) gets over 100 pages and Kandinsky and Mies 40-odd. Weber can write with informed passion, but when stuck for a metaphor has a tendency to resort to cliché (as when Gropius compensated 'in spades' for his father's professional setbacks but inherited 'a windfall of money' from a great-aunt). Some pages read like summaries of passages from other people's books, while this large volume is almost devoid of historical context. Thus, we are told of specific financial problems faced by individual *Bauhauslers* in the early years but nothing of the ferocious hyperinflation that afflicted all of Germany at the time, nor is there more than the most cursory reference to the all-important rise of right-wing politics during the 1920s. At times the narrative style verges on the tabloid: Alma Mahler, the composer's widow and the notoriously lubricious lover and sometime wife of Gropius, was 'the Madame Pompadour of the twentieth century' we read, and 'a vixen of fantastic sexual capabilities'. Good gossipy stuff. But a book about the Bauhaus by Nicholas Fox Weber, author of a number of previous books on artists and architects and friend of the last of the *Bauhauslers*, raises high expectations. If you allow him his idiosyncrasies, and have plenty of time on your hands, you won't be disappointed.

Final Solution: The Fate of the Jews, 1933–49
David Cesarani (Macmillan, 2016).

History Today, May 2016.

There are a great many studies of the Holocaust, but few scholars have relayed as graphically or in as much detail as David Cesarani the crimes and cruelties committed by Hitler's Third Reich against the Jews of Europe. Throughout *Final Solution*, he quotes the vivid personal testimony of those who were present as they recall almost indescribable barbarities, and he often caps such a section with a brief recital of the most chilling statistics. Cesarani died last October at age 58 and, in his absence, was the recipient of this year's Longman-History Today Trustees' Award. His previous books include penetrating studies of the lives of Arthur Koestler and Adolf Eichmann while his active advocacy helped lead to the Holocaust galleries at the Imperial War Museum and the establishment in Britain of Holocaust Memorial Day. By the time of his death, Cesarani had completed the main text of *Final Solution* and he spent his final days and weeks going through the detailed references (which take up nearly 100 pages at the end of the book). He did not live to check the final proofs.

***

Until forty or so years ago, few historians of World War II focused on the Nazi mass-murder of Jews, the whole subject tending to be subsumed within a narrative more likely to be predominantly political or military. People wrote (and read) biographies of such figures as Hitler, Stalin, Churchill and Roosevelt and there was a widespread appetite for books recounting the great battles and the men who led them. Then, as the wartime horrors gradually receded into the past, many who had survived them, hitherto often reluctant to talk about their painful experiences, came in old age to feel the urgent need to do so. Personal memories were recorded and videoed, archive banks accumulated, educational courses installed, exhibitions and museums inaugurated. The collapse of Soviet communism, furthermore, led to the opening up of previously unavailable sources in Russia and its former satellite territories, thus helping extend the centre of gravity for research from Germany itself to incorporate Eastern Europe where many of the most heinous crimes had been committed.

Meanwhile, a new generation of historians – not least in Germany – was trying to confront the large question of responsibility. How far could

Hitler personally be held to account for the mass murder of European Jews? He had made his views, hopes and intentions about the Jews clear ever since publication of *Mein Kampf* in 1925 if not earlier. Maybe, argued some, the horrors of Nazism were essentially the implementation by Hitler and his henchmen of a carefully pre-planned policy. In contrast to this 'intentionalist' view, other scholars tended towards what came to be dubbed a more 'functionalist' interpretation of Nazi crimes. This held that, while the overall politico-philosophical outlook of Hitler and his followers had indeed been known from the outset, the detailed unfolding of their actions and their descent into the moral abyss could better be understood if seen against the constantly shifting (and rapidly deteriorating) military circumstances in which the Nazi leadership eventually found itself.

The deeper truth, as always in such complex issues, no doubt contains elements of both but Cesarani aligns himself resolutely with the functionalists. He is in good company, alongside such distinguished German scholars as Martin Broszat and Hans Mommsen as well as Christopher Browning, Ian Kershaw and others. But, more than most, Cesarani is at pains to emphasise (over-emphasise at times?) this approach. Thus, while Hitler had an overall view about, for example, the desirability of combining Austria and Germany, 'it was characteristic that he had given little thought to the practical details of how this was to be accomplished'. Again and again – including at the notorious Wannsee conference of January 1942 – the 'Jewish Question' was left unresolved, says Cesarani, something of a 'sideshow': it was 'ill-planned, under-funded and carried through haphazardly'. This is not of course to deny that Hitler and his followers had an obsessive hatred towards the Jews. But the *leitmotif* that runs throughout the book is that it was 'Germany's economic exigencies, strategic priorities, military successes and setbacks (that) would decisively influence how Jews were treated'.

In Cesarani's view, Hitler thought of himself as a warrior and it was above all the experience of the First World War and of Germany's ignominious defeat – engineered, he was convinced, by 'international Jewry' – that shaped his subsequent thinking. In the 1930s, the Nazi desire to render Germany free of Jews had included the possibility of getting them to move to Palestine (which Eichmann visited in 1937). Once war had broken out and Nazi forces were moving eastwards across Poland, Jews came to be regarded as an available, invaluable, malleable and much-needed workforce. As such, they were concentrated in specially commandeered camps and ghettos from which those too old or sick to work could be systematically 'removed': a brutal policy which, as the Nazi regime found itself confronted by ever-increasing military pressure, especially from Soviet Russia, came to be applied in a somewhat desperate way to Jewish populations wherever they were encountered. Cesarani leads us right across the map of Europe in his quest to cover the detailed unfoldings of the Nazis' *Judenpolitik*. And unlike many another work on the war and Holocaust, *Final Solution* takes us beyond 1945 as Cesarani reminds us of the continued sufferings of millions who remained 'deported' and homeless in the years following the official end of war.

The book is not an encyclopaedia, and there are aspects of the wider story that Cesarani has not investigated or documented in any detail: the thoughts and feelings of the countless ordinary 'perpetrators', 'bystanders' and 'collaborationists', for example, or the fate of other (non-Jewish) victims of the Holocaust. But with its focus on the fate of European Jewry, *Final Solution* is an important and impressive book, extraordinarily wide ranging in its coverage and sources. It will go down as the *magnum opus* of a much-lamented and greatly admired historian of modern Jewish history.

The 2003 Scouloudi Lecture

The Hitler Emigrés: The Cultural Impact on Britain of Refugees from Nazism

This lecture was delivered in Beveridge Hall, Senate House, London on 12 June 2003 on the invitation of the Director of the Institute of Historical Research, David Cannadine. Below is an expanded (and sourced) version of the text that was subsequently published by the IHR where, in 2004, I was made a Senior Research Fellow.

The essay (and lecture) arose from work undertaken for my book The Hitler Emigrés: The Cultural Impact on Britain of Refugees from Nazism *(Chatto & Windus, 2002; Pimlico, 2003). The book was primarily a study of British cultural and intellectual history since the 1930s, focusing on the impact of the 'Hitler Emigrés'. But many reviewers and interviewers also read the book as (variously): a contribution to the history of Nazism, the Holocaust and the Second World War, a record of the specifically Jewish contribution to the arts and culture or an argument for a liberal immigration policy. Why?*

I was delighted and honoured when invited to deliver this year's Scouloudi Lecture. Irene Scouloudi was born in this country in 1907. Her parents were both from families of Greek origin; Irene was made to attend Greek Orthodox services which she didn't find particularly inspiring, and she seems to have grown up with a distaste for religion in general. But something in her personal lineage – perhaps including her obviously non-native name – drew her to the study of immigration and what we would now call ethnicity. At the London School of Economics, she read history as an undergraduate and went on to do a Master's degree for which she wrote a thesis on 'Alien immigration into and alien communities in London 1558–1640'. Irene Scouloudi completed the thesis in 1936 – precisely at a period when London was becoming home to a new wave of immigrants, or 'aliens', some of whom we will go on to discuss.

What interested Irene Scouloudi was the positive impact on British life that immigrants had been able to make over the years. Many know of the enormous contribution to British life and culture of the Huguenots, for example, who came here from France in the years following the revocation of the Edict of Nantes, and this is in no small measure due to Scouloudi's work as Honorary Secretary and Editor to the Huguenot Society of Great Britain from 1951 to 1987. In 1988 she became the first recipient of an

Honorary Fellowship of the Institute of Historical Research. It is altogether appropriate, therefore, that the biennial Scouloudi Foundation Lecture, of which this is the second, should take place here at the University of London and under the auspices of the IHR – and I would like to thank Professor Cannadine, the Director of the Institute, and the Foundation, for inviting me to be this year's lecturer.

***

It is even more appropriate, in a way, that we are meeting in Beveridge Hall. Let me begin with a story about the man after whom it is named. In March 1933 – precisely when Irene Scouloudi was at the London School of Economics working on her MA about immigrants and aliens – Beveridge, then Director of the LSE, happened to be visiting Vienna.

'Lionel Robbins, one of my colleagues at the School, was also in Vienna at the time,' Beveridge recalled later, 'meeting fellow economists. He and his wife and Ludwig von Mises and I, sitting in one of the Vienna cafes, were talking of things in general, when an evening paper was brought in, with an announcement that a dozen leading professors of all faculties were being dismissed from posts in German universities by the newly established Nazi regime, either on racial or political grounds. As Mises read out the names to us our wonder grew, and with it grew indignation.'[1]

That night, Beveridge made an astonishing decision. Robbins recalled the evening in his memoir and was generous in his assessment.

'This was one of Beveridge's great moments,' Robbins wrote, 'his finest hour I would say. Slumped in a chair, with his great head characteristically cupped in his fists, thinking aloud, he then and there outlined the basic plan of what became the Academic Assistance Council – later the Society for the Protection of Science and Learning.'[2]

The SPSL was an organisation to which hundreds of émigrés, many of them of great distinction and including a clutch of subsequent Nobel Prize winners, owed the preservation of their careers and in many cases their lives. Robbins wasn't always so flattering about Beveridge's generous instincts. I'd love to have been a fly on the wall the day Beveridge mentioned to Robbins that he was planning to bring over *en bloc* the entire body of the Frankfurt Institute for Social Research. Robbins, knowing the Frankfurt School's reputation as a stronghold of Marxism, was exasperated and tried to dissuade his Director against so rash a step. Robbins consulted his conservative comrade in arms, Friedrich von Hayek, himself an Austrian émigré, and also the LSE's aged co-founder Sidney Webb. Eventually Beveridge decided against – and had the grace to thank Robbins for his wise counsel.[3] But it was a damn close-run thing, and I have often wondered what the consequences might have been had Beveridge gone ahead. Who knows? If some of the famous Frankfurt refugees such as Marcuse, Adorno and Horkheimer had found a permanent base here in London rather than in the United States, maybe the great spearhead of New Left radicalism in the 1960s would have been not in Berkeley or Berlin but right here in the University of London.

My theme this evening is the 'Hitler Emigrés' who came to this country. 'Emigrés' note; not 'Refugees'. The word 'refugee' (*réfugié*) was first used about the French Huguenots who fled to this country after the revocation of the Edict of Nantes in 1685. But not all the 'Hitler Emigrés' were refugees, at first at any rate. Hayek did not come to Britain as a refugee. Nor, for example, did the architect Berthold Lubetkin, the film producer Alexander Korda or the art historian Ernst Gombrich. These, in each case, initially came to Britain to work; then, as the situation in Central Europe deteriorated, it became increasingly obvious that this was the place to stay. The Vienna-born biochemist Max Perutz came to Britain as a student, while the historian Eric Hobsbawm arrived from Hitler's Germany as an adolescent not as a refugee but with a British passport and under the care of an uncle who had work here. Some – the philosopher Karl Popper comes to mind, or the conductor Georg Solti – were refugees elsewhere during the war before later on settling in Britain. And a tiny handful of people arrived in this country after the war having miraculously survived Nazism: people like the musicians Rudolf Schwarz and Anita Lasker Wallfisch, or Rabbi Hugo Gryn.

While we're on the subject of terminology, you'll notice I also haven't used the word 'exile'. Maybe I should. There is a thriving industry in 'Exile Studies'; this university has a 'Research Centre for German and Austrian Exile Studies', and I have been happy to make use of some the excellent work they have produced. But Hobsbawm, Korda, Perutz, Gombrich - these were not exiles. Nor even were those who were authentic refugees: the filmmaker Karel Reisz, the publisher George Weidenfeld, the musician and broadcaster Hans Keller or the three members of the Amadeus Quartet who came to Britain as teenagers from post-*Anschluss* Austria. An exile, one of the people I interviewed put it to me, is someone who hangs up his harp on the willow tree and yearns for his homeland, his *Heimat*. 'I spent the first fifteen years of my life in Germany,' said another, 'but I've spent the next sixty-five in Britain. This is my homeland.' Many who settled here but retained the vestige of an accent found it irritating when, after many years, people still asked them: 'Where are you from?' when the answer, of course, was Hampstead, Swiss Cottage or St John's Wood![4] A few of the 'Hitler Emigrés' did go back to live in Central Europe, particularly communists who were attracted (as was Brecht) to East Germany. Some, such as the physicist Max Born, felt it their duty to help build up the new post-Hitlerian Germany (like the lawyer in the recent film *Nowhere In Africa*). But many thought you could do this just as well from Britain. Think of Weidenfeld, who made a point of publishing English-language editions of books by bright young Germans and Austrians, or the Amadeus Quartet who for many years had a recording contract with Deutsche Grammophon.

So today, for want of a better term, we are talking about the 'Hitler Emigrés' and, in particular, about their impact on British cultural life. And by 'cultural' life, I mean primarily what they would have meant by the word 'culture' – that is, the intellectual life and the high arts (the old-fashioned, rather than the more current, anthropological use of the word 'culture'). My focus, therefore, is on what the 'Hitler Emigrés' brought to British art, architecture, film, photography, music, literature, the press, broadcasting and the academic humanities, sciences and social sciences, and on how their contribution fitted in with the wider background of British cultural history as a whole: the war, the development of the Welfare State (more Beveridge!), the Arts Council, the BBC Third Programme, the Festival of Britain and so on. What resulted when people schooled in the high culture of pre-Hitlerian *Mitteleuropa* began to mix their labours with the rather different culture they encountered in Britain (initially, of course, the – to them – alien world of Bloomsbury, Garden Cities, John Reith's BBC, the pastoralism of Holst and Vaughan Williams)? When people raised in Culture 'A' encountered people raised in Culture 'B'? This is what interests me. For it was the admixture of the two that helped create the rich cultural milieu from which I – and I suspect you – have so greatly benefited.

***

The primary focus of my research, therefore, was on the past sixty-odd years of British cultural history. But, at least by implication, my book *The Hitler Emigrés* was about a lot of other things as well. In some respects, it was a study of 'Cultural Transfer': what happens when people raised in one intellectual environment encounter, and live among, people imbued with another? How far do they assimilate, integrate, acculturate or remain in a cultural ghetto? It was also in part a generational study: older migrants, such as the Berlin theatre critic Alfred Kerr, found it harder to adjust to a new country and an unfamiliar language than his children Michael and Judith (one of whom later became a distinguished judge and the other one of our leading writers for children and adolescents).[5] Another of the themes in *Nowhere In Africa*.

Did German and Austrian refugees leave a different mark on their new homeland? Perry Anderson once argued that the German émigrés tended to be the more radical and gravitated towards the United States (he had in mind people like Brecht, or some of the Frankfurt philosophers), whereas those raised in old Austria-Hungary such as Popper, Gombrich and Hayek found conservative, class-bound Britain more of a magnet.[6] I find this too schematic. I can think of many conservative figures who made their homes in the United States (Hayek himself in later life) and plenty of radicals who settled in the UK (think of Isaac Deutscher, Eric Hobsbawm or the cartoonist Vicky, for example). Apart from which, most émigrés simply fetched up wherever they had a friend, a cousin, a contact, the chance of a job; few had the luxury of choosing where they would go.

I would argue that there was, nevertheless, a difference between the *impact* of the emigration from Nazism on British and American cultural life and that, overall, it was probably greater here in Britain. It's not only that the numbers who came to the UK were proportionately larger. In addition, Britain was a comparatively homogeneous society in the 1930s in which a sudden wave of migrants made more cumulative impact than in the USA which, after all, had historically been built up by waves and waves of immigrants. In America, too, the émigrés were soon dispersed all over the country – to New York and New Haven, Boston and Black Mountain College, Los Alamos and Los Angeles.[7] In the UK, by contrast, they were more concentrated, forming something like what the physicists among them would have called a 'critical mass'.

Which is why, in my work, I have concentrated largely on London (with occasional forays to elite places like Oxford and Cambridge, Edinburgh and Glyndebourne). It has been pointed out that I have mentioned relatively few women in my book. And, to compound the political incorrectness, that I have homed in on indisputably tall poppies, an intellectual and cultural elite, purveyors of high excellence. If there are any members of the Thought Police present, I would humbly submit (as Hans Keller used to say) that, firstly, in pre-Hitlerian Central Europe, high culture was a predominantly masculine pursuit; and, secondly, that, like it or not, the tall (mostly male) poppies of my narrative did mostly settle in places like Northwest London and not equally around the country.

Each of these topics warrants a lecture in itself – food, no doubt, for lively historiographical disputation. But I want to put them momentarily aside and consider three further factors that seem to have growing contemporary resonance. Some have seen *The Hitler Emigrés* as a contribution to Nazi and Holocaust Studies. Others have read it as being about what people a generation ago would have called 'the Jewish contribution to civilisation'. And, thirdly, as I know from the thrust of just about every radio, television and press interview since the book came out, *The Hitler Emigrés* has been widely regarded as a case study illustrating the benefits of a generous immigration policy. Let me try and concentrate on these three topics.

***

First, Nazism and the war. In recent years we have experienced an extraordinary resurgence of interest in the Hitler era. A succession of films, books and television programmes on the subject sprang up, like the endless progeny of Banquo (TV's History Channel, indeed, became popularly renamed the 'Hitler Channel'), while hardly a week went by without prominent press coverage of yet another Nazi-related story: 'Nazi gold' in Swiss banks, Jorg Haider and the Freedom Party in Austria, the uncovering and arrest of yet another elderly alleged war criminal, what to do with art works looted by the Nazis, how far Pope Pius XII (or Britain's Duke of Windsor) gave unwarranted support to Nazi plans, the David Irving trial and the issue of 'Holocaust denial', whether to mark Hitler's birthplace, the inauguration in various countries (including Britain) of Holocaust Memorials, Museums and Days and the performance of Beethoven's Ninth Symphony on the site of the Mauthausen concentration camp.

There are of course good reasons why the Nazi era retains so powerful a purchase upon the collective imagination. The unprecedented barbarity unreined by the Hitler regime continues to hold a ghoulish fascination, while the epic struggle by which it was overcome provides inexhaustible material for inspiration and research. This greatest war in history was widely perceived as one in which forces of monumental evil had to be utterly eliminated if civilisation were to survive. This, surely, was what medieval theologians and Renaissance jurists meant by a 'just war'. Such a war inevitably cast a giant shadow over all of subsequent history, and continues to do so in our own times. But there are further reasons why the Nazi era returned to particular prominence at the end of the 20th century and the beginning of the 21st.

The very method by which World War II had been ended, the dropping of atomic bombs, gave notice of a new threat to civilisation, potentially every bit as conclusive as the one just defeated, and for forty-odd years the world lived under another shadow, the threat of nuclear annihilation. The eventual end of the Cold War and the dissolution of the USSR caused people to rub their eyes with disbelief as they gradually realised that thermonuclear holocaust had been avoided, at least for the time being, and saw the Soviet Union revealed as a sham, a charade, a chimera that dissolved, like a magician's stage set, in a puff of smoke.

The elimination of the USSR was widely seen in the West as a great triumph, the final removal of the 'evil empire'. One incidental result was the opening up of Soviet archives. This, as Ian Kershaw[8] and others have pointed out, helped shift the centre of gravity for historical research from Germany itself to Russia and Eastern Europe – the very epicentre of the Holocaust. A very practical reason, perhaps, for the growth of interest in the Holocaust over the past decade or so.

More generally, the end of the Cold War removed many of the geopolitical certainties of the previous half century, a bipolar world of good guys and bad. In the post-Cold War era, such certainties were no longer available as the world settled into a period of moral relativism, or what might be termed geopolitical post-modernism. In such a climate it is not perhaps surprising if there was a renewed hankering for the black-and-white certainties of yesteryear.

It seems that people need a 'hate figure' as part of a healthy psychological tool kit. Think how, over the years, we lapped up almost incredible stories about a succession of 'evil' characters – Idi Amin, Colonel Gaddafi, Radovan Karadzic, Slobodan Milosovic, Osama bin Laden, Saddam Hussein – each of whom was demonised, routinely compared with Hitler, and then dropped for a while as other stories took over. And it's said that the British were well-adjusted to reality and unusually lacking in neurosis while fighting World War II – a war in which, more than any other, pretty much every participant believed in the cause for which he or she was fighting.[9] It is hardly surprising then, if robbed of the psychologically convenient ogre of the Soviet Union, popular attention in the West in the 1990s reverted once more to the Nazi period.

In Germany, where historians had long struggled to comprehend the nature of Nazism, reunification brought about renewed public debate. In East Germany it had been common to portray Nazism as a barbarous form of capitalism that only communists had consistently opposed, while many in West Germany had found comfort in regarding the twelve years of Nazism (and the entire Hitler gang) as uniquely abhorrent and aberrant and therefore, in a sense, outside history. Clearly, such politically self-serving and often simplistic explanations would no longer suffice – just as Austrians can no longer take comfort from the illusion that their innocent nation was 'annexed' by the Third Reich.[10] In America, too, there were particular reasons why the war grew to great prominence several decades after the event (you can read some of them in Peter Novick's thought-provoking book *The Holocaust and Collective Memory*[11] in which he considers how and why the Holocaust gradually emerged to become absolutely central to the self-definition of American Jewry).

And in Britain? The recurrent interest in the Nazi era is also in part a reflection on subsequent history. The war was the last time the UK played a unique and pivotal part in world affairs (a fact pinpointed a few years later by the former US Secretary of State, Dean Acheson, when he said that Great Britain had 'lost an empire and not yet found a role'). As Britain slipped ever further from those heroic days when she had 'stood alone', many fell back on myths and memories of wartime heroism for solace and inspiration. Politicians were not immune from the temptation, as successive leaders evoked the spirit of Churchill (and Hitler) when ordering troops to foil the evil machinations of ruthless foreign dictators in the Falklands, the Gulf (twice!) or Kosovo.

But I think there is a further reason why the Nazi era has returned once more to prominence. By the turn of the millennium, the war was receding from living memory. Many with personal experience of it had died and, for their grandchildren's generation, it was gradually becoming consigned, almost like Agincourt or the Armada, to the fusty realm of myth. But the events and impact of World War II had been so momentous that many of the older generation became determined that first-hand knowledge of this of all wars should be preserved. Personal memoirs were recorded and videoed, archive banks accumulated, educational courses installed and museums opened. The more curious of the younger generation – like the boy Raleigh – became keen to learn what things had been like when giants and demons stalked the earth. Just as our Victorian ancestors would ask their pliant grandparents about Waterloo so, today, as the last participants in World War II approach the end of their lives, there is an almost palpable desire – by people of all ages – to spin out for as long as possible the direct legacy of that epochal era, soon to be lost to memory, as if anxious to retain the chain until the last link is finally broken.

Thus, as the 20th century crept towards its end, politicians and media indulged in an orgy of retrospection, marking with due solemnity and a plethora of reminiscences from the elderly, the anniversaries of the Munich Agreement, the outbreak of war, the arrival of Churchill in Downing Street, the Battle of Britain, the D-Day landings, the discovery of the concentration camps, VE and VJ Days. By the turn of the century, nobody in Britain could doubt that this, their 'finest hour', had also been the furnace in which the lives of all who lived thereafter had been tempered. So I suppose it was inevitable that any book with a title like *The Hitler Emigrés* – even if primarily about British cultural life – would be seen as a contribution to the vast literature about Germans, Nazism and the Second World War.

***

It has also been read as being about Jews, Jewry and the Jewish 'contribution'. Here again, I don't so much want to demur as to reflect. The question here is: what was the relevance – if any – of the Jewishness of so many of the 'Hitler Emigrés' to what they went on to achieve?

The first thing to say is that many of the 'Hitler Emigrés' were not Jewish. So far as I know, the artistic founding fathers of Glyndebourne, the director Carl Ebert and the conductor Fritz Busch, weren't Jewish. Ebert had been *Intendant* of the Charlottenburg Opera in Berlin (predecessor of today's *Deutsche Oper*) and Busch Artistic Director of Dresden's Semperoper. These were powerful, independent-minded figures who couldn't stand a regime that burned books and told them which works they could and couldn't perform, which musicians or set designers they could and couldn't employ. Hayek, who had come to the LSE in 1931 and was to stay for twenty years, was not Jewish but from a quasi-noble Viennese family which had produced strings of scientists and civil servants. Kokoschka wasn't Jewish, nor Fritz Schumacher, author of *Small is Beautiful*. Nor were Walter Gropius or Rudolf Laban, both of whom tried to make some adjustment with the Nazi regime in its early years but found this increasingly impossible.

Many of the 'Hitler Emigrés' were of course Jewish, but often only nominally so. 'To my parents, especially my father' (this was Claus Moser reminiscing to me) 'being German came first. He thought of himself as a German, and only then as a Jew'. Lord Moser's father was a wealthy banker in pre-Hitlerian Berlin. He had fought in World War I and he and his wife, like so many others in their position, thought of themselves as proud and patriotic Germans. 'That's why so many of them thought – tragically wrongly – that things would be all right,' their son told me, 'that this Hitler thing would pass over and they would be OK. They thought it wouldn't touch people like them because they were such good Germans!'

Lord Moser's memory was shared by many other refugees from Nazism who came from Jewish backgrounds. 'This terrible thing cannot last. Germany is a civilized nation and these barbarians will soon be out.' This was the father of the artist Milein Cosman (wife of the musician and broadcaster Hans Keller). Peter Frohlich, who went on to become the American historian Peter Gay, had two uncles called Siegfried. We were the real Germans, he recalled thinking when he was young. 'The gangsters who had taken control of the country were not Germany – we were.' The real Germany, after all, was 'the most civilized of countries'.[12]

And here is Fred Uhlman, in his semi-autobiographical novella *Reunion* about a young Jewish boy brought up in Stuttgart in the 1930s.

> … All I knew then was that this was my country, my home, without a beginning and without an end, and that to be Jewish was fundamentally no more significant than to be born with dark hair and not with red … [13]

The boy's father is a proud patriot and his Iron Cross, First Class, hangs over the bed alongside a picture of the Goethe-Haus in Weimar. One day, a Zionist visits the family home to collect money for the new cause. 'My father abhorred Zionism,' says the narrator. 'The whole idea seemed to him stark mad.' Doesn't Hitler shake your confidence, asks the Zionist? Not in the least, replies the boy's father, a popular doctor, respected (he is sure) by his Jewish and Gentile patients alike.

> 'I know my Germany,' says the boy's father. 'This is a temporary illness, something like measles, which will pass as soon as the economic situation improves. Do you really believe the compatriots of Goethe and Schiller, Kant and Beethoven will fall for this rubbish?'[14]

The cultural references are significant. Again and again, it is music, art, literature, that people, later émigrés from Hitler, mentioned when reflecting on what had made them and their families so proudly German. And I'm talking not just of German nationals but of people from all over German-speaking Central Europe. Nor was the culture they admired and imbibed exclusively German but included a knowledge of languages (ancient and modern), of the fine arts and a willingness to cross artistic boundaries. Thus, Schoenberg was a fine painter, Kandinsky interested in theories of music. The art historian Ernst Gombrich and the philosopher Karl Popper both adored music (and had mothers who were excellent pianists). Popper indeed – like Claus Moser – dreamed as a boy of becoming a professional musician. Martin Esslin, for many years BBC Radio's Head of Drama and world expert on Brecht and the Theatre of the Absurd, learned Greek and Latin at age twelve and by the time he was an adolescent had added reasonable French, English, Italian and Spanish. In Britain, Lord Moser told me in a sentiment shared by countless others, 'culture was the icing on the cake, whereas in Central Europe we were raised to think it was the cake!'

I don't want to give the impression that German Jewry en bloc was oblivious to its *Jewish* legacy. Far from it. There was a thriving religious life throughout the German-speaking world; one only has to recall the number of synagogues and other avowedly Jewish premises destroyed during *Kristallnacht*. Or the huge contribution later made to Anglo-Jewish life by people like Immanuel Jakobovits, Chief Rabbi during the Thatcher years or, in the Reform and Liberal communities, Leo Baeck, Ignaz Maybaum, Hugo Gryn, John Rayner and Albert Friedlander. And, of course, many Central European Jews became ardent Zionists. Zionism, said, George Weidenfeld, became his guiding beacon.[15]

The interesting question is not why Immanuel Jakobovits or Hugo Gryn retained their Jewish faith and Weidenfeld his Zionism but why so many of the Jews of German-speaking Central Europe, even though more or less oblivious of their Jewishness, seemed to excel in the professional, intellectual and cultural worlds. Was there anything specifically 'Jewish' about their achievements?

There are what you might call both positive and negative answers to that question. Throughout Jewish history, from Biblical times really, great emphasis had been placed on learning. The mythologised figures in the Jewish past had been Men of God, Rabbis, scholars. Daniel and his friends are praised for their devotion to their studies, Solomon for his wisdom.

From the Biblical Moses to Moses Maimonides in the 12th century to Moses Mendelssohn in the 18th, it is the prophets and philosophers, the scribes and the scholars quite as much as the kings and generals who are the role models. In the Russian and Polish Pale, in the *shtetl* and synagogue, the pivotal figure is the Rabbi and he is not so much a preacher or prayer leader as a teacher and scholar, the person responsible for the education of the next generation, the only figure in town capable of solving difficult questions of Jewish law. Even Jews who were not particularly conscious of their Jewish ancestry, or believed they had transcended or disavowed it (like Heine, Marx, Mahler, Schnitzler or Freud), tended to gravitate towards achievement in the intellectual and cultural worlds. Devotion to learning is a constant theme throughout much of Jewish history, one that was much in evidence in pre-Hitlerian Middle Europe. In *fin-de-siècle* Vienna, Jews made up about 10 per cent of the population (200,000 in a population of around 2 million), but they accounted for something like 30 per cent of the pupils enrolled in those elite grammar schools known as *Gymnasien*.[16]

It would be foolish to read too much into this admiration for learning or to apply it indiscriminately to all Jewish communities in the past. At certain times and places, it was the Jewish merchant or moneylender, for example, who became the archetype rather than the scholar or thinker. However, at least until the establishment of the State of Israel, Jews were not especially distinguished for their agricultural or military skills. But as writers and musicians, thinkers and mathematicians, people of Jewish origin and background had long been disproportionately prominent. To some extent, as I have suggested, this probably derives from the age-old emphasis on the value of learning, perhaps going back to Rabbinic and even Biblical times.

But I suspect it also arises from other, what you might call 'negative', causes as well. If you were a young Jewish man in late 19th-century or early 20th-century Vienna or Berlin, you would have known without it being spelled out to you that the upper ranks of certain professions were, in effect, barred to you. You would have been unlikely to aspire towards a career in the army, diplomacy, politics or (obviously) the church, for example. These professions tended to lend themselves to the sons of the social elite, and a young Jew, however gifted and ambitious, would probably have been courting rejection if he had set serious sights on them. 'A diplomat!', Fred Uhlman's father expostulates cruelly when his innocent son suggests the profession he thinks he might enter. 'Why not a Pope? Has anybody ever heard of a Jew in the diplomatic service? Do you think I am Bismarck?'[17]

It was partly a question of anti-Semitism; one only has to read the prose works of Wagner or the political speeches of the mayor of Vienna at the turn of the century, Karl Lueger, or to recall the fate of Alfred Dreyfus, a Jew who entered the army service in France, to be reminded that anti-Semitism was not invented by Adolf Hitler. Far better to gravitate towards those fields in which Jews (with all that *Gymnasium* education behind them) tended to be more widely accepted – the law and medicine, economics and philosophy, music, literature, journalism and publishing. Steven Beller suggests that over half of those teaching in the Medicine Faculty at the University of Vienna in 1910 and over a third of those teaching Law were of Jewish descent.[18]

So: the reasons why so many Jews moved into such fields probably included both the traditional 'pull' towards learning as well as the 'push' of exclusion from the upper reaches of the army or politics. 'Culture', in other words, provided a gateway to social mobility.[19]

There is a further point. Many of the leading figures in these liberal, cultural professions may have been Jewish but, as we have seen, would have considered themselves no more than nominally so. Some had even been converted to Christianity, though conversion fooled no-one. Jewish converts were often uncomfortable with their adopted faith and unlikely to tempt providence by trying to 'pass' in a traditionally closed profession. In any case, one of the main reasons for conversion was usually to help the proselytising family to keep out of the spotlight. Many more were neither converts nor practising Jews but, rather, thought of themselves as thoroughly 'assimilated'. And assimilation presupposed almost by definition the rejection of partisan ideology, separatism, exclusivity, dogma – Jewish, or any other – and, in their place, the aspiration to cross boundaries, embrace universal truths and the whole of humanity. These were the sentiments of the press and the academy, not of the army, church or politics. 'All Men are Brothers', Schiller had written, a cry famously hymned by Beethoven and echoed for a century thereafter by liberal intellectuals – including many assimilated Jews – who were neatly able to marry their cultural Germanism with a belief in universal values.

Many of these liberal-minded German Jews of Central Europe had roots further east, in the villages of Poland and Russia, Moravia, Hungary and Romania; but, if so, most were proud of having shaken the mud from their ancestral boots, thrown off their kaftans and *yarmulkes*, and moved upwards (and westwards) to a comfortable life of urbane sophistication in Breslau and Berlin, Munich and Vienna. To such people, Eastern Jews (*Ostjuden*) represented the past, those who had not made it, people without culture who clung on to outmoded attitudes and rituals. Silvia Rodgers, brought up in Berlin by Polish parents, was taken on a visit to Poland in 1934 and later recalled seeing a country and a Jewish community that 'to me, brought up in Germany, did look bizarre, as if from a previous century or another world'.[20] Germany, by contrast, stood for urban and urbane life rather than the fields and the ghetto, emancipation and enlightenment rather than atavistic obscurantism. Perhaps it was not so surprising after all, nor particularly reprehensible, that so many cultured families in Hitler's *Mitteleuropa* were 'more German than the Germans'.

***

Was there *nothing* specifically Jewish, then, about the later work in Britain of Gombrich, Popper or the Amadeus Quartet? Gombrich, to the end of his long life, denied that his Jewishness had anything to do with his art history. Who cares, he asked, whether this or that historian or philosopher happened to be Jewish? – adding pointedly that he'd rather leave such questions to the Gestapo. From the opposite corner, as it were, Immanuel Jakobovits, Chief Rabbi during the 1980s, told me with equal vehemence that he too could see nothing in the ideas of Marx or Freud (or Mahler or Einstein for that matter) that arose in any way from their Jewish backgrounds. As an orthodox rabbi, Lord Jakobovits regarded the historical importance of such people as lying outside Jewish history and therefore neither influenced by nor contributing to it.

Another very different figure who tried to grasp this thorny issue was Isaac Deutscher, biographer of Trotsky and author of an essay entitled 'The Non-Jewish Jew'.[21] Here, Deutscher considered what he called the great Jewish 'heretics' – he added people such as Spinoza and Heine to the familiar litany of Marx, Freud and the rest – and wondered what if anything they had in common. To Deutscher, it was not a question of vestigial, or subconscious religiosity. He argued that these, and people like them, gained their special strength from the fact that they dwelt on the borders of various civilisations, religions and national cultures and were born and brought up on the borderlines of epochs. 'Their mind matured where the most diverse cultural influences crossed and fertilised each other,' says Deutscher. 'They lived on the margins or in the nooks and crannies of their respective nations. Each of them was in society and yet not in it, of it and yet not of it.' Steven Beller, writing about Jews in *fin-de-siècle* Vienna, showed how they inhabited 'the centre of culture but the edge of society'.[22]

In other words, the very fact that Marx, Mahler, Freud and the rest transcended their Jewishness and reached out to cross boundaries of mind, place and even time, itself arose – paradoxically – from deep within Jewish history and tradition. It has sometimes been suggested that (from the wanderings in the Sinai desert, indeed!) Jewish achievement is, at core, that of a scattered diaspora, of a world-wide, cosmopolitan people linked by the shared legacy of settlement, upheaval, flight and resettlement (by this account, Israel becomes something of an historical by-way rather than the aspiration towards which Jewish history had always been leading). 'If there was anything specifically Jewish about it,' Eric Hobsbawm wrote in his autobiography, reflecting on the scattered family of his childhood, 'it was the assumption among all of them that the family was a network stretching across countries and oceans, that shifting between countries was a normal part of life.' The Jews, he agreed with a French colleague, were '*un people en diaspora*'.[23]

There's been something of a 'Diaspora Boom' recently; my bookshelves include a clutch of new titles like *Scattered Among the Peoples, Diasporas and Exiles, Jewries at the Frontier.* You may have come across the essay by Sander Gilman, 'The Frontier as a Model for Jewish History', in which Gilman attempts to reconcile the competing claims on Jewish identity of Israel and the Diaspora – centre and periphery – and argues that, post the creation of Israel, it's the idea of 'living on the frontier' that provides the key to understanding the modern Jewish experience. The 'frontier' in Gilman's formulation is no longer the outpost – the 'periphery' – that it was, say, to Frederick Jackson Turner, or regarded as a place of temporary exile. On the contrary, almost everyone nowadays lives on frontiers, on margins, on intellectual borderlands, in worlds that cross cultures – so that the Jewish experience of 'Diaspora' (archetypally perhaps in pre-Hitlerian Central Europe) has therefore led the way to the modern world we know today. This 'diasporic' view of Jewish history is, if you like, a kind of positive gloss on the old image of the Wandering Jew.[24]

As I studied the life and work of the 'Hitler Emigrés', I repeatedly encountered a sense that, certainly in the modern, 20th-century world, homelessness was almost regarded as a virtue, that the only true culture was one that crossed boundaries. 'The bags are always packed' – at least intellectually. Anthony Julius, in a stimulating exploration of what is Jewish about Jewish art, refers at one point to the painter Mark Rothko, who was born Rothkovich in Russia but lived as an émigré in the United States. You'll know all those wonderful big, tranquil abstract canvases that he did. Rothko, suggests Julius, reveals himself as a painter of Jewish origins in his 'insistence upon the universal character of art,' and his quest for (a form of representation) 'which unifies all human experience'. Jewish universalism again.[25]

And indeed, many of the 'Hitler Emigrés' gravitated towards international, multicultural or cross-disciplinary areas of interest. I think of journalists (such as Hella Pick) who gave British readers a broad international perspective on the stories of the day, publishers like Weidenfeld or Deutsch who consciously acted as bridges between languages and cultures, historians (Eric Hobsbawm is the classic example) who helped us to study historical processes across national boundaries. Gombrich brought to art history insights from psychology and anthropology. The excellent recent biography of Arthur Koestler by David Cesarani is entitled *The Homeless Mind*. Is the diasporic experience the norm? Isaac Deutscher is not, I suspect, alone in believing that this very process of travel – and travail – across constricting boundaries is precisely what had defined Jews from time immemorial.

***

It is also, of course, what defines the émigré, the exile, the refugee – the 'asylum seeker' in today's jargon – my final topic. I'll start with a couple of quotations, both of which may sound familiar. The first is from the Home Secretary, who said in the House of Commons:

> While ... it is proposed to pursue the policy of offering asylum as far as is practicable ... it is essential to avoid creating an impression that the door is open to immigrants of all kinds. If such an impression were created would-be immigrants would present themselves at the ports in such large numbers that it would be impossible to admit them all, great difficulties would be experienced deciding who could be properly admitted, and unnecessary hardship would be inflicted on those who had made a fruitless journey across the Continent.

My second quotation is from *The Daily Mail*.

> To be ruled by misguided sentimentalism ... would be disastrous ... Once it was known that Britain offered sanctuary to all who cared to come, the floodgates would be opened, and we should be inundated by thousands seeking a home.

Both quotations date from March 1938,[26] a week or so after the *Anschluss* when Hitler entered Vienna in triumph, adding Austria to the Third Reich. It is often thought that the 'Hitler Emigrés' who applied to come to Britain were highly favoured asylum seekers, afforded special status and welcomed with open arms. Not so. Not, at least, by everybody; or at first.

The total number of émigrés from Hitler's Central Europe who came to Britain, and settled here (as opposed to those who went on to the United States and elsewhere), was probably not a lot over 50,000. Not many, when you consider that in recent years we have often been getting over 70,000 asylum applications a year. And make no mistake. Many of those we are talking about were asylum seekers; think of those 10,000 youngsters who came over with the so-called Children's Transports in the final year or so before war broke out – people like Siegmund Nissel and Peter Schidlof, later of the Amadeus Quartet, or the film maker Karel Reisz. Should – could – Britain have been more generous? Before we rush to judgement we should perhaps remember that Britain, like America, was going through severe economic recession in the 1930s, and of course nobody at the time could have imagined the horrors, the death camps, that came later.[27]

As we speak, refugees are again knocking at the door asking for asylum in Britain, this time from Asia, North Africa, Eastern Europe and the Balkans. All over the world, indeed, people are trying to migrate in ever-greater numbers from the poorer or more unstable regions of the world to the wealthier, while governments such as our own struggle to find policies that they think will be wise, just – and politically acceptable: a difficult juggling act, not helped by a popular press happy to fuel rampant xenophobia. So what's new? you may think. Immigrants everywhere have always appeared to present a threat; they are by definition foreign, alien, 'Other'. Anarchists, terrorists, foreign spies – yes, immigrant groups have traditionally contained these too, and the Churchill government in summer 1940, fearful lest there might be some lurking among the 'Hitler Emigrés', infamously 'collared the lot', interning artists and architects, musicians and mathematicians, filmmakers and physicists in the Isle of Man and elsewhere.[28]

In Britain, ambivalence towards the 'Other', the outsider, runs deep. Always has, I suspect – particularly ambivalence towards the continent. On the one hand, the traditional panorama of British history tends to highlight this country's insular independence from the continent, how Britain has never been successfully invaded since 1066, how we beat off the Armada, Napoleon and Hitler. But when it comes to 'culture' – well, the British always thought Europe rather good at this. Think of the continental scholars at the court of Henry VII or the Venetian musicians – or Holbein – at that of his son Henry VIII. Think of Rubens, Van Dyck or Handel. In the 18th century, no gentleman was considered properly educated unless he spoke French and had undertaken the Grand Tour; in the 19th and into the 20th, any British musician worth his salt had to study in Germany, any decent artist needed exposure to Paris.

The story of the 'Hitler Emigrés' can be seen as, among other things, one chapter in that long story of British ambivalence towards arrivals from the continent, similar in a way to the story of the Huguenots who fled Louis XIV and came to Britain in the late seventeenth century. Some in Britain were hostile, questioning the wisdom of letting them in but in retrospect we can see that the new arrivals added greatly to the cultural mix which we have inherited. The Huguenot contribution is now very well-known – thanks in part to the efforts of people like Irene Scouloudi. As for the 'Hitler Emigrés', I think we can say that, by mixing their labours with what they found when they got here, they helped professionalise aspects of our cultural life. Consider, for example, the transformation of art history from a genteel, Sunday-afternoon pursuit seventy or eighty years ago preoccupied with questions of aesthetics and connoisseurship, to the highly professionalised academic subject of today as pioneered by Gombrich and his colleagues at the Warburg Institute. Or the somewhat amateur atmosphere at the Royal Opera House that upset George Solti when he arrived as Music Director and which he swore he would eradicate. At his first press conference, Solti said he'd turn the place into the finest opera house in the world – which I think it was by the time he left in 1971.[29]

The 'Hitler Emigrés' also helped cosmopolitanise British cultural life, creating new links with that of resurgent continental Europe. It was largely through the émigrés that a British generation raised on neo-Tudorbethan architecture and the Garden City became familiar with the Modernism pioneered by Gropius and the Bauhaus, music lovers with the work of Schoenberg and his protégés, theatregoers with Brecht and Ionesco.

Whenever George Weidenfeld talked about 'we', his friends would joke, you never quite knew if he meant the British, the Europeans, the Jews or the whole of humanity!

In some ways the 'Hitler Emigrés' were an unusual group of asylum seekers. Many were from educated, well-connected (and reasonably moneyed) middle- or upper-middle class families: not, by and large, your huddled masses yearning to be free. But, like many groups of migrants before and since, they did want to do whatever they could for their country of adoption. I have heard countless touching stories of people who, having found refuge in Britain, made Herculean efforts to become as British as possible: to hide their foreign accent and speak good English, roll their umbrellas, eat porridge and put milk instead of lemon in their tea, and learn to love 'cricket'. One man waited years to get British naturalisation. Finally, his papers came through – and he promptly burst into tears. 'But why now of all times are you crying?' his friend asked. 'I know I should be happy,' blubbed the new British citizen. 'I am crying because – why did we have to lose India!'[30]

Fifty, sixty years ago, many émigrés found they could comfortably doff one nationhood and enthusiastically embrace another. Nowadays, partly because of the very extremes of nationalism associated with Nazism, earnest expressions of patriotism have become unfashionable, at least in our part of the world. People tend to emphasise not what unites but what differentiates them. Region, religion, colour, ethnicity, sexual orientation or age bracket: these are nowadays asserted, with accompanying demands for appropriate respect and cultural provision. Today, as people tell you they are Black or Asian, Welsh or Scottish, straight, gay or lesbian, senior citizens or single-parent welfare claimants, it almost seems there are as many Brit*ains* as there are Brit*ons*. Thus, many of the more recent arrivals to these shores identify more closely with the culture they and their parents have come from rather than that they have come to. It would be wrong to blame them if they are less inclined than the 'Hitler Emigrés' of the 1930s to identify themselves as 'British'; this is no longer the fashion. But if the 'Hitler Emigrés' made a contribution to the life and culture of their new homeland, this was undoubtedly eased by the fact that most tried to identify with its values, speak its language and subscribe to its civic structures and traditions.

Today, history has moved on. I have a couple of children in their mid-twenties (in 2003), and they're not particularly interested in the legacy of

Expressionist film or Modernist architecture, the paintings of Kokoschka or the essays of Koestler. Why should they be? They and their contemporaries are growing up in a new, 21st-century world of Brit-art, postmodernism, computer-graphics, Afro-Caribbean influences and World Music. And I don't want to suggest that the contribution of the 'Hitler Emigrés' was the be-all and the end-all of the immensely rich and varied cultural world of 1950s and 1960s Britain in which I was raised. Of course it wasn't. I was brought up in a world of Laurence Olivier and Peters Brook and Hall, of Tippett and Britten, of Francis Bacon and Henry Moore, of Wain, Braine and Amis (that's Kingsley of course!).

So I don't want to exaggerate. But the work of the 'Hitler Emigrés', and the way it intermixed with what was already here, did provide an important part of that world. And I'm glad to think that it's been caught (as it were) when it was. Thirty years ago, it would have been impossible to have undertaken a book like *The Hitler Emigrés*. Most of the people I have written about were in mid-career, and wouldn't have reflected on their lives and work as candidly as they were to do later. Thirty years hence, the story will have gone. Indeed, many of those I interviewed have since died. Today – virtually as we speak – the story of the 'Hitler Emigrés' is moving from Memory into History.

And I don't want to suggest false analogies with today's asylum seekers. The bedraggled beggars on our streets from Bosnia, Baghdad or Bucharest are not filling a labour shortage as did the Caribbean arrivals in the 1950s, nor do most of them have the educational accomplishments of the 'Hitler Emigrés'. But let's think positively. Who knows what they and their descendants might contribute to life in a thriving, multicultural Britain as the past and present yield to the unchartable future? If there is one thing about our new era of which we can be reasonably certain, it is that growing world population, allied to increasingly cheap and accessible means of communication and transportation, will stimulate ever larger movements of people and ideas across national boundaries.

***

So: the Nazis and the war; Jews and Jewishness; and immigration and asylum. Three topics, all of which have risen once again to the top of the agenda. In the first place, our world, in the aftermath of the attacks of 9/11, and subsequently on centres of Western activity and enterprise around the globe, have faced us once again with forces apparently as destructive in their avowed intent as Nazism. Second, the very nature of Jewishness and Jewish identity is once more being urgently questioned, re-examined, re-defined, in both Israel and the Diaspora – partly in response to a resurgence of virulent anti-Semitism. And thirdly, new waves of migrants are seeking asylum, in Britain and elsewhere, fleeing oppressive regimes – and anxious about the kind of reception they will receive from ambivalent governments and a frequently antipathetic press and public. The topics are of course interconnected – and worldwide in their implications. So they were sixty years ago.

As we gradually adjust to the hatreds, fears, anxieties and opportunities of our strange new 21st century, therefore, we might do well to ponder once again the startling silver linings that can encircle even the darkest historical clouds. In particular, the cultural enrichment from which Britain benefited thanks to migrations of the past such as the Huguenots who fled Louis XIV in the 18th century – and the 'Hitler Emigrés' admitted into Britain in the 20th.

And of course this is not just a British story. Last year (2002) I went on a 2-month, round-the-world lecture tour. Everywhere, people told me about émigrés from Nazism who had brought their gifts to this or that particular city, region or nation. Indeed, it is one of the great ironies of history that Hitler, by trying to stamp out a cosmopolitan culture that he abhorred, succeeded in the long run in bringing it to the entire world.

So I'd like to end with a quotation – not from a Brit but from an American. In addition to providing refuge for great luminaries such as Einstein, Brecht, Thomas Mann and Schoenberg, for example, the United States also became home to many of the most distinguished artists who fled from Nazism: painters like Chagall, Max Ernst and George Grosz, art historians of the calibre of Erwin Panofsky, and virtually all the great figures from the Bauhaus. In the 1930s, the Director of the New York Institute of Art was Walter Cook. He used to enjoy going up to people and saying: 'Hitler is my best friend: he shakes the tree – and I collect the apples!'[31]

***

Notes

NB: The following people, referred to and/or quoted in the text (and notes), were among the many 'Hitler Emigrés' I interviewed between 1997 and 2002: Norbert Brainin (Amadeus Quartet), Milein Cosman Keller, Martin Esslin, Sir Ernst Gombrich, Eric Hobsbawm, Lord Jakobovits, Lord Moser, Siegmund Nissel (Amadeus Quartet), Max Perutz, Peter Pulzer, Karel Reisz and Lord Weidenfeld.

1. Lord Beveridge, *Power And Influence* (Hodder and Stoughton, 1953), pp. 234–5.
2. Lionel Robbins, *Autobiography of an Economist* (Macmillan, 1971), p. 144. Beveridge writes of the origins and early history of the AAC and SPSL in *Power and Influence*, pp. 234–8, and in his later book *A Defence of Free Learning* (OUP, 1959).
3. Robbins, *op cit*, p. 140.
4. See, for example, the charming memoir by Carl F Flesch (son of the celebrated violinist), which he entitles *Where do you come from? Hitler refugees in Great Britain then and now: The happy compromise!* (Pen and Press Publishers Ltd, 2001)
5. Marion Berghahn examines the question of the 'assimilation', 'acculturation' etc. of the 'Hitler Emigrés', as well as the generational issue, in *German-Jewish Refugees in England: The Ambiguities of Assimilation* (Macmillan, 1984). Alfred Kerr is transparently disguised as the wise father in *When Hitler Stole Pink Rabbit* (Collins Modern Classics, 1998) by his daughter Judith Kerr, and is evocatively described in George Weidenfeld's autobiography, *Remembering My Good Friends* (HarperCollins, 1995), p. 106. For a longer English-language consideration of the life and work of Alfred Kerr after his arrival in Britain, see the article by Deborah Vietor-Englander in William Abbey *et al.* (eds), *Between Two Languages: German-speaking Exiles in Great Britain, 1933–45* (Verlag Hans-Dieter Heinz, Akademischer Verlag Stuttgart, 1995).
6. Perry Anderson, 'Components of the National Culture' in *New Left Review* (no. 50, July–August 1968, pp. 3–57).
7. There is a large bibliography on the intellectual and cultural impact of the 'Hitler Emigrés' who went to the USA. In addition to countless individual biographies and memoirs (and Christopher Hampton's play *Tales from Hollywood*), these include: Mark M Anderson (ed), *Hitler's Exiles: Personal Stories of the Flight from Nazi Germany to America* (The New Press, New York, 1998); Stephanie Barron (ed), *Exiles+Emigres: The Flight of European Artists from Hitler* (Los Angeles County Museum of Art, 1997); Laura Fermi, *Illustrious Immigrants: The Intellectual Migration from Europe, 1930–41* (University of

Chicago Press, 1968); Donald Fleming and Bernard Bailyn (eds), *The Intellectual Migration: Europe and America, 1930–1960* (The Belknap Press of Harvard University Press, 1969); Anthony Heilbut, *Exiled in Paradise: German Refugee Artists and Intellectuals in America from the 1930s to the Present* (Viking, 1983); H Stuart Hughes, *The Sea Change: The Migration of Social Thought, 1930–1965* (Harper and Row, 1975); Jarrell C Jackman and Carla M Borden (eds), *The Muses Flee Hitler: Cultural Transfer and Adaptation, 1930–1945* (Smithsonian Institution, 1983); Claus-Dieter Krohn, *Intellectuals in Exile* (University of Massachusetts Press, 1993); Abraham J Peck, *The German-Jewish Legacy in America 1938–1988* (Wayne State University Press, Detroit, 1989); Friedrich Stadler and Peter Weibel (eds), *The Cultural Exodus from Austria* (Springer Verlag, 1995); John Russell Taylor, *Strangers in Paradise: The Hollywood Emigres 1933–1950* (Holt, Rinehart & Winston, 1983).

8. Ian Kershaw, *The Nazi Dictatorship: Problems & Perspectives of Interpretation* (Arnold, 2000), p. 269.

9. Angus Calder records that statistics for suicide and drunkenness fell during the war. Angus Calder, *The People's War, Britain 1939–45* (The Literary Guild, 1969), p. 223.

10. Ian Kershaw, *op cit*. See, in particular, Chapters 1 ('Historians and the problem of explaining Nazism') and 10 ('Shifting perspectives: historiographical trends in the aftermath of unification').

11. Peter Novick, *The Holocaust and Collective Memory* (Bloomsbury, 2001).

12. Peter Gay, *My German Question: Growing Up in Nazi Berlin* (Yale UP, 1998), pp. 111–112.

13. Fred Uhlman, *Reunion* (The Harvill Press, 1997), p. 39.

14. *ibid*, p. 40.

15. For the impact on Anglo-Jewish religious life, see Werner Mosse et al (ed), *Second Chance: Two Centuries of German-speaking Jews in the United Kingdom* (J C B Mohr (Paul Siebeck) Tubingen), 1991), pp. 405–462. George Weidenfeld's Zionism is a recurrent theme in his *Remembering My Good Friends*.

16. Steven Beller, *Vienna and the Jews 1867–1938: A cultural history* (CUP, 1997), p. 52.

17. Fred Uhlman, *The Making of an Englishman* (Gollancz, 1960), p. 60.

18. Beller, *op cit*, p. 36.

19. The (Vienna-born) Peter Pulzer discussed the 'push' and 'pull' that led German and Austrian Jews towards the liberal and intellectual professions in his Fritz Thyssen Lecture, 'What Shall I Put in my Luggage? Thoughts on the Cultural Migration from Central Europe' delivered in Jerusalem in June 1999.

20. Silvia Rodgers, *Red Saint, Pink Daughter* (Carcanet, 1997), p. 108.

21. Isaac Deutscher, *The Non-Jewish Jew and Other Essays* (OUP, 1968).

22. Steven Beller, *op cit*, pp. 216–7.

23. Eric Hobsbawm, *Interesting Times: A Twentieth-Century Life* (Allen Lane The Penguin Press, 2002, pp. 15, 25)

24. Allan Levine, *Scattered Among the Peoples: The Jewish Diaspora in Ten Portraits* (McClelland and Stewart, Toronto, 2002); Howard Wettstein (ed), *Diasporas and Exiles: Varieties of Jewish Identity* (University of California Press, 2002), Sander L Gilman and Milton Shain (eds): *Jewries at the Frontier* (University of Illinois Press, 1999). Gilman's essay 'The Frontier as a Model for Jewish History', originally the Introduction to *Jewries at the Frontier*, is reprinted with modifications in Sander L Gilman, *Jewish Frontiers: Essays on Bodies, Histories and Identities* (Palgrave Macmillan, 2003).

25. Anthony Julius writes of Rothko in *Idolizing Pictures: Idolatry, Iconoclasm and Jewish Art* (Thames & Hudson, 2000), p. 98. Silvia Rodgers – a red-haired Jewess born to Communist Polish parents – writes sensitively of the 'betwixts and betweens' of her Berlin childhood. This multiple 'marginality', she says, was dangerous in Nazi Germany – but after migration, it became a strength. In England, says Rodgers, 'I have come to glory in it as a gift' (Silvia Rodgers, *Red Saint, Pink Daughter*, p. 12). But she adds a sting in the tail, pointing out that, in German, the word *Gift* also means poison!

26. The Home Secretary, Leslie Hore-Belisha, was speaking in the House of Commons on 22 March 1938, while the quotation from *The Daily Mail* is from the issue of 23 March 1938. Both are reproduced in A J Sherman, *Island Refuge: Britain and Refugees from the Third Reich 1933–1939* (Elek, 1973), pp. 93–94.

27. The most recent book about the Children's Transports is Mark Jonathan Harris and Deborah Oppenheimer, *Into the Arms of Strangers: Stories of the Kindertransport* (Bloomsbury, 2000). The most substantial recent study of British policy towards the refugees from Nazism is Louise London, *Whitehall and the Jews* (CUP 2003).

28. The first important book on internment was Francois Lafitte, *The Internment of Aliens* (Penguin, 1940, reprinted 1988). More recent studies include Peter and Leni Gillman, *'Collar the Lot!' How Britain Interned and Expelled its Wartime Refugees* (Quartet Books, 1980) and Ronald Stent, *A Bespattered Page: The Internment of 'His Majesty's Most Loyal Enemy Aliens'* (Deutsch, 1980). One of the most vivid descriptions of internment is in an essay, originally for *The New Yorker*, by the biochemist and Nobel laureate Max Perutz, most recently reproduced as 'Enemy Alien' in his collection *I Wish I'd Made You Angrier Earlier* (OUP, 1998).

29. Solti thought so, too. See his autobiography, *Solti on Solti: A Memoir* (Chatto & Windus, 1997), p. 157. For the supposed amateurishness he found when he arrived, see p. 152. For Solti's incomprehension at 'English ways', see John Tooley, *In House: The Story of Covent Garden* (Faber and Faber, 1999), p. 26. Sir Georg Solti was far from being the only Central European emigre to

rail at what he saw as English amateurishness. Nikolaus Pevsner pronounced that 'the amateur (was) altogether characteristic of England', a country that has produced 'a nice crop of amateur painters from maiden aunts to Prime Ministers' (Nikolaus Pevsner, *The Englishness of English Art*, Penguin ed, 1997, p. 80). Geoffrey Elton condemned the amateur historian for finding the past, or parts of it, 'quaint', while the professional, quite incapable of this, 'lives in it as a contemporary … equipped with immunity, hindsight and arrogant superiority' (GR Elton, *The Practice of History*, Collins Fontana edition, 1969, p. 30). George Weidenfeld, noting that he and his partner Nigel Nicolson both lacked business training when setting up their publishing firm, said that he 'considered it a regrettable shortcoming (while) Nigel was secretly proud of it' (George Weidenfeld, *op cit*, p. 125).

30. I first encountered a version of this frequently-repeated story in Paul Tabori, *The Anatomy of Exile: A Semantic and Historical study* (Harrap, 1972). Not everyone went so far as to weep on becoming British. But consider the contribution of Alexander Korda to his new homeland. The Hungarian-born film producer named his company 'London Films', adopted Big Ben as his trademark and placed a couple of conspicuous Union flags outside the main entry. Korda went on to produce a string of self-consciously 'British' feature films, such as *The Private Life of Henry VIII*, *The Drum*, *Elephant Boy*, *The Four Feathers* and *That Hamilton Woman*, became close to Churchill (and is believed to have done intelligence work for him in the USA) and was later knighted. See Karol Kulik, *Alexander Korda: The Man Who Could Work Miracles* (Virgin Books, 1990).

31. Walter Cook is quoted in the Epilogue ('Impressions of a Transplanted European') of Erwin Panofsky, *Meaning in the Visual Arts: Papers in and on Art History* (Penguin, 1993), p. 380.

Insiders/Outsiders

Introduction.

Insiders/Outsiders *was a nationwide festival, created in 2019 by the art historian Monica Bohm-Duchen, to examine and celebrate the rich contribution of refugees from Nazi-dominated Europe to the visual arts across the UK. Originally intended to last for a year, the festival proved of widespread interest and was extended (largely by Zoom) throughout and beyond the Covid pandemic of 2020–23.*

I was consultant to the project and the text included here – a shorter, less academic article than the one above – is largely based on my Introduction to the book that accompanied the festival, published by Lund Humphries in 2019 (and a similar article written for the magazine Jewish Renaissance*).*

All migrations bring 'culture' with them, as much of British history testifies: consider the legacy of the 400-year Roman occupation, the Angles and Saxons, Normans, Huguenots, the Irish following the Great Famine, Jews escaping Russian pogroms in the later 19th century and many another migration. So what of the culture brought to Britain by the refugees from Nazism? What resulted when people schooled in Expressionist art, Bauhaus architecture, Schoenbergian Modernism, Brechtian drama and Weimar-era cabaret began to mix their labours with the arguably more genteel culture they found in Britain: a world of Bloomsbury, Garden Cities, the BBC and the olde-worlde revivalist architecture of Edwin Lutyens or the musical pastoralism of Holst and Vaughan Williams? It is important to know, for the admixture of the two contributed mightily to the richly-textured cultural milieu of Britain over the decades that followed.

The story is primarily a story about men, notwithstanding the elegant pottery of Lucie Rie, the paintings of Marie-Louise von Motesiczky, the photography of Dorothy Bohm, the outstanding designs of Dorrit Dekk and the creative output of numerous other women, many of whom deserve further research and recognition. To add to the political incorrectness, I should add that the story is also predominantly (but not entirely) London-based: northwest London in particular, as many of the émigrés settled in and around Hampstead, Swiss Cottage and St John's Wood.

***

London was to prove for many the perfect place from which to set out on their new post-war lives. Much of Europe had been under the control of the Third Reich during the war and countless cities severely bombed. In Britain, despite the horrors and privations of war, many felt now was the time to build on the civilised values for which 'we' had fought. And the émigré community – musicians in particular, perhaps – were among those to benefit. An 'Arts Council' was established to provide public funds for music and the arts, and the BBC established the 'Third Programme', a radio network devoted to high-quality music and culture. Covent Garden reopened to opera and ballet (its first opera director a former Schoenberg pupil, Karl Rankl) and audiences for classical music were boosted by members of the refugee community eager to recapture something of the life they had been forced to flee. One way and another, London was becoming the centre of the musical world. Literally so. Former musical capitals such as Berlin, Munich, Vienna, Prague or Budapest, struggling to shake off the debris of war, found themselves on the frontiers of the emerging Cold War, while the introduction of the jet plane soon enabled London to be reached from New York in a mere seven hours. What better location for a new string quartet such as the Amadeus to launch itself or for Otto Klemperer to take up the reins – or the baton – of the Philharmonia Orchestra!

***

To what extent are we talking about 'Jewish Refugees from Germany'? Many of the émigrés were from countries other than Germany that had been taken over, all or in part, by the Third Reich: from Austria (especially Vienna), from Hungary, Czechoslovakia, Poland and elsewhere. Nor, as we have seen above (pp. 136 et seq) were all the émigrés Jewish: the artistic founding fathers of Glyndebourne, Carl Ebert and Fritz Busch, for example, or the choreographer Rudolf Laban, all of whom initially tried to make some accommodation with the Nazi regime but soon found this impossible.

Most were of course Jewish, but many only nominally so. As Claus Moser told me in the 1990s, his father thought of himself as 'a German, and only then as a Jew', while the art historian Ernst Gombrich denied that his Jewishness had anything to do with his scholarly interests. Who cares, Gombrich would ask defiantly, whether this or that historian or philosopher happened to be Jewish? – adding pointedly that such questions were more the domain of Hitler. In Isaac Deutscher's essay 'The Non-Jewish Jew', he argued that the very fact that Marx, Mahler and the rest transcended their Jewishness and reached out to cross boundaries of mind, place and time arose from deep within Jewish history and tradition: a view of Jewish history that put a modern gloss on the old image of the Wandering Jew. In Judith Kerr's semi-autobiographical novel *When Hitler Stole Pink Rabbit*, the little girl asks her father when on their way to exile in Britain: 'Do you think we'll ever really belong anywhere?' The father replies gently: 'I suppose not ... But we'll belong a little in lots of places, and I think that may be just as good.'

***

In some ways they were an unusual group of migrants. Many were from educated, well-connected middle- or upper-middle class families: not, by and large, your huddled masses yearning to breathe free. But, like many migrants before and since, most wanted to do whatever they could for their country of adoption. By mixing their labours with what they found when they arrived in Britain, they helped professionalise aspects of British cultural life. Art history, for example, became a highly professionalised academic subject as pioneered by Gombrich and his colleagues at the Warburg Institute, while the somewhat amateur atmosphere at the Covent Garden opera house that upset George Solti when he arrived as Music Director in 1961 was transformed under his leadership to become, by the time he left a decade later, one of the world's finest.

Furthermore, the émigrés helped cosmopolitanise the still somewhat insular culture of Britain, acting as a bridge between British cultural life and that of resurgent continental Europe. Pevsner, in a succession of writings, introduced the ideas of Gropius and the Bauhaus to a generation raised on the Tudorbethan revival and the Garden City ideal while Hobsbawm examined historical processes across national boundaries and Martin Esslin at the BBC brought the work of Central European playwrights to British audiences. The émigrés may have become 'Insiders'; but their special strength was the way many of the most talented were able, at the same time, to retain the vision of the 'Outsider'.

***

Today, most have passed away and the whole subject is moving from 'memory' into 'history'. The refugees from Nazism, like other migrant groups, played a part in the cultural life of their adopted homeland, but did not dominate it. They helped irrigate the cultural current, immeasurably enriching it; but they did not constitute the river itself.

In Britain, ambivalence towards the 'Other', the outsider, runs deep. On the one hand, the traditional panorama of British history tends to highlight the nation's insular independence from the continent, how Britain has never been successfully invaded since 1066, how 'we' beat off the Armada, Napoleon and Hitler. But when it comes to 'culture' the British have always thought foreigners rather good at this. In the 18th century, no gentleman was deemed fully educated unless he spoke French and had undertaken the Grand Tour, while in the 19th and into the 20th any British musician worth his salt had to study in Germany and any decent artist needed exposure to Paris.

The story of the 'Hitler Emigrés' can thus be seen as, among other things, just another chapter in that long story of successive waves of immigrants from Europe to Britain. In retrospect, however, we can also appreciate how, by melding elements of their own culture with that of their adopted homeland, they helped enrich the overall mix that subsequent generations were to inherit. Fifty years ago, a project like 'Insiders/Outsiders' would have been impossible to undertake: the story was ongoing and most of the individuals highlighted were in mid-career. Fifty years from now, the story will have slipped into an ever-receding past, just one historical episode among many. Now, therefore, is the perfect moment to take stock of its overall significance.

Truman's 'decision' to drop the atomic bomb

A recent film about J Robert Oppenheimer (the 'father of the A-bomb') attracted widespread attention and gave rise to a recurrent wave of public debate about whether Hiroshima was a 'good thing' (it brought World War II to a rapid end with minimum loss of life), or one of the most abhorrent political decisions in history. How did Truman reach his decision to drop atomic bombs on Hiroshima and Nagasaki in August 1945?

During the Kennedy years (1961–63) I was a postgraduate student at Cornell University in the USA where I did an MA degree on the issue of presidential decision-making and, in particular, Truman's to drop the bomb. In addition to the academic research involved, I contacted Oppenheimer and interviewed several of his atomic scientists as well as many of the influential political figures of the time. Above all, I had a substantial conversation with Truman himself which, in variously edited forms, I went on to publish in later years in a number of outlets.

I had worked assiduously on my MA thesis throughout much of the 1962–63 academic year, examining the history of the Manhattan Project and the extraordinary confluence of scientific, military and political considerations that led to Hiroshima. Then, while planning the outlines of a summer trip across the USA to the West Coast and back, I realised I would – or could – pass through Missouri. I wrote to ex-President Truman telling him of my work and asking if I might meet him. A letter came back, addressed to me at the Department of Government, Cornell University. The envelope included no stamp; just the printed signature of the ex-President:

> Dear Mr Snowman:
> Mr Truman will be glad to see you when you are in this part of the country. If you will telephone when you arrive in the area, a time will be set up for you to come in.
> Sincerely yours,
> (signed) Rose A Conway
> Secretary to Mr Truman

I called his office from St Louis, Missouri, on 14 July 1963, and was told to present myself at the Truman Library in the President's hometown of Independence, just outside Kansas City, at 9 am two days later (the 18th anniversary of the first atomic bomb test in Alamogordo, New Mexico).

***

I was shown into an open-plan office. Rose Conway was working at a desk in the corner and told me that Mr Truman came in every day; he was currently working on a new book: *History for Teenagers*. A few minutes later, Truman appeared. He was dressed in a lightweight, loose-fitting, blue-and-white striped cotton suit that gave his seventy-nine-year-old tummy plenty of room to expand. He looked at me with an open-mouthed, jaw-protruding grin as though slightly amused by my temerity. We shook hands and he beckoned to me to sit down.

I told him, with what I took to be appropriate respect, that I had been studying American politics at Cornell and his immediate riposte was that I 'should've come and learned it out here ringing doorbells. They know more about politics out here than in those big East Coast schools,' he grinned.

My particular project, I said, had been a study of presidential decision-making and, in particular, his decision to drop the atomic bomb. He broke through my deferential manner with a guffaw.

'That was no decision!' he said, demolishing with a single pre-emptive strike the entire basis of my thesis.

Truman, who had become President barely four months before Hiroshima upon the sudden death of Franklin D Roosevelt, had been convinced by FDR's advisers, notably the venerable Secretary of War, Henry L Stimson, that dropping the atomic bomb on people was the one initiative that might bring the war in the Pacific to a rapid end without the need for a protracted and bloody invasion of the Japanese islands, which might have cost a million lives. In other words, Truman had had little option other than to order the bomb project to proceed. Indeed, if he had been the kind of person to have said 'No' to such a proposal, he would hardly have been elected Senator from Missouri in the first place or been chosen to run with FDR as Vice-President.

'That wasn't a decision!' Truman repeated, with added emphasis. 'Do you know about those bombs the Germans were developing in World War I? The big ones that were designed to fall on Paris?'

I nodded.

'That's all the atomic bomb was. A big bomb to end the war. And it did end it too! I had given the Japanese a warning of what we were going to do and received a sassy reply. Well, they knew what was coming, and it came.'

As I understood it, the USA at the time had manufactured only two atomic bombs: the Uranium-235 'Little Boy' bomb, dropped on

Hiroshima on 6 August 1945, and the plutonium 'Fat Man' bomb dropped on Nagasaki three days later.

'We had lots of 'em,' Truman told me with another wicked grin.

'Did you? I know you said they'd rain upon the Japanese if they didn't surrender, but I thought that was just to frighten them.'

'Well, once the first one was made, others could be easily constructed.'

I asked him about the great secrecy that surrounded the Manhattan Project. During the war, before his nomination as FDR's Vice-Presidential running mate in 1944, Missouri Senator Truman had been Chairman of the Senate's Special Committee to Investigate the National Defense Program. Later, in his *Memoirs*, he had mentioned that he nearly found out about the Manhattan Project but was persuaded by Stimson not to send investigators into certain war plants. Was this true?

'Yes, Stimson asked me if I would be good enough to call off the investigations. But I knew about the project.'

'Through the Committee?'

'Sure. That's what it was for – to investigate large wartime expenditure. This thing cost two billion dollars, you know.'

Did Truman really know about the Manhattan Project before becoming President? Or was I hearing a combination of bravado, hindsight and the right of the elderly to embroider the facts? If Truman's Senate Committee had found out about the Manhattan Project, who else was in the know? What about all those Congressmen who had had to vote for the appropriations? Did they know what all that money was for? It seems not. Truman told me that Stimson and others (he mentioned General George C Marshall) had persuaded the Congressional leaders of the importance of this funding.

'You mean they voted for all that money and didn't know where it was going?' I asked.

'Yup. But you must remember – this was wartime.' He reminded me of the importance of secrecy during times of war, and how this was a concept perfectly familiar in the UK. A cue, I felt, to ask about British participation in the Manhattan Project. How much did Churchill know?

'As much as he wanted to know.'

I tried to press the former President. 'You mean he preferred to leave all the responsibility with you, the Americans?'

'No. But he wanted to be able to report fully to Parliament.'

Churchill, at least according to Truman, didn't want to know what he didn't want to know.

Truman made a few complimentary remarks about Churchill and various other European contributions to the atomic bomb project – especially those of émigré physicists. Then it was time for another Truman squib.

'Of course, the dropping of the bomb wasn't the biggest decision I had to make as President.'

'But surely it had the biggest effect.'

'No. It wasn't the biggest or the most important. The biggest decision was to go into Korea.'

I reflected that I had obviously chosen the wrong topic for my thesis and should have picked on the 1950 intervention in Korea. How, I wondered aloud, does a President reach a decision of such importance?

'You simply look at the facts,' Truman told me. 'Nobody had access to all the facts except the President.'

'True. But on many issues, you must have had doubts. You'd come to a decision, change your mind, wonder whether all the information before you was accurately reported and so on?'

'Yes, of course. But I'd check up on the facts, and then come to a decision – and then go on to the next one. I've never lost any sleep over any decision I've had to make.'

And that clearly included the bombing of Hiroshima and Nagasaki. By now emboldened, I told Truman I had always had visions of the President of the United States pacing the corridors of the White House, like Lincoln during the Civil War, weighed down by the pressure of the job.

'I was never under any pressure in the White House.'

My scepticism must have shown, for Truman leaned forward and added, confidentially: 'Your Winston Churchill was the same, you know.'

Clearly, this was a man keen to appear decisive, even unreflective, the man who famously told people that 'if you can't stand the heat you should keep out of the kitchen'. It was almost as though he thought that weighing the pros and cons was a sign of indecisiveness, of weakness – something of which President Kennedy was at the time being frequently criticised. A great many decisions, Truman told me, have to be made by the President and by him alone. I mentioned the famous motto on his desk: 'THE BUCK STOPS HERE'. Did he acquire that attitude in the White House?

'Nope. Why, I ran this county (Jackson County, Missouri) the same way years ago'. Truman looked out of the window and mused about his early days in politics as part of the legendary Prendergast machine. And he emphasised once more how he ('and your Winston') always got on with whatever was the next job in hand.

Eventually it was time to go. 'Well,' he laughed, as I made to stand up, 'it's nice that you youngsters are able to think about these things long after the event and decide what should or shouldn't have been done at the time!' He doubtless had in mind historians like Gar Alperovitz who had argued that the bomb was an unnecessary, unmitigated evil. Or the scientist Patrick Blackett who believed that Truman, aware that Stalin was shortly planning to enter the war against Japan in order to gain credit for the inevitable victory, decided to bomb Hiroshima at the earliest possible opportunity as an anti-Soviet warning in the run-up to what soon became the 'Cold War'.

Not at all, said Truman dismissively. Warm but provocative to the end, the old man pulled his portly frame out of his seat, shook my hand and waved me a cheery goodbye.

***

By this stage in his life, Truman was a benign, grandfatherly figure. He was getting a good press and was widely held up as a shining contrast to his 'bumbling' successor in the White House, Dwight D Eisenhower and to his successor, the 'inexperienced' John F Kennedy. Our meeting took place at the height of the Cold War, two years after the erection of the Berlin Wall and just a few months after the Cuban missile crisis. Widely credited with the vision and decisiveness that led to the Marshall Plan, the creation of NATO and the 'Truman Plan' that helped keep Greece and Turkey from Communism, Truman was something of a national icon by now. And he clearly enjoyed telling incredulous 'youngsters' about the old days when giants stalked the land and he, Harry Truman, had stood up to them and made the world safer (as he saw it) for the rest of us.

There was no hint of doubt or regret in anything he said to me about any of his actions as President, and he undoubtedly went to his grave a few years later confident that his 'decision' to drop the atomic bomb was the right and inevitable one. All debate about the dangers of nuclear radiation, for example, or whether the bomb was really used to impress or scare the Soviets, was dismissed out of hand as the dreamings of people who had nothing better to do than speculate about matters which they weren't competent to judge. As far as Truman was concerned, the bomb was intended to end the war with minimum loss of life (that is, no American loss of life) – and it did so.

I returned to my hotel in nearby Kansas City, invigorated by the spirit of that feisty old man in the striped cotton suit, and straightaway wrote down, as accurately as I could recall, precisely what had been said. I didn't tell Clinton Rossiter that my MA thesis on presidential decision-making was based on a 'decision' that wasn't. He might have made me write an entirely new one on the decision to enter Korea. But I did send a telegram to London a couple of days later to congratulate my cricket-loving father on his 50th birthday:

> WELL BATTED FOR HALF CENTURY. STOP.
> HARRY SENDS REGARDS.

My parents later told me they were thrilled with the telegram but found 'Harry' a mystery. In some ways, so did I.

History and the Arts

FROM THE PULPIT

History and the Arts should get together more often

Literary Review, June 2010.

Sometimes, I think I'm a jack of many trades and master of none. But on a good day I tell myself that, as an historian, there may be some merit in this. History – of all disciplines – surely invites cross-fertilisation with others. Yet I sense that much historical research continues to be relentlessly specialist and, in general, to marginalise the arts (especially 'classical' music), preferring to leave these to the experts. And that for its part, much arts history continues to be largely preoccupied with its own in some ways esoteric and isolated subject matter.

Things used to be a lot worse. When I was at Cambridge half a century ago, 'history' concentrated on great public trends and events and the men (sic!) responsible for them. By the later 1960s and 1970s, the historiographical barometer was swinging towards the story of 'ordinary' people. This new 'history from the bottom up' was revolutionary and welcome, but had little time for the 'high' arts. Nor did cultural history, which emerged a little later. Indeed, if there was one thing 'culture' did not mean to most cultural historians it was precisely what the term had probably meant to their grandparents: the Western tradition of painting, architecture, literature and 'classical' music.

Today, many historians primarily concerned with more traditional fare do draw the arts into their writings, citing literary works, for example, to help illustrate a point or to evoke the spirit of an earlier age or reinforce a particular view of the past. Many art historians, similarly, no longer regard paintings simply as objects 'out there' but also try to understand the motivation of the artist in creating them and the circumstances surrounding their subsequent reception. And where art history has led, music history has followed (if with a limp of reluctance) thanks to a few courageous pioneers – particularly in the USA but also in Britain.

Yet I am still struck how, to many historians, the arts (especially Western 'classical' music) remain consigned to the margins and regarded as the domain of the specialist. Or, at best, the glacé cherry on top of the icing on top of the real thing. But of, course, any art form – like political or economic systems, religions or what we call 'science' – is also a social construct. And this applies to music: both the 'works' and the 'events', that is the musical scores *and* their performance history and subsequent reception. Surely the arts should be seen not as sugary decoration on the outer edges of the main historiographical cake but as an essential ingredient and therefore incorporated into the study of the past, like any other data. Ideally, we historians should try to achieve a kind of Hegelian synthesis drawing together the specialist insights of the history of art and music with those arising from more mainstream historical research in the hope that something mutually enhanced might emerge. While writing my book about opera history, for example, I tried to keep in mind five broad, constantly intersecting themes: the politics of the time, finance and economics, the social context, the scientific and technological advances and, of course, the shifting ways the arts were produced and perceived. (For more on each of these see below pp. 200–202.)

None of this, of course, is to argue that the greatest operas or other artworks, or their creators, were 'merely' the products of their time and place. When scholars attempt to understand Mozart's works in historical context – his financial problems as he tried to live as a freelance before the advent of decent copyright laws, the expense and discomfort of travel, the limited opportunities for performances once the Habsburgs were back at war with the Ottomans – the result is surely to enhance, not to reduce, the stature of what he achieved. As for the other side of the divide, as it were, historians examining (say) sexual attitudes, immigration patterns or forms of work and leisure in 19th-century London or Paris might learn more than they think if they include in their researches the musical life of these cities.

I have no magic bullet, no single formula about how best to achieve the overarching, all-embracing historical *Gesamtkunstwerk* I am advocating. But I am sure that, if historians are to be true to the past, it is important for us to try.

Historians and the Arts, 1950–2010

History Today, 2 February 2011.

In 2010 contributors to History Today *were invited to look back over the changes that had taken place in their field of interest in the sixty years since the founding of the magazine. I focused on new approaches to the study of the history of culture and the arts – and of music in particular.*

When I was a child, shortly after the war, my father took me to my first opera. I was eight and the work was Verdi's *Rigoletto*: a rip-roaring masterpiece about sex and murder, two topics I did not yet know much about. However, I was perfectly capable of recognising big, bold passions as they came pouring across the footlights: that night I laughed with the lascivious Duke, loved with the vulnerable Gilda and wept at the end with her bitter, bereaved father. Over the years that followed I went to more operas and began to go to concerts, discovered museums and art galleries, read Dickens and Dostoevsky and pretended I could enjoy the films of the French *nouvelle vague* without bothering to look at the subtitles. In Cambridge for a week of exams and interviews for a history Open Scholarship, I relaxed one evening by going to the cinema. What was on? A recent film of *Aida* in which the main attraction (I just about admitted to myself) was the heaving bosom of Sophia Loren, who was miming the title role to the voice of Renata Tebaldi.

I was rather earnestly learning to be 'cultured'. In my spare time, that is. The serious work of the day was devoted to earning degrees and then going on to prepare others a little younger than myself to do the same. At Cambridge I found that 'history' tended to concentrate on great political, constitutional, diplomatic and military trends and events and the men responsible for them. I learned something about the Peloponnesian wars, the mediaeval (sic) conflicts between church and state, the Tudor and Stuart monarchies, Hobbes, Locke, Napoleon, Gladstone and Disraeli. At Cornell during the Kennedy years I added 'Government' to my intellectual portfolio, studied the 'functions and structures' of JFK's live press conferences and wrote a thesis on the 'presidential decision-making process' and, more specifically, why Truman decided to drop atomic bombs on Japan (which, Truman told me with a provocative grin when I met him in 1963, was 'no decision' since there had been no serious counter-arguments). Meanwhile, the vast surveys of American history I consumed would include 'culture and the arts' – if at all – at the back of the book as a kind of sweet course after the main meal (or, in Trevelyan's evocative metaphor, 'hanging at the end of history books like the tail from a cow').

Something of a divided life, you might think: one hemisphere bursting with undigested excitements about art and culture, the other trying to master the facts, processes and theories of history, society and politics. The twain scarcely met. When I found time to read about the life and works of Beethoven, Verdi or Wagner, this was time off from serious scholarship. Meanwhile, the histories of the Napoleonic Wars or Italian or German unification that I encountered had little or nothing to say about music. Trevelyan, a historian I greatly admired (and author of a wonderful study of Garibaldi and the Risorgimento), said in a famous 1945 lecture that 'some understanding of the social and political scene' would help us appreciate the works of Chaucer, Shakespeare, Dickens et al. But, he went on: 'Music needs no such historic introduction to be fully appreciated.'

The message was clear: history and the arts were separate fields, the boundaries between them marked by wire fences and closed gates rather than well-trodden pathways. Historians might use works of art to back up a point: a Reynolds painting here, a Wordsworth quote there. But the history of the arts as such was shunted off to be the preserve of those with specialist interests. And, if this was true of literature or painting, it was doubly the case with music: the exclusive realm of the musicologically trained. Mainstream scholars had more important things to get on with, such as understanding how human history had got to where it was and where it might be going.

This division of labour bothered me. Intelligence, I thought, was the capacity to see connections and that meant daring to cross dangerous boundaries. We tried to do this at the new University of Sussex where Asa Briggs talked refreshingly about 'redrawing the map of learning' when I was a young lecturer. At Sussex we had no academic departments; rather cross-disciplinary 'Schools of Study' and an interdisciplinary course structure. At the BBC, similarly, where I worked later, it was the opportunity to seek links between ostensibly separate intellectual territories that excited me. History, surely, did not have to restrict itself to the sayings and doings of great men and their institutions.

***

Many others were thinking along similar lines as, concomitant with the new radicalism of the 1960s and 1970s, the historiographical barometer swung towards the story of 'ordinary' people, the great majority of whom history had hitherto marginalised or ignored. Edward Thompson's *The Making of the English Working Class* (1963) became a classic. Eric Hobsbawm's early writings on British social history and those of George Rudé and others on France (influenced by their *Annales* colleagues) appeared around this time, while a little later Raphael Samuel and his History Workshop comrades began to collect what everyone else presumed did not exist: actual documentation by the 'ordinary' people of the past such as sailors in Nelson's navy, factory girls during the early years of industrialisation, Victorian fairground performers and travellers. This new 'history from the bottom up' was revolutionary and welcome (and historians such as Thompson, Samuel, Rodney Hilton, Christopher Hill and Asa Briggs were among the contributors to the twenty-six-part BBC radio series I co-produced in the early 1970s called *The Long March of Everyman*). But it seemed the new history had little time for the 'high' arts except, occasionally, as a somewhat peripheral social phenomenon. Maybe there was a vestigial class bias at work as historians intent on elevating the role of 'ordinary' people disdained what they regarded as 'elite' pastimes. Even avowedly feminist historians often ignored the fact that opera provided one of the few opportunities for a woman with talent (and luck) to become independently wealthy and internationally celebrated at a time when women could not even own property.

***

Social history was later augmented by the emergence of 'cultural' history. Here historians learned much from anthropologists such as Clifford Geertz and brought to the fore issues of ritual, gender and ethnicity. What (asked Natalie Zemon Davis, Carlo Ginzburg and other pioneering scholars) can we reasonably surmise about the daily texture of life as experienced by an 'ordinary' man or woman living long ago? What did people think, feel or even know about in times and places with, by our standards, limited levels of travel, literacy or social interaction? This approach greatly enriched our knowledge of the past as the documentary 'facts' about people long dead and the lives they had led were augmented by evidence-based speculation about their values, attitudes and *mentalités*. If there was one thing 'culture' did not mean to most cultural historians, however, it was precisely what the term had denoted a generation or two before: painting, architecture, literature and 'classical' music. The arts were not ignored. But they tended to be regarded as socio-cultural phenomena rather than through the prism of aesthetics.

***

Thus the 'cultural turn', like that to 'social history', seemed to eschew discussion of the high arts. Music in particular, it seemed, tended to be marginalised by mainstream history. There were some good reasons for this. We can all look at a painting or read a novel, but only those capable of reading a music score, it was widely presumed (on both sides of the divide), could really write music history. Unlike a painting or a novel, moreover, music was 'non-representational'; that is, it was not normally intended to represent some aspect of the real world as we experience it. It might do so, if the composer added a storm sequence or bird noises – or (in opera) words, characters and a story line. But it is not difficult to see why what used to be called 'absolute' music was widely regarded as obeying rules of its own, not easily susceptible to verbal description, whether you read or heard it, and why its historical reception – even more than that of painting or literature – tended to be left to experts. If a music historian chose to examine the details of a score, its melodic or harmonic progression and so on, this would have been genuinely difficult terrain for the non-expert historian. Against this, however, one might argue that all forms of historical research require some degree of special expertise. Few of us, after all, have the skills required to make sense of a document from the courts of Charlemagne, the Renaissance popes or Catherine the Great, or explain the symbolism embellishing a vase or coin from Ancient Greece or Rome. But music is also (like documents and coins) a social construct. As such, it is surely equally susceptible – in principle at least – to historical description and analysis.

Maybe there is a further inhibition. Two or three hundred years ago most people thought of those who composed and performed music as craftsmen responding to the practical needs of the court, church or popular entertainment. Craftsmanship can be comprised relatively straightforwardly within a historical framework; thus, we have a pretty good idea how and why Bach and Haydn produced the works they did. But in the 19th century music came to be seen as a quasi-autonomous, elevated form of 'art' and a composer like Beethoven an inspired genius who, through heroic struggle, was capable of producing ennobling masterpieces. In this more romantic view, art is harder to comprehend historically. The work of art becomes a kind of Rorschach test, with consumers seeing or hearing the qualities they personally impute to it, finding this or that symphony, for example, 'magisterial', 'contemplative' or 'unsettling'. Is the Mona Lisa objectively 'beautiful' or the finale of Beethoven's Fifth Symphony 'uplifting', or are we simply repeating positions we have inherited? Such questions (and the answers you choose to give) go to the very heart of the dilemma faced by any historian of the arts.

So does a further, related issue – the idea that certain iconic works of art express the deep inner concerns of their creators. That the transcendent power of Mozart's Requiem, for example, arises from the composer's premonition of his own imminent death or that Verdi's great chorus 'Va pensiero' from *Nabucco* was a covert expression of his desire for Italian independence. Of course, artworks reflect in part the personal preoccupations of their creators. So do most of the things we choose to do during the course of our lives. But remember that Mozart's Requiem was a commission (like *Die Zauberflöte*, the comic opera about priests, princes and birdmen he was writing around the same time), while the quasi-political status of what has become known as the Chorus of the Hebrew Slaves was not really cemented until many decades after its composition.

It has clearly not been easy for historians to incorporate the high arts into their researches or for experts in the arts to embrace historical context. But some scholars have made heroic efforts and in recent decades the fences between the two fields have lowered appreciatively and the pathways become better trodden. I have in mind, for example, the work of art historians such as Ernst Gombrich or Francis Haskell, who taught us not to regard artworks simply as objects 'out there' but to try to understand the motivation of the artist in creating them, the social, economic and ideological circumstances in which they were created and the psychological and cultural baggage through which they have subsequently been perceived.

Where art history led, music and musicology followed, sometimes with a limp of reluctance, but at a sprightly and inspiring pace among a few courageous pioneers, particularly in the United States but also in Britain. I think, for example, of the 1987 book *Music and Society*, edited by Richard Leppert and Susan McClary (and of McClary's own typically forthright contribution). John Rosselli's writings on the operatic professions in 19th-century Italy were ground-breaking, as were William Weber's analysis of the emerging middle-class audience for concerts of classical music and the work on early operatic life in Venice by Ellen Rosand and by Beth and Jonathan Glixon. Robert Hume and Judith Milhous opened up the hitherto largely unexamined topic of the finances of opera in 18th-century London, while Tim Blanning, concentrating primarily on France and Habsburg Central Europe, traced the transition from a mainly court-centred culture to a newly emergent 'public' sphere and argued for the 'triumph of music' vis-à-vis the other arts. James H Johnson investigated why opera audiences in France behaved so differently in 1750 and 1850, while aspects of the opera 'business' in 19th-century Paris were further illuminated by scholars such as William Crosten, Anselm Gerhard and Steven Huebner and in London by Jennifer Hall-Witt. Meanwhile, a number of economists and economic historians with an interest in the arts – William Baumol, Cyril Ehrlich, Bruno Frey, FM Scherer – greatly enriched our understanding of the historical relationship between music and money, while thinkers from Theodor Adorno to Lydia Goehr speculated about the philosophical issues raised by music and its history.

***

Artworks and the ways they are created and consumed are products of historical time and place: not just the works themselves, but (for example) the idea that 'classical' music is 'classical' or that Mozart's operas are 'great' or that Beethoven was a 'genius'. Indeed the very idea of the artist as 'genius' is better understood if examined (as Tia DeNora has done) in historical context. And from the other side, as it were, social historians examining (say) sexual attitudes, immigration patterns or forms of work and leisure in 18th- or 19th-century Paris or London might learn more than they think from studies that have been produced about the operatic life of these cities. Opera in particular, perhaps, because opera, in its origins and much of its history – and virtually by definition – has been an attempt to combine all the arts (a *Gesamtkunstwerk* in the Wagnerian terminology). Opera is, therefore, of all the performing arts the most complex and ambitious: the hub of a wheel with spokes leading in every imaginable direction.

Is there a danger here of historicising the arts and their creators, of reducing Mozart or Verdi and their works by seeing them as 'merely' the products of their particular time and place? Of course, and any study of *Don Giovanni* or *La Traviata*, say, that explains no more than why the first was premiered in Prague and the second in Venice, or why *La Traviata* or

Madama Butterfly were failures on their first nights, tells only a fraction of the truth. What is remarkable about the Mozarts, Verdis, Wagners and the rest is that they were real human beings, struggling as we all do with the demands of everyday life, who nonetheless managed to produce artworks that transcended immediate circumstances and continue to speak to us today. Mozart is the greater precisely because he was not a smart little marble bust atop the pianoforte. To understand his works in historical context seems to me not to reduce their stature but to increase it.

The two sides of this equation, the aesthetic and the historically conditioned, have always been deeply intertwined. You only have to glance at Mozart's or Verdi's letters to see this tension in practice; or at the detailed (and still unpublished) diaries of Frederick Gye, the man who ran the Covent Garden theatre from the late 1840s until the late 1870s, as he struggled to balance the conflicting demands of political and social acceptability, newsworthy showmanship, economic solvency and artistic excellence. The time has surely come when the arts should be regarded not as a sugary decoration on the outer edges of the main historiographical cake but as an essential ingredient. Therefore (if I may mix metaphors in the spirit of true multidisciplinarity) they should be brought into the mainstream of research and, where appropriate, incorporated, like any other data, into an all-embracing study of our shared past.

'Guerra! Guerra!' – War and the Arts, 1800–2000

As the British passed the 200th anniversary of the Battle of Waterloo and the centenary of the First World War (and approached the 80th of the end of the Second) I reflected on the historical relationship between War and the Arts. This essay was published in a variety of forms and magazines and became the basis of a frequently commissioned lecture for the Arts Society (formerly 'NADFAS').

'I sing of arms and the man.' The opening words of the Aeneid, the great epic poem by Virgil about the Trojan warrior Aeneas who had already, many centuries earlier, been a central figure in the Iliad by Homer. Arms and the Man. Men at arms. War has been a central theme in art – all the arts – since earliest times and, probably, in all cultures. You only have to read the bible, or look at surviving artefacts from ancient Egypt or China (the terracotta army for example). Or Ancient Greece or Imperial Rome, with all those triumphal arches. Try to envisage the Battle of Hastings and what comes to mind is the Bayeux Tapestry. Or move on to Benjamin West's Death of Wolfe (1770) and of Nelson (1806) and the American and French Revolutionary wars.

How and why have the arts responded to warfare over the course of history? Not just painting and sculpture but also architecture, poetry, film, photography and music. Many national anthems are uplifting musical settings of somewhat militant texts. The Marseillaise, for example, is a blatant call to arms while in Britain we beseech God not only to 'Save the Queen' but (in the second verse) to 'Scatter her enemies and make them fall'. The Italian anthem, its words penned in the heated run-up to the 1848 Revolutions, proclaims that 'We are ready to die' for a united Italy. As for the American anthem, this was inspired by US resistance to the British in the war of 1812:

…The rocket's red glare, the bombs bursting in air
Gave proof through the night that our flag was still there …

Opera is full of scenes hymning the glory of war. In the opening scene of Verdi's *Aida* – a grand opera composed at the height of the Franco-Prussian War and whose most famous scene features a celebratory military march – the chorus sing ecstatically as they set off to 'War! War!' ('Guerra! Guerra!'). Bellini's *Norma*, composed forty years earlier, is a wilting story about love between a Gallic priestess and a Roman general, but it contains a positively ferocious Guerra! Guerra! chorus. War is exciting, especially perhaps, to young men, and there are any number of artistic evocations of crowds cheering as the menfolk go off to war or return in triumph.

But music and the arts can remind us, too, that war involves suffering and loss, defeat and death. Think of the profound sadness evoked by Elgar's *Nimrod* every November at the Cenotaph. Alongside the centenary of the Great War, many returned to the poignant poetry of Wilfred Owen, the Lutyens war memorial at Thiepval and the many bleak portrayals of battlefield destitution, while familiar war-related artworks from later in the 20th century included Picasso's *Guernica* and Henry Moore's huddling masses in the underground stations, and uplifting films such as Noel Coward's *In Which We Serve* and much else.

The relationship between war and art is a vast subject which can be no more than touched on here. So let's restrict ourselves to (merely!) Europe over the past couple of centuries or so. First, a brief trot around the battlefield, after which I'll train the telescope on a few revealing examples.

***

During the opening decades of the 19th century much of Europe continued to tremble under the impact of the Napoleonic Wars. French troops and authority had spread their tentacles across the map, from Madrid to Moscow, leaving behind them a trail of triumphs (depending on which side you were on) and disasters (ditto). Napoleon himself was portrayed in every imaginable way: from hero crossing the Alps to grasping politico carving up the world with Britain's William Pitt to a bedraggled failure leading his troops in humiliating retreat, while it took a revolutionary Spanish artist, Goya, to portray the blatant horror of war.

By the time of the 1830 revolution in France, was liberty leading the people (as portrayed by Delacroix)? Or base anarchy?

In 1848/9, a number of European regimes were severely shaken and some overthrown before returning to crush and oust the popular forces that had tried to replace them. Before long, several of the major powers of Europe were at war in the Crimea, returning home to further volcanic eruptions which, in time, led to demands from some of their minority peoples for national independence. Italian and German unification, both of them heroically portrayed by the victors and their sympathisers at the

Painting by Goya: The Third of May, 1808. *(Alamy)*

Painting by Delacroix: Liberty Leading the People, *1830. (Alamy)*

time, were only achieved as the outcome of warfare; a few decades later, both nations lurched into fascism. By then, of course, all of Europe and parts of the wider world had been plunged into the catastrophe of the 'war to end all wars', only to undergo even greater carnage a generation later. Memorials to the fallen in both world wars provide moving landmarks across both eastern and western Europe. In our own time, apart from the horrors in former Yugoslavia in the 1990s and occasional acts of what we nowadays dub 'terrorism', serious warfare in Europe has been blessedly rare.* But wars of various kinds, many of them scarcely reported in Europe, have continued, and continue, to cause (literally) untold suffering in many parts of the wider world.

***

Pretty much everything summarised above has been represented in art. Some of it is positive: the songs of cheery soldiers as they march into battle, the paintings and sculptures of heroic generals and brave troops, great vistas of victorious battlefields such as that at Austerlitz or Waterloo. At the opposite end of the scale there are the images of grieving mothers, the bleak memorials, the musical and poetic dirges for the fallen. And let us not forget the wit and wisdom – and sometimes the cruelty and sheer bloody-mindedness – of caricaturists and satirists from (to stick to Britain for a moment) James Gillray back in Napoleonic times to David Low during the Second World War and Joan Littlewood's *Oh, What a Lovely War!* of 1963. We like to think of the 19th century as a more decorous age than our own. But no modern cartoonist has been more irreverent than when Isaac Cruikshank portrayed the lascivious Duke of Wellington crudely 'Exercising his Ordnance'!

Many war-related artworks have been produced in the presence, or the direct aftermath, of the events they portray. With the advent of photography, and later of film, new technologies developed that positively required the artist to be present. The Crimean war (1853–56) stimulated the earliest examples of high-quality war photography by pioneers such as Roger Fenton, and by the 1930s a sharp-eyed photojournalist like Robert Capa could illustrate the Spanish Civil War, using the latest Leica camera, with what came to be called 'action shots'. Paintings and literature, too, if not quite so 'immediate' in style and impact, could also embody something

---

* This article was written before the Russian invasion of Ukraine.

of the personal experience of the artists. The war paintings of Paul Nash or Christopher Nevinson, for example, or the poems of Wilfred Owen, RC Sherriff's play *Journey's End* or the novel *All Quiet on the Western Front* by the German author Erich Maria Remarque all build upon the potent recollections of the men who created them.

More often, war art is created by people inspired by events at which they were not personally present. Beethoven was in faraway Vienna when he composed a bombastic orchestral piece to celebrate Wellington's 1813 victory in the Battle of Vitoria (a military triumph that helped lead to overall victory in the Peninsular War). Forty-odd years later, Tennyson was in England, not the Crimea, when he penned his great poem *The Charge of the Light Brigade*. Composed to a galloping rhythm, it is a hymn of patriotic praise to a body of cavalrymen who, on orders from above, rode heroically against their Russian foe at the Battle of Balaclava despite knowing the odds against them were insuperable.

> Half a league, half a league,
> Half a league onward,
> All in the valley of Death
> Rode the six hundred.

The men of the Light Brigade knew it was nobler to fail in a good cause than to avoid the fight.

***

During the decades following the Crimean War, the map of Europe was bespattered by a succession of wars and near-wars, including those that led to Italian and German unity and to ever more powerful dreams of national independence among Hungarians, Poles, Czechs and others. As new futures seemed to loom, countless artworks across Europe called upon a mythologised past for political succour: in particular, the revival of folk myths plucked from a supposed 'national' history or pre-history, much of which incorporated the idea of battle. In the process, any resemblance to historical authenticity often became severely modified or frankly discarded. One thinks, for example, of the militant Nordic – i.e. quasi-Germanic – heroes and villains of Wagner's *Ring*, or of the Finnish epic the *Kalevala* which was to inspire Sibelius and his fellow cultural patriots. In Prague, the new (Czech) National Theatre was inaugurated in 1881 with a new opera by Smetana focusing on the mythic queen Libuše who, in an ecstatic trance at the culmination of the work, sings of her vision of a future Czech nation. In Russia around this time, the painter Ilya Repin, an influential figure in the reassertion of his nation's Slavic roots, worked on and off for nearly a decade perfecting his portrayal of an incident when the Cossacks two centuries before, supposedly confronted by the political demands of the Ottoman Empire, sent a vulgar and disrespectful reply. In Britain, these are the years that witnessed the revived cultural prominence of King Arthur and his knightly warriors, while in Paris a proud new equestrian statue of Joan of Arc was erected in the Place des Pyramides as a calculated boost to national morale in the wake of France's military defeat at the hand of the Prussians.

More recent history, too, was often recruited and adapted to serve the national cause. Tolstoy's *War and Peace*, first published in 1869, heroised the figure of General Kutuzov whose calm patience had enabled the Russians to see off the Napoleonic invasion earlier in the century (an event later celebrated by Tchaikovsky in his '1812 Overture'). In Britain, Lady Butler's famous portrayal of the Scots Greys at the Battle of Waterloo (*Scotland Forever!*) dates from 1881 while Richard Caton Woodville Jr's *Charge of the Light Brigade* is from 1894, shortly after the by now frail and aged Tennyson recorded his poem onto a scratchy wax cylinder.

***

By the time of the First World War, much had changed. As the technology of warfare became more sophisticated, images of tanks and swooping aeroplanes began to replace those of generals on horseback. To Marinetti, the pro-Fascist founder of Italian Futurism, an art of power, movement, speed and violence was paramount. 'We will glorify war,' wrote Marinetti: 'the world's only hygiene.' Yet for most involved in real wars, opportunities for individual heroism plunged as the range and scope of horror increased. Otto Dix, a loyal (and decorated) German soldier in the First World War, survived to portray its traumas, notably the grotesque skull-like faces of his gas-masked comrades as they advanced upon the foe. And in Britain? There was nothing heroic about John Singer Sargent's *Gassed*, or such bitterly ironically entitled works as Nevinson's *Paths of Glory* or Paul Nash's *We Are Making a New World*.

Rather (in Wilfred Owen's immortal words) the 'pity of war' and the

John Singer Sargent: Gassed. *(Alamy)*

'old Lie' that it is a good thing to die for one's country…

A generation later, and the world was at war again. All the combatant countries produced artworks and, as Monica Bohn-Duchen has shown in her book on art and the Second World War, the results everywhere reflected, in part at least, the political imperatives under which they were produced. In Britain, Kenneth Clark's War Artists' Advisory Committee encouraged artists to help boost national morale, portray ordinary people rolling up their sleeves and pulling their weight and if possible to avoid anything too obviously upsetting. In America, too, and in the USSR, many artists turned their hand to morale-boosting imagery, portraying battlefield buddies and a resolute and supportive home front. It is easy to dismiss Nazi and Fascist art as having been no more than crude propaganda; much was subsequently confiscated ('looted'?) by the victors as dangerously inflammatory. But it is at least arguable that some of the sculpture of Arno Breker, for example, or the films of Leni Riefenstahl or Albert Speer's architectural plans for central Berlin all embodied the highest aesthetic standards of the time, place and circumstances in which they were conceived no less than did (say) the works of Noel Coward and Henry Moore mentioned earlier.

And what of artworks produced by victims of the Holocaust, such as the composer Hans Krása or the painter Charlotte Salomon (both of them murdered at Auschwitz)? As Bohm-Duchen rightly says, it would seem almost blasphemous to assess their work purely in aesthetic terms. Indeed, if any single message emerges from a study of war-related art, it is perhaps that artworks can never be judged exclusively according to some kind of universally applicable aesthetic principles. In China, Mao Zedong proclaimed (in 1942) that art was 'intended for the masses of the people', while Britain's war-time arts supremo Kenneth Clark was on record as having said, with equal conviction, that popular taste was, ipso facto bad taste. In their own terms, both were probably right.

***

Nearly half a century after the outbreak of the Great War, the 'war to end all wars', and after an even more catastrophic world war, a remarkable integration of all the arts came together in a small industrial town in the English Midlands. In 1962, a new cathedral was inaugurated in Coventry to replace St Michael's, the old Gothic cathedral that had been largely destroyed by German bombing back in 1940. Designed by Basil Spence, the new cathedral was built alongside the ruins of the old: a moving and symbolic link between past and future. Spence (also the architect of the University of Sussex) wanted Coventry Cathedral to embody and contain symbols of forgiveness, of reconciliation, a quest which drew on the talents of many of the major artists of the time, among them John Piper, Graham Sutherland and the sculptor Jacob Epstein.

To mark the consecration of the cathedral, Benjamin Britten was

Coventry Cathedral. (Alamy)

commissioned to write a new piece. A committed pacifist, Britten composed his *War Requiem*, one of the most powerful and moving pieces in his entire oeuvre. Created at the height of the Cold War, it was written with three soloists in mind – one English, one German and one Russian: the tenor Peter Pears, the baritone Dietrich Fischer-Dieskau and the soprano Galina Vishnevskaya (in the event, Vishnevskaya was prevented by the Soviet authorities from participating and the soprano part was sung by Heather Harper). The work is scored for a large orchestra, a semi-separate chamber orchestra, a large mixed choir and an ethereal offstage boys' choir. Subtly alternating the poetry of Wilfred Owen and the words of the Latin Mass, the piece resonates with the cruelty and absurdity of war. It begins quietly, a pair of bells tolling that epitome of musical anxiety, the tritone (or augmented fourth). The chorus sings the opening words of the Requiem and, over the course of the eighty-five minute piece, of the day of anger, that terrible day when sinful man will come before his judge, and the soprano soloist pronounces herself trembling with fear. The tenor and baritone soloist, meanwhile, sing settings of Owen's war poems:

'What passing-bells for these who die as cattle?' asks the tenor, quoting Owen's poignant Anthem for Doomed Youth:

> Only the monstrous anger of the guns.
> Only the stuttering rifles' rapid rattle
> Can patter out their hasty orisons.

Later, the baritone sings a terrible evocation of the great destructive cannon:

> Be lifted up, thou long black arm,
> Great gun towering toward Heaven, about to curse.

And the two men tell the story of Abraham, about to sacrifice his son Isaac as proof of his devotion to God. An angel intervenes at the last moment, to sugary harp sounds, to provide instead a ram caught in a thicket. But in Owen's horrific version, the old man goes ahead and slays his son. 'And half the seed of Europe, one by one' – a phrase repeated by Britten's soloists again and again, as though incomprehensible at first in its sheer dreadfulness.

And, most terrible of all, perhaps, there's Owen's 'Strange Meeting' of two men in a deep, dark underground tunnel. They seem to recognise each other. 'I am the enemy you killed, my friend,' says one at last.

After all the horror, the Requiem ends with a glimmer of optimism:

the hope of liberation, paradise, peace and genuine, eternal rest that leaves audience and performers alike immobile and silent. Wilfred Owen was killed in France at age 25 in November 1918, a few days before the armistice that brought that terrible war to an end.

Britten was born just before the war, in 1913, on St Cecilia's Day (the patron saint of Music). To mark Britten's 50th birthday, BBC television scheduled a special mid-evening programme about his life and work which would feature the recently premiered *War Requiem*. The date was 22 November 1963. A few hours before transmission the President of the United States was shot and killed.

. . . and Music in Particular

Vauxhall Gardens: A History

by David Coke and Alan Borg (Yale University Press, 2011).

Literary Review, June 2011.

I have a terrible confession to make: I scribble in books – especially those I review. Well, not scribble exactly. But I sometimes underline bits of text I think interesting or important, add a comment here and there in the margins and, so doing, deface objects I was taught as a child to revere. I do this not because I despise books but because, on the contrary, I love them, devour them, live off them. They are my intellectual foodstuffs. In order to squeeze all that is nutritious from a book I am reading, I have to chew on it, roll it around in my mind, render it more palatable by mixing its subject-matter with my own intellectual juices; only then can I digest it properly and recall over the longer term what it had to say.

But here, for once, is a book even I dare not deface. *Vauxhall Gardens* is, like its subject, a huge, multi-faceted and carefully crafted work of art which takes time to absorb properly. You can if you like pick and choose, sampling an entertaining story or picture here or sitting down to consume more solid fare there. In some ways, an encounter with this superbly researched and richly illustrated book is what you choose to make of it. Like the pleasure gardens it documents, it is probably better re-visited many times than at a single sitting. It is also a Big Book. Reading, as Roy Porter famously pointed out, can be bad for your health and (how shall I put this delicately?) my lap is just recovering from having supported, day after day, some three concentrated kilos of *Vauxhall*. I did wonder at one point whether it might not be safer to chain the book up like a medieval Bible and read it standing up. Then, after a few days of respite, I returned to my quarry reinvigorated, filled up my punchbowl, and read on with fresh enthusiasm. David Coke, the book's principal author, has been working towards this book for decades. A distinguished scholar and museologist (and son of Gerald Coke whose Handel Collection provides the core of the display at London's Foundling Museum), Coke has been patiently collecting all manner of Vauxhalliana, sleuthing sources, identifying images and crafting captions and texts. Teaming up with co-author Alan Borg, former director of the V&A, Coke's dream has at last become reality.

Vauxhall Gardens was long the most popular place of public entertainment in Britain, lasting from 1661 until finally closing in 1859. The name of the gardens and surrounding area derived from 'Falke's Hall', the home of a Gascon mercenary in the service of King John, and underwent many spellings in later centuries. Pepys was a regular visitor to 'Fox-hall', mentioning the gardens in his diaries twenty-three times between 1662 and 1668. The heyday was during the middle decades of the 18th century when the gardens were under the inspired management of Jonathan Tyers (and after his death in 1767 his immediate family). Every evening throughout the summer, the gardens with their walkways, musical performances and supper-boxes, would typically play host to a thousand or more people who would stroll, eat, drink, socialise, flirt and, in general, enjoy a carefully managed combination of 'Virtus' and 'Voluptas'.

Parts of the gardens were extravagantly illuminated, others enticingly dark, and people from all stations in life were welcome provided they could pay the low price of admission (held at a shilling through much of the century). Frederick Louis, the Prince of Wales, was a frequent visitor, as were titled gentry, soldiers, dandies, servants and apprentices, plus the inevitable smattering of pickpockets and prostitutes whose presence doubtless added a frisson of excitement. Tyers, with the help and active encouragement of friends such as Hogarth and Handel, had a mission: he would bring together large numbers of people who would never normally encounter each other as equals, and provide them all with a seductive combination of high art and sensual pleasure.

By the turn of the 18th and 19th centuries, as war in the American colonies was followed by the French Revolution and Napoleonic Wars, carefree entertainment at Vauxhall lost some of its appeal while many among London's rapidly rising urban population gradually found alternative distractions more to their taste. A succession of managers attempted to revive Vauxhall's fortunes with the introduction of what a later generation would have regarded as circus acts – tightrope walking, juggling and the like, and Vauxhall finally sank towards its final exit despite the best efforts of Frederick Gye (and his son Frederick Gye Jr who went on to become manager of the Covent Garden theatre).

Some of the most absorbing sections of the book concentrate on the artwork at Vauxhall, the music and musicians a visitor could hear and the way Tyers and others developed the gardens as a business. In addition to the entry fee, you might want to eat in one of the elegant supper-boxes on the outer edges of the gardens. These were covered over but open on the side facing the gardens, rather like theatre boxes, and the upper part of each was decorated with a largescale mural. This was usually of ordinary people doing ordinary things – strikingly innovative at a time when most commissioned paintings were formal landscapes or official portraits. Everywhere, it was the informality of the art, allied to its quality, that Vauxhall strove to promote. Thus, the music, performed out into the gardens from the upper tier of a building called 'the Orchestra', might include the popular songs and medleys of the day or the latest works by Arne or Handel. The most famous artwork at Vauxhall was the statue of Handel that Tyers commissioned in 1738 from the young French sculptor François Roubiliac. The statue was a sensation, showing the composer relaxed, wigless, his legs crossed and wearing a pair of sandals one of which has slipped off his foot.

For all the informality of the statue, however, there was no doubting its message. As Handel plucked at a lyre, a little angel or *putto* at his feet taking down the master's composition, this was a statement of both the immediate accessibility and of the eternal appeal of his music – the combination of sensual pleasure and moral seriousness for which Tyers (and Handel) constantly strove. If erected anywhere other than at Vauxhall the statue might have been greeted with derision. Placed where it was, it became one of the principal attractions of the gardens, doubtlessly boosting further the reputations of Tyers, Roubiliac and the composer himself in the process. When the 'Fireworks Music' was given a public rehearsal at Vauxhall in April 1749 prior to its official premiere, an estimated crowd of 12,000 fought and shoved and tied up much of London's traffic in order to attend. And for all the apparent frivolity of Vauxhall, a perennial favourite was the stirring 'Dead March' from Handel's oratorio *Saul*.

Vauxhall Gardens is an artwork in its own right, its scholarly text woven subtly around the images. But the book is also a triumph of historical detective work, as we read detailed accounts of how people travelled to and from Vauxhall, what happened when it rained, the story of Vauxhall's various buildings, the income and costs of those in charge, the changing social composition and behaviour patterns of its visitors, the differences between Vauxhall and its competitors (notably Ranelagh and

Vauxhall Gardens. (Alamy)

Handel: Roubiliac statue.

Marylebone) and the repercussions of new bridges across the Thames and the arrival of the railway. Vauxhall finally slid into history, but not before a couple of grainy photographs recorded its dying days. And its legacy lived on, transmuted by changing circumstances into a variety of new forms, among them the circus, the music hall, alfresco dances, popular concerts such as the Henry Wood Proms and a range of international derivations ranging from Copenhagen's Tivoli gardens to Disneyland to Woodstock. What price 'Virtus' and 'Voluptas' today?

Nuremberg Chronicles

In search of Mastersingers and Minnesingers.

OPERA magazine, February 2015.

An historically-based piece which I drafted (with the detailed help of Lucie Skeaping).

I still remember the first time I found myself in Nuremberg. It was everything I'd imagined a real old German town to be. A fairytale silhouette of pointy roofs and rounded towers, wood-beamed houses, and here and there fountains with life-like statues of the city's great and good: the powerful burghers and civic guildsmen who remind us of Nuremberg's proud past as the home of some of Germany's most important merchant families. Just up the hill towards the medieval castle you can visit the house that once belonged to Albrecht Dürer, his kitchen and printshop now beautifully recreated. And a little further down, near the Pegnitz river, stands the statue of Dürer's younger contemporary, the shoemaker, poet and master songsmith Hans Sachs who, three hundred years later, would become the pivotal figure in one of the 19th century's most beloved works, Wagner's *Die Meistersinger*.

Most of Wagner's operas are based on more or less mythological stories and characters. *Die Meistersinger*, however, is rooted in history. Two strata of history, in fact: the Mastersingers of post-Reformation Nuremberg and, by implication and sometimes explicitly, the Minnesingers who had flourished three hundred years earlier still. What we see and hear today, therefore, at a performance of Wagner's opera, is a layer-cake of German cultural history: a 19th-century recreation of a 16th-century community who were themselves inspired by their 13th- and 14th-century predecessors.

***

The Hans Sachs of Wagner's opera, and the guilds of cobblers, tailors, bakers and the rest that make up a large part of the opera's personnel, were an integral part of town life in 16th-century Nuremberg, as was the song competition, judged by the masters and guildsmen, which forms the dramatic backbone of the work. Like many groups who earnestly try to fill the footsteps of revered forebears, the Mastersingers could at times be punctilious to a fault concerning what they deemed to be the correct modes of behaviour – including in their case the criteria to be fulfilled by anyone hoping to join one their ranks. Thus, a new song by an aspiring guild member would be assessed not as a form of individual artistic expression but as a kind of application form whereby its author would attempt to show that he was worthy of admission into a select body of craftsmen committed to upholding the highest standards of earlier times. The song had to be constructed and performed in strict accordance with a prescribed set of rules and regulations: essentially, an AAB pattern (called 'Bar-form') in which an opening tune, the *Aufgesang*, is performed twice and is followed by a third stanza to a different 'aftertune' (*Abgesang*). No place here for flights of fancy or spontaneous bursts of inspiration. Every tiny error was recorded, every misplaced note or syllable ticked off and added up at the end, and a successful applicant was rewarded with what was, in effect, a badge of honour to be worn with pride. In the hands of the honest, upwardly aspiring artisans of small-town Nuremberg, these songs and song contests could easily take on what to a later generation could look like an eccentric, provincial quality, a workmanlike obsession with outdated rules, titles and tradition.

Wagner wrote a first prose draft for *Die Meistersinger* in the mid-1840s when he was music director at the royal court in Dresden. His initial idea was that this might become the basis for a comic afterpiece to *Tannhäuser*, the rather more earnest 'song contest' opera he had just completed. Both were loosely derived from (often heavily romanticized) versions of earlier German history. But Wagner also delved into the works of the finest scholars, including (in the case of *Die Meistersinger*) his slightly older contemporary, the historian Georg Gottfried Gervinus. In a recently published multi-volume work, Gervinus had shown how the development of German cultural identity was in many ways embodied in its literary heritage. He saw a marked contrast between a medieval tradition in which poets had to go begging at court and the emergence of 'Mastersong' which Gervinus celebrated as an altogether more independent form of poetry penned by poets who no longer had to depend upon their writings in order to live. And he pointed to Hans Sachs as a pivotal transitional figure between the two eras.

Later, when Wagner came to rework his *Die Meistersinger* text, he turned to the late 17th-century ecclesiastical historian Johann Christoph Wagenseil. Much of Wagenseil's work consisted of collections of supposedly subversive works by Jewish authors. But in his 'Nuremberg Chronicle' of 1697, he gave accounts of the real mastersingers of Nuremberg, and it is in no small part due to Wagenseil that Wagner came to know something

Hans Sachs statue in Nuremberg.

about the history and customs of the guilds, their music and the detailed rules of composition they followed (what came to be called the *Tabulatur*, an amusing version of which Wagner has the apprentice David outline in the opera). Singing competitions among aspiring young mastersingers were held in church on Sundays or holidays, with the singer seated while presenting his song and a group of four markers curtained off in a box where they would list the errors he committed.

All this would no doubt have been familiar to the real Hans Sachs who was born in Nuremberg, the son of a tailor, towards the end of the 1400s. After travelling, Sachs began work as a shoemaker and then took up an apprenticeship to become a poet and mastersinger. Sachs suffered more than his fair share of personal tragedy (his wife and children all died, possibly of the plague, and Wagner portrays him as a widower). In one of his earliest and most famous poems, *Silberweise*, Sachs wrote: 'I greet thee, Lord Jesus. Thou art life's source, you guide all our hope – help us out of all our woes'.

But some of his writings have a cheeky streak to them which may well have touched a raw nerve or two with his fellow guild members. In one, he writes of a Venetian merchant whose work takes him abroad for some four years. On his return he finds a two-year-old child in his house: 'Whose boy is this?' he asks his wife. 'Listen,' she says. 'One night when I was asleep and thinking of you an icicle touched my lips and made me pregnant – now isn't that a miracle!' The merchant pretended not to catch on, but a dozen years later he got his revenge. 'Wife,' he announced, 'I'm bound for a foreign land and will take the boy with me to learn my trade'. In Turkey he sells the boy to a merchant and returns home without him. 'Where is my son?' cries his wife. 'Well,' replies the merchant, 'the sun was so hot that it melted him into water, just as would have happened to his father, the icicle!' The wife gulped but spoke not a word. And the moral? He who travels far and wide should see that his wife doesn't eat an icicle while he's away!

Sachs was clearly a prolific and inventive writer, and he was to bequeath to posterity a large body of work by himself and others. But he and his contemporary mastersingers were, for the most part, no more than amateur poets, members of the town's aspirant middle and lower-middle classes whose creative writing was essentially a hobby. By no means all of them would have been musically literate, and most surviving manuscripts contain only the texts of the poems. Thus, we find 'songs' on such diverse subjects as religion, storytelling ballads, historical themes, fables and even riddles – all doubtless sung to melodies that were already widely known: in effect, the popular tunes of the day.

If Sachs flourished at the very height of the mastersong tradition, some surviving texts date from several generations earlier. The barber-surgeon Hans Folz, born in Worms in 1437, later settled in Nuremberg (and appears as 'Hans Foltz' in Wagner's opera as a coppersmith). In his Meisterlieder, Folz frequently touches on sin, sickness and death and the ultimate possibility of salvation through Christ. In one, he reminds us how Jesus announced that 'a bitter death will come to all those down here who have lived in lust'. But not only to those.

> Oh death, how harsh art thou! Even a man who seems to live in peace, who does his job right, is not burdened by sorrow and enjoys his food and drink – even to this man death will be terrible!

If this reads something like a Lutheran rant *avant la lettre*, other mastersongs (such as Sachs's *Icicle* poem) were livelier, catchier. 'I always have an eye for the Frankish *Fräulein*' writes an anonymous poet (from the mid-15th century *Lochamer-Liederbuch* collection), and he goes on to outline the attractions of the girls from Swabia and the Rhineland before finally, with a little sigh, admitting he's now an old man whose only company is a bottle of wine!

***

Wagner was looking back some 300 years in his country's history when composing *Die Meistersinger*. But the mastersingers themselves were looking back for their own inspiration. In forming their town singing guilds they were in effect honouring the famous old poets of medieval Germany: the 'Minnesingers' of the 13th and 14th centuries whose work mirrored the courtly troubadour tradition of Provence. As in late medieval France, the German *Minnesang* was cultivated, not so much by 'wandering minstrels' of the vagrant variety as we often think of them, but by educated and erudite musicians, often those of noble birth. One early Minnesinger was a mid-13th century courtier named Tannhäuser.

The word *Minnesänger* literally referred to someone singing 'in service to love' or 'courtly love'. The idealized image of Love, indeed, was the central theme of the poesy, the knight striving for the favour of some unattainable lady and subjugating himself to her – a form of allegiance nicely analogous in some ways to that of the feudal system of the day. These poet-singers, after all, were bound in service to powerful patrons. The earliest *Minnesang* of the 1100s were pretty well straightforward love songs, sometimes from the woman's point of view as well as the man's: folksong-like and often based on simple dance carols. Gradually, the influence of the French troubadours came to be felt as the man alone became the protagonist, yearning for his lover, while the idea of Love itself became less overtly sensual and more contemplative. The songs became more complex and varied, and by the late 12th century and the early 13th they were coming to embody a more courtly form of expression, the self-conscious chivalric style we associate with the 'Romances' of late medieval Europe.

Some of the earliest Minnesinger songs have survived: the *Palästinalied*, for example, by the poet Walther von der Vogelweide. Born around 1170, Walther is one of the traditional competitors in the tale of the song contest atop the Wartburg. He was to make his mark in both of Wagner's 'song contest' operas: in *Tannhäuser*, he is one of the characters onstage, while in *Die Meistersinger* Wagner has his young hero Walther von Stolzing cite von der Vogelweide as his early master and inspiration in the Act I monologue *Am stillen Herd*.

By the time Wagner came to read about Walther von der Vogelweide, the poet was chiefly celebrated as an early champion of Germany – the state – as against the Papacy. Historically, however, Vogelweide was rather broader than this. Good medieval Christian that he was, he penned his *Palästinalied* as a politico-religious celebration of the Fifth Crusade (1217–1221), the Crusade in which the original Tannhäuser may well have participated.

> From the moment my sinful eye looked upon this noble land I have been living in a noble manner for the first time in my life. I have reached the place where God walked in the flesh. Here a maiden bore a child, lord over all the angels. Was that not a perfect miracle?

This 'Palestine Song' by Walther von der Vogelweide is unusual in that not only the text but also the original tune managed to survive over the centuries. Even more unusual was that the poet acknowledges that all the Abrahamic religions might be said to have had some claim to the Holy Land. However, he has no doubts about the ultimate righteousness of the Christian cause. 'Christians, Jews and Heathens claim this to be their heritage,' he writes. 'God has to assign it in the right way, for His three names. The whole world is coming battling here – our cause is right. It is right that He is granting it to us.'

A slightly later Minnesinger whose work also was known in Wagner's time was Heinrich von Meissen, often dubbed *Frauenlob* ('In Praise of Women') – not so much for his interest in the flesh as for his devotion to the Virgin Mary. On his death in 1318, the women of Mainz are said to have carried his bier to the cathedral in appreciation of his lifelong chivalrous devotion to their sex. His tomb was restored in 1783, and in 1842 (by which time Wagner was of course already active) a monument was erected to his memory by the women of Mainz. One of Heinrich von Meissen's best-known lyrics was one composed on hearing of the death in 1287 of one of the most revered Minnesingers of the time, Konrad von Würzburg. With Konrad's passing, he wrote, the Poetic Art too was now also dead. Konrad of Würzburg was probably the first in the Minnesinger tradition to earn his living from his music and poetry, and he has left us a song which compares the seasons – the harsh winter followed by the brightness of spring – with, respectively, the pain and then the joy of Love. 'Nevertheless,' he tells us at the end, 'the man without honour fades. He who has spent his life wrapped in sin cannot bathe his heart in the dew of valour which glimmers in the first sunlight.'

The Minnesinger tradition was a long and fruitful one but by the mid-14th century, with the rise of towns and of a tiny but emergent bourgeoisie, the courtly poet gradually became bypassed. The man who is widely regarded as the last – and arguably the greatest and most colourful of them all – is Oswald von Wolkenstein. A poet and composer whose lifestyle was, by all accounts, as lively as his verses, Oswald came from the German-speaking area of the southern Tyrol. Born in the 1370s into an aristocratic landowning family, his early life seems to have been taken up with various legal squabbles over inheritance, disputes that, in what were dangerous times, could lead to violence and bloodshed. Of these, Oswald appears to have had his fair share. Prison, torture and financial disputes were all part of his life; a famous portrait shows him with an eye missing, which I suppose suggests one way of settling a family argument!

Oswald was something of a globetrotter. He was just 11 when he first left the grand family residence, probably in the service of a knight whom he accompanied around the Mediterranean and the Near East. Being of noble birth himself, he fitted naturally into the court scene and later went on all sorts of diplomatic missions abroad on behalf of his king, on the way gaining a first-hand knowledge of foreign music and, in particular, of French chanson. Like other Minnesingers, Oswald would write words for pre-existing popular melodies, many of them no doubt picked up on his extensive travels, or perhaps from the many musicians who regularly made their way back and forth along the nearby Brenner Pass. But what he made of these tunes could be (literally!) breathtaking. One surviving Oswald song, dating from as late as the early 15th century, is a wonderfully virtuosic tongue-twister which, by incorporating the colourful and evocative names and sounds of multifarious bids, celebrates the arrival of spring.

Until the time of Oswald, the Minnesinger would typically set his poetry to a single-line melody. Oswald seems to have been one of the first to turn his hand to polyphonic settings. One of his songs, while remaining an old-fashioned tale of knightly chivalry with a nobleman declaring his love for his lady, features three different voices. But don't look for innovation in the poetry itself. 'I am a poor wretch,' cries the knight, 'abandoned by all joy. I beg your mercy, no other woman on this earth has ever pleased my heart so much.' She replies: 'How could you want me? I am ugly and twenty-four years old'. Obviously well over-the-hill in pre-Reformation Germany!

***

Maybe it's a shame that, although the Mastersingers of Nuremburg and other cities took inspiration from great creative figures from their past – people like Oswald von Wolkenstein – their own musical repertoire nevertheless remained firmly monophonic, and on the whole unaccompanied. But theirs was really more of a poetic tradition than a musical one and, as mentioned, they were for the most part not free-roaming courtiers but busy family men trying to practise their various crafts and earn their living as best they could in a small, somewhat enclosed commercial community. The Mastersingers reached their peak in Nuremberg during the time of Hans Sachs. And one can see why, in light of their reverence for their poetic predecessors, Wagner could place in the mouth of Sachs the powerful and eloquent plea with which his opera concludes: that the good folk of Nuremberg should continue to honour their German Masters of earlier times and thereby help preserve 'holy German Art'.

Sachs lived a long and rich life, dying in 1576 in his eighties. But he would have been gratified to know that the tradition he did so much to uphold far outlived him. The last Nuremburg guild appears to have been disbanded in 1774. But it was still possible to encounter mastersingers in other German towns right up until the early 20th century, and it is reported that the very last Meistersinger died, in Memmingen, in 1922.

Matters Operatic

Introducing *The Gilded Stage*

Most histories of music concentrate on composers and their
works. But Daniel suggests a different approach.
NADFAS Review, Winter 2009.

Here, nothing is played, sung or whistled but *Figaro*. No opera is
drawing like *Figaro*. Nothing, nothing but *Figaro*.

Mozart's 1787 letter from Prague to a friend in Vienna nicely conveys the
breathless excitement of his first protracted visit to the Czech capital. So
popular was *Figaro* that its composer was commissioned to write a new
work – *Don Giovanni* – which would have its premiere here.

But was everyone in Prague really playing, singing and whistling
Mozart's music? If so, how would most people have known it, or even
known who he was, in an era before photography, recording, radio, TV
and a mass press? In London earlier in the century, Handel's operas were
produced in a theatre (the King's, Haymarket) capable of holding an
audience of under a thousand; did crowds of people stare at him in the
streets and point him out with awe to their children? How familiar had
the works of Leonardo or Raphael been to their contemporaries? And was
it really true that in 19th-century Italy everyone hummed the latest Verdi
arias and revered the composer as a national hero? Aren't we in danger of
exaggerating the celebrity our favourite artists were able to enjoy in their
own day?

Most histories of the arts concentrate on revered creators and their works;
there are many excellent studies of famous operas and their composers,
just as there are of Baroque architecture or the art of the Impressionists.
But what interested me in *The Gilded Stage* was to go beyond this and to
examine opera – an art form that attempts to combine all the others – in
its wider historical context.

The result was an intoxicating operatic odyssey during which I found
myself feasting on a rich diet of art, architecture, music, literature and
drama. This magnificent Grand Tour of the mind required me to stop
over in the courts of Renaissance Italy, Louis XIV's Versailles, the London

of Hogarth and Handel, Habsburg Vienna, the Paris of Delacroix and Chopin, Verdi's Italy, Wagner's Germany and much else. By the mid-19th century, opera was no longer a European monopoly; out on the American frontier, gold rush millionaires flaunted their flamboyant claims to high culture while New York's *nouveaux riches* set up the Metropolitan Opera and established a vogue for high-quality opera that thrives across the USA to this day. In the 20th century, opera managed to survive and surmount the tragedies of two world wars to become a truly global art form: today, the most famous building in the entire southern hemisphere is an opera house.

Throughout, I found myself confronting further questions. How did a supposedly 'elite' art form take root in such self-consciously egalitarian societies as the USA or Australia? When did theatre audiences start to give more attention to the stage and less to their fellow audience members? How did the *prima donna* get her fiery reputation? Which have been better for opera (and the arts in general), dictatorships or democracies – and how far has art been influenced by the sources of its finances?

Today, everyone knows who Mozart was (and what the Mona Lisa looks like), and more opera is performed, financed, seen, heard, filmed and broadcast than ever before, and its leading performers are worshipped and paid like pop stars. Yet the art form is widely derided as 'elitist', and parts of the classical recording business appear close to bankruptcy. But the world of opera has always had to face crisis and uncertainty, and the resulting struggles – social, political, economic and above all artistic – have often proved every bit as vivid as those portrayed onstage.

Let's Get Together

Daniel urges musicologists and historians to join forces.

My book, The Gilded Stage: A Social History of Opera, *was first published in autumn 2009. By way of anticipation, I drafted the following article (published in* OPERA *magazine, November 2009). The additional section towards the end, about the Covent Garden fire of 1856 and the theatre's manager Frederick Gye, was derived from research I undertook while writing the new book.*

I have been firmly inside the operatic tent ever since I was taken to my first opera, *Rigoletto*, in October 1947. Later, I doted on Gigli at the Royal Albert Hall, watched Callas rehearsing for her Covent Garden debut in *Norma* and in recent decades have attended opera at all the world's major centres. And I have consumed the pages of *Opera* magazine almost from its inception and still eagerly await each new edition, impatient to find out who has been doing what and how far the opinions of its reviewers tally with my own.

Something has been worrying me, however. No: not the advent of surtitles or *Regietheater*, not the apparent incapacity of most new works to retain a place in the repertoire nor inadequate funding for the arts. It is deeper than all of these, and concerns the very way in which we regard opera.

***

'Are you starting with Monteverdi?' A question frequently posed by people who had heard I was writing a book about opera history. Monteverdi would certainly come into it, I replied, adding that I'd probably give more attention to the Gonzaga court for whom he worked. Mozart and his operas would be there, of course; but I also hoped to highlight the kind of audiences his works could attract or the hazards of pursuing a freelance career in 18th-century Vienna. It was not so much the operatic stage itself and what went on within its gilded confines that I wanted to concentrate on; many others have done this, and my bookshelves – like those of every opera lover – are packed with their work. Rather, I aimed to explore the broader context in which opera has been created, financed, produced, received and perceived. Not so much the supply side, in other words, but the demand, not just the production of opera but also its consumption and the many chains linking opera houses and impresarios, monarchs and money makers, art, artists and audiences.

In doing so, I found myself working with two rather different historiographies. First, there was a large and growing volume of excellent scholarly material on aspects of opera history, often by people trained as musicologists. Much of this tended to be fairly close-focused, with books and articles concentrating primarily on the traditional trio of composers and their works and performers. And second, a vast corpus of research delving into aspects of social, political and economic history. It will be no surprise to toilers in either field if I say that wire fences and closed gates rather than well-trodden pathways often marked the boundaries between the two. Of course, the standard biographies of the great operatic composers included something of their family background and the social and political context in which their works were created. No study of Mozart would make sense without reference to his extraordinary childhood or the Habsburg capital in which he lived and worked, while Verdi's prominence in *Risorgimento* Italy was long a standard feature in any study of the man and his operas. However, one could read otherwise excellent composer biographies by the fistful, or books about great singers, and search in vain for anything more than cursory consideration of the wider context of their subjects' lives and work. There were often good reasons for this. Music historians might point out, for example, that while anyone can read a document or look at a painting, no one without specialist expertise can understand a musical score. The autograph of a Mozart or Verdi opera, like a Latin court deposition or papal encyclical, is thus a core historical 'document' and only those who can read it can be considered equipped to write its history.

Mainstream historians could be just as territorial – and often for equally valid reasons. 'That's not my field,' says the Bismarck scholar pressed for a view on Frederick the Great or the Medievalist when asked about the Renaissance. Why should an historian of the Napoleonic Wars or the *Risorgimento* be expert on *Fidelio* or *Un ballo in maschera*? None of us is omniscient and we all have to defer to experts in 'fields' not our own. Moreover, historical data about many aspects of operatic history are unavailable. We simply do not know enough about life at the Mantuan court when Monteverdi's *Orfeo* was first produced, or even with absolute certainty where in the palace it was performed, while there were no polling organisations in the early years of opera to provide impresarios with socioeconomic profiles of their audiences. How widely known would

Handel and his music have been in early Hanoverian London, or Mozart and his in Habsburg Vienna, and who precisely played in their orchestras and sang in their choruses? Did the Italian immigrant community in late 19th-century New York provide a substantial proportion of the audience at the new Metropolitan Opera? Perhaps; but there are no accurate data to substantiate or contradict what must remain a hunch.

In recent years, the fences have begun to be breached and the pathways become better trodden than before. A lead came from historians of the fine arts such as Gombrich and others who taught us to look at sculptures and paintings not simply as objects 'out there' but to try and understand the motivation of the artist in creating them, the ideological and economic circumstances in which they were created and the psychological and cultural baggage through which they were subsequently perceived. Music history has followed suite, often with a limp of reluctance, but at a sprightly and inspiring pace among a few pioneers such as John Rosselli, Robert D Hume, Cyril Ehrlich, Tim Blanning and others.

Moreover, important advances have been made in recent times in how we try to unravel the past. History as taught in the academy used to concentrate on the great political, diplomatic and constitutional events of the past and the men who effected them. Much of this changed during the 1970s as the historiographical barometer swung towards the story of 'ordinary' people whose history had hitherto been marginalized or ignored. Today, social history has been augmented by the emergence of cultural history; here, historians have learned much from anthropology and have brought to the fore such issues as gender, ethnicity and ritual. 'Culture' has come to mean many things. What it does not mean to most historians nowadays, however, is precisely what it probably meant to their grandparents: the high arts, including opera. Just as music history often gives short shrift to the wider context in which composers composed and performers performed, social or cultural history tends to give minimal attention to the so-called 'high' arts. Perhaps there is a vestigial class bias here as historians intent on elevating the role of ordinary people disdain to consider such 'elite' pastimes as opera while opera historians prefer to concern themselves with 'great art'.

All historical scholarship is necessarily selective, limited by the capacities of the historian and the availability of data. But the difficulties lying in the way of an ambitious and worthwhile project are rarely strong enough reasons for not attempting it. My plea is for a kind of Hegelian synthesis drawing together the specialist insights of traditional opera history on the one hand with, on the other, those arising from more mainstream historical research. The results, if judiciously integrated, might stand to enrich the insights of both. *The Gilded Stage* makes no claim to have achieved this ideal synthesis; rather, an attempt to pull together into a single volume some of the disparate elements of a large story. While writing it, I tried to bear in mind, and interlink, five recurrent themes.

***

* The first was *political.* When a Gonzaga or Wittelsbach duke or a Bourbon monarch promoted opera, the aim was usually to impress someone (a rival ruler, perhaps), while 'popular' opera could often be more subversive. Napoleon appeared at the opera to show himself to 'the people' whose cause he was supposedly upholding abroad. Later, much of central Europe became immersed in a rising tide of cultural nationalism, a theme that many of the producers and consumers of opera embraced and which survived well into the 20th century – notably and notoriously under the Third Reich. In our own times, public debate about the supposed 'elitism' or 'popularity' of opera has sometimes taken a fiercely political turn.

* Alongside politics is *finance.* It is impossible to talk about an art form that aspires to combine all the others, and is therefore liable to be the most expensive, without discussing money and management. Opera has rarely been self-financing, and if there is one issue that recurs like a rondo theme throughout the story it is the question of who pays. Or, rather, who picks up the deficit. The story of opera is therefore in part that of a succession of dukes and monarchs, risk-running impresarios, syndicates of bountiful bankers and industrialists, grants from local or central governments, and latterly of various ingenious, more or less tax-exempt schemes to raise money from sponsorship and private donation.

* Opera has always been a *social* phenomenon, too. The shifts in the nature of the audience parallel other historical changes as power and money moved from the aristocracy, church and higher soldiery to the emergent bourgeoisie and, latterly, to a wider social spectrum. Equally remarkable is the changing social status of those in the operatic professions – especially among talented women singers to whom opera offered a rare opportunity for substantial social and economic improvement at a time when

women were not permitted to own property and a 'good' marriage was almost the only socially acceptable way to guarantee long-term economic wellbeing. Otherwise, a woman might become a nun, like several of the sisters of Francesco Rasi, the first Orfeo, or three centuries later, Puccini's sister Iginia. Or a singer – or courtesan (two professions widely associated in the public mind, both being seen as giving sensual pleasure in exchange for money). For a woman with the right combination of talent, willpower and good luck, therefore, opera held out the possibility of genuine liberation from gilded cage to gilded stage and beyond.

* Alongside these changes was a succession of advances in **technology** that transformed the nature of opera. From earliest times, opera flaunted magical stage effects as Eros flew overhead, Jove or Juno descended from heaven or the plot's wicked miscreant was dragged, Don Giovanni-style, down into a fiery hell. 'Scenes' and 'machines' were as much remarked as the music or drama. Thus, the attention of the opera historian might turn to candle, gas and electric lighting, to gauzes and swimming machines and the arrival of laser lighting and surtitles, not to mention developments in music publishing and copyright law and the successive invention of photography, recording, film, TV, video and the latest satellite and digital technologies.

* Finally, of course, opera is an **art form**. Broadly speaking, two strands weave their way in and out of the narrative. The first, which one encounters in the courts of late-Renaissance Italy, in Handel, Wagner, Verdi and Britten, is what we might dub 'serious' opera, usually through-composed and dealing with heightened emotions, situations and characters. The other, a more 'popular' style of music theatre with catchy tunes and vernacular dialogue, can be traced in Italian *commedia dell'arte*, *The Beggar's Opera* and *The Magic Flute* through to Viennese operetta, Gilbert and Sullivan and beyond. The music of operas, meanwhile, shifted from stylised recitative and aria towards more integrated music-drama, thence perhaps to psychodrama (and, in parallel, the popular 'musicals' of recent decades). As for the interpreters, the singer has always provided an essential ingredient, and opera history is replete with the supposedly extravagant behaviour, funding and achievements of vocal superstars. But everyone else's weight on the scales of relative significance has shifted over time as the story has lurched from what might loosely be labelled 'Patrons' Opera' (the

courts of Louis XIV or Joseph II), to 'Composers' Opera' (from Mozart to Puccini and Strauss), to 'Conductors' Opera' (the Mahler/Toscanini era) to 'Producers' Opera'.

In earlier times, opera goers liked to attend something new, rather like today's cinema audiences. By the 20th century, they were coming to prefer a standard repertoire of acknowledged classics, an emerging 'canon' to which few new works were subsequently added. Running alongside this fundamental change was the way operatic plots and productions altered focus over the centuries from high authority and quasi-mythical heroes, via the grand operas of the 19th century with their powerful rulers and vociferous crowds, to those of the mid-20th (*Wozzeck, Moses and Aaron, Peter Grimes, The Rake's Progress*) portraying the frustrations and anxieties of anomic individuals at odds with those around them.

***

Clearly, operatic history, if fully investigated 'in the round', can be found to interlink with what we learn from other kinds of source. I am not calling for a kind of historicist reductionism that sees great works of art merely as manifestations of personal and historical circumstance. Nor is my argument necessarily with opera historians. On the contrary, I am more disturbed by the opposite problem: the way much mainstream history has tended to disregard or marginalize the arts. Social historians examining (say) sexual attitudes, immigration patterns or forms of work and leisure in 18th-century London or 19th-century Paris might learn more than they think from studies that have been produced about the operatic life of these cities. Let me cite an example from my own researches that might help clinch the point.

***

In the early hours of 5 March 1856, towards the end of a somewhat riotous and drunken *Bal Masqué*, fire broke out in London's Covent Garden theatre. There was a rush for the exits, and half an hour later the roof collapsed. Later that day, condolences poured in from all directions, visitors to the site including the Queen and Prince Albert. The destruction of Covent Garden was a calamity but far from unique. During the 19th century, opera houses were destroyed or severely damaged by fire in virtually all the world's great opera centres, including Barcelona, Berlin, Dresden, Moscow,

Fire at Covent Garden theatre, 5 March 1856.

Statue of Frederick Gye (entry to Royal Opera House).

Munich, Naples, New York, Paris, Prague, St Petersburg and Venice.

The man in charge of Covent Garden from the late 1840s for some thirty years was Frederick Gye. Gye kept detailed diaries, and these have survived and are packed with revealing details about the operatic world in mid-Victorian London. There was no round-the-year opera or opera company at the time. Gye's season would normally last about four months, from mid-April until mid-August – a period of operatic force-feeding during which the theatre would typically stage three or four performances of some fifteen or more works with overlapping casts. Artists, including famous foreign soloists, were contracted for the season and required to sing a total of (say) fifteen performances in five different operas. For much of the rest of the year, Gye would typically let his theatre to a succession of temporary tenants who would promote various non-operatic entertainments – such as the masked ball that eventuated in its destruction.

When the fire occurred, Gye was on the continent finalizing his casts and repertoire for the season that was due to begin a month later (there was no nonsense in those days about superstars being booked years in advance!). Like many opera managers, Gye leased his theatre, paying a ground rent to its owner (the Duke of Bedford), and had a considerable personal stake in its financial success. Without a theatre in which to house his season – and with top opera stars contracted – Gye faced ruin. So his diary for March 1856 is packed with anxious visits to various other theatres (including Her Majesty's on the Haymarket, run by his rival Lumley). He finally settles on the Lyceum, just down the road; but the Lyceum has fewer seats than Covent Garden, so Guy arranges a series of concerts at the Crystal Palace to help amortize overall costs. He also has several meetings with Queen Victoria's private secretary, well aware that an encouraging word from the monarch could be translated into money. And he dashes back to the continent to beg his artists to accept a reduced fee.

On 9 April, just over a month after the fire, Gye announced his season in *The Times*. It would open on the 15th with a repertoire of seventeen operas (including 'Verdi's new opera *La Traviata*') and showcase some of the world's finest singers. Gye had worked fast. He continued to do so. Two years later, a new theatre was inaugurated on the Covent Garden site, designed by Edward Barry (son of the architect of the Palace of Westminster). This was essentially the house we know today.

***

Gye remained at the helm for another twenty years. The diaries reveal him constantly trying to refresh his repertoire and casts while remaining deeply aware of the appeal of the tried and tested. He is bold in his introduction of new French works but slow to recognize the rising popularity of Wagner. And he knows a starry soprano might fill the house (and attract the Prince of Wales to attend) but demand an exorbitant fee. The diary entries take us in and out of banks and law courts and illustrate the importance of retaining contacts in government and at court. We read of Gye's meetings with the great, the good and the bad, and we frequently accompany him abroad where he records what he picks up about operatic life in continental Europe while keeping regularly in touch with all that is going on back home. Britain may not have produced outstanding opera composers or singers; but all of any consequence came to London, and the diaries teem with the minutiae of Gye's dealings with major composers of the time such as Meyerbeer (whose works he championed) and celebrated singers like Mario, Grisi and Patti.

***

Gye's diaries reveal a man constantly struggling to balance the conflicting demands of artistic excellence and economic solvency. The two sides of the equation – the aesthetic and the practical – were deeply intertwined. They always have been, and of course remain so today. As the study of the operatic past shows signs of becoming increasingly cross-disciplinary, let's hope that its wider context will advance closer towards centre stage and come to share more of the limelight with the all-important history of the art form itself.

Opera in America – New World Overtures

This article combines material from an excerpt in Opera Now *in 2007 with a longer essay published in* History Today *in January 2010.*

There was opera of a sort in America before independence, but it had a chequered history. Theatre of any kind was condemned by the Pilgrim Fathers. Life in Puritan New England, they preached, was tough and the daily fight for food, shelter and survival rendered virtually any form of entertainment superfluous, not a part of the European cultural heritage they were keen to transplant to their City on a Hill. Music may have been permissible, but only if reserved for liturgical purposes. Further south, a somewhat more tolerant attitude developed. Travelling theatrical troupes began to appear up and (mostly) down the Atlantic seaboard, and productions including music were commonly dubbed 'operas'. Gay's *Beggar's Opera*, produced in New York in 1750, fed a vogue for 'ballad operas' that strung together a sequence of popular airs linked by rudimentary dialogue and a simple, feelgood plot. By the time of the Revolution, a few cultured enthusiasts would have known the works of the current European masters: Thomas Jefferson played the latest airs on the fiddle and Benjamin Franklin invented the glass harmonica and devised a theory of melodic and harmonic consonance. But to most, the hymns of Isaac Watts, Charles Wesley or William Billings would have been more familiar than the compositions of Gluck or Haydn. As the Revolutionary troops went into battle against King George's Redcoats, Billings's four-part hymn *Chester* became something of a rallying cry, as psalms had been for Cromwell's Ironsides.

In the decades after independence, musical theatre emerged most strongly in New Orleans, a European outpost sold to the newly-sovereign USA by Napoleon in 1803 along with the rest of France's vast Louisiana territories. Here, French *opéra comique* thrived for a while, alongside an occasional Italian or German work in French translation. When there was opera in Philadelphia, Boston or New York, it was usually by a touring company from New Orleans. And Italian opera – in Italian? Lorenzo Da Ponte, famous as Mozart's librettist but in the 1820s an elderly professor living in New York, was distressed to find it almost totally lacking. That is, until the arrival of Manuel García.

***

García has many claims to operatic fame, not least as father of two of the 19th century's most celebrated singers, Maria Malibran and Pauline Viardot. Born in Seville in 1775, García gained early renown as a versatile singer and composer, later honing his skills in France and Italy. In Rome in 1816, he sang the role of Almaviva in the premiere of Rossini's *Barber of Seville*. In 1824, we find García in London, and it was from here that he and his family-based opera troupe set sail for America the following year. Also on board was the socialist idealist, Robert Owen, en route to set up a utopian colony in New Harmony, Indiana. Owen's son kept a diary in which he describes what he refers to as 'our Italian party' singing what he supposes to be:

> ... Italian catches, glees and humorous songs, in the highest spirits, apparently extemporizing with the most perfect ease and harmony. Amongst other amusements they imitated the Scotch bagpipes to perfection.

Arriving in New York in early November 1825, García recruited an orchestra and chorus from whatever talent he could find. Standards were patchy, García past his vocal best and many Americans regarded opera as an expensive, foreign-bred form of elite entertainment still carrying something of the aristocratic patina of its courtly origins. How would opera go down in the commercial capital of the most self-consciously egalitarian nation on earth?

The Garcías opened in New York's Park Theatre, near the Battery, in late November, performing Rossini. The *New York Evening Post* reported that the first-night house was full. One senses a touch of relief: the local citizenry had not disgraced themselves by refraining from attending an event so elevated, so 'European'.

> ... An assemblage of ladies so fashionable, so numerous & so elegantly dressed, was probably never witnessed in our theatre ...

wrote *The Post*. And not only fashionable ladies. In the boxes were some of New York's most prosperous merchants, plus a scattering of prominent intellectuals. The novelist James Fenimore Cooper was there, as was Napoleon's brother Joseph Bonaparte, the exiled former king of Spain, while the less elevated strata of the European immigrant community poured into the dollar-a-seat pit and the twenty-five-cent gallery. As the year turned, however, and the novelty wore off, houses were not as full or enthusiastic as at the outset, and by the spring Da Ponte was suggesting to

García that he might like to vary his repertoire – for example, by putting on 'my *Don Giovanni* set to music by the immortal Mozart'. And so, on 23 May 1826, *Don Giovanni* had its North American premiere, to Da Ponte's original text, in the presence of its elderly librettist.

The Garcías stayed for nine months, after which many (including Da Ponte) believed that opera had at last taken root. But it was one thing for wealthy New Yorkers to part with a few dollars in order to attend a passing show; quite another for these embodiments of the profit motive to put big money into something so predictably *un*profitable as a permanent opera company or a dedicated opera house. Manuel García left New York as lacking in Italian opera as he had found it. He came, was seen, was applauded and paid – and he left.

***

In 1847, the Mexican province of Alta California was ceded into American hands; the USA now stretched from coast to coast, and people across the Union rejoiced in the 'manifest destiny' evidenced by their spectacular new acquisition. In 1849, gold was discovered and a year later California celebrated its formal entry into the Union as the 31st state.

In this golden environment, people craved entertainment. There were a dozen or more theatres in San Francisco alone, all lit by candles or whale oil (gas didn't arrive until 1854); many burned down but were promptly rebuilt. On offer was a variety of popular vaudeville shows at which dancers, instrumentalists and operatic vocalists might alternate with acrobats, tightrope walkers, fire eaters and the occasional performing animal. When 'opera' was on the bill, this usually meant edited excerpts (with no chorus), to the rudimentary accompaniment of a honky-tonk piano and perhaps a flute, harp or guitar. Acting was rudimentary: hand on heart to signify love and/or sincerity, hand on brow to indicate emotional pain and arms out wide to milk applause at the end of an aria; costumes and sets, too, tended to be multi-purpose standard issue. Performers found travel to be perilous, pricey and uncomfortable while hotels could be insalubrious and dangerous, rooms (and even beds) often shared with strangers and food and water risky to ingest.

But the potential rewards were enticing. The British soprano Anna Bishop made an arduous journey down from New York, across Nicaragua and then up the Californian coast, but recouped all her expenses at her first San Francisco concert in 1854, while Catherine Hayes ('The Swan of

Erin') sang songs and arias to hordes of sentimental Irishmen and retired on the proceeds. Many of the singers were Italian, their presence having been stimulated not only by gold but also by the failed revolutions of 1848. Sometimes, complete operas would be assayed, and performers took their talents up from San Francisco to Sacramento or, in the wake of the Comstock lode, to Eureka or Piper's Opera House in Virginia City in Nevada.

As more 'opera houses' were built, new audiences emerged. People dusted down their best hats for the opera, sometimes wearing them throughout the performance (perhaps in part to keep their hair free of candle drippings from the chandeliers above). A successfully executed aria might be rewarded by gentlemen twirling their hats on their sticks and a burst of yelling, stamping and whistling, while a bad performance would elicit hisses and catcalls. Germans go to opera, wrote Mark Twain, because they like it 'with their whole hearts'. Americans, by contrast, go 'in order to learn to like it' or 'to be able to talk knowingly about it', often humming along with the music 'so that their neighbors may perceive that they have been to operas before'.

***

Back in New York, meanwhile, the Irish-born William Niblo was putting on public entertainments in 'Niblo's Garden' on lower Broadway, a kind of Vauxhall Gardens with open-air music and ice cream in summertime and an enclosed theatre for more serious theatrical fare. Then there was Castle Clinton, built in 1811 as a fort off the Battery on the southern tip of Manhattan Island. Later joined to mainland Manhattan by landfill, 'Castle Garden' as it became known functioned from the 1820s as a place of public entertainment, was roofed over in the 1840s, and until 1855 functioned as a concert hall and theatre until it was requisitioned as an immigration reception centre (the predecessor to Ellis Island). It was here that Jenny Lind, the 'Swedish Nightingale', made her American debut in 1850 before 6000 adoring fans.

There were also recurrent attempts among the city's elite to establish fully-fledged opera in New York. 1847 saw the opening of the Astor Place Opera House, between Broadway and Fourth Avenue, strategically placed at the top of Lafayette Place where some of New York's wealthiest had their mansions. But in 1849, as revolution continued to smoulder across Europe, Nativist supporters of the American actor Edwin Forrest, furious that his English rival Macready was starring at Astor Place, marched on the theatre. The national guard was called in, and by the time the mob

Castle Garden, NY: scene of first US appearance of Jenny Lind, September 1850.

was quelled the opera house was pock-marked with bullet holes and in the street outside more than twenty people were dead. With them, serious theatre and opera in Astor Place also died.

The tragedy of Astor Place was quickly exorcised, however, with the inauguration in 1854 of a new opera house, the Academy of Music. The Academy was a little further uptown, in the fashionable neighbourhood of 14th Street and Irving Place, near Union Square. Walt Whitman was a frequent attendee, and the opera left a deep impression.

> Across the stage with pallor on her face, yet lurid passion,
> Stalks Norma brandishing the dagger in her hand …

The Academy soon ran into financial difficulties. Impresarios were replaced, concerts of popular classics promoted and the building leased out for social and charitable events. The hard fact was that, apart from a few rich people keen to buy themselves some social standing and European culture, plus a few *cognoscenti* like Whitman, European grand opera had limited appeal – even in New York, the most cosmopolitan city in America. The Academy boxes on opera nights may have been packed with the great and the good, but there were frequently rows of unfilled seats.

On the face of it, you might have expected an old-fashioned, upper-class

European art form like opera to make little impact in a self-consciously egalitarian society like the USA, a nation set up in deliberate opposition to old-world elitism. Yet America went on to have well over 100 professional or quasi-professional opera companies, among them some the finest in the world such as the New York Metropolitan. Why? The short answer is that the establishment and early popularity of an opera company like the 'Met' resulted from the intersection of three great forces: mass immigration, Gilded Age wealth and the coincidental invention of several new technologies each of which helped to spread the word (or song).

***

Migration to America was nothing new, of course. Many Germans and Scandinavians, for example, had come in the 1840s and 1850s; all Americans except those of native 'Indian' blood had foreign forebears. Two things were different, however, about this new wave of migrants. The first was its size. From about 1880 until the outbreak of war in Europe in 1914, an average of some half a million people fetched up every year on America's shores. By the early 20th century, the annual number was sometimes close to a million. The advent of steam shipping had rendered trans-oceanic travel faster and more efficient than ever before, while steerage costs fell once shipping companies began fitting out their steamers for passengers rather than freight. The second unprecedented feature was the geographical distribution from which they came. Increasingly, the bulk were from eastern and southern Europe. Jews escaping from the pogroms of Russia and, above all, Italians – especially from the *Mezzogiorno*: young men (and some women) who had picked themselves up from the parched fields of Calabria and Puglia or the disease-infested slums of Palermo or Naples and somehow found the wherewithal to make the epic journey from the old world to the new. In 1880, Italian arrivals alone totalled about 12,000; by the eve of the First World War the annual figure had climbed to more than 300,000.

New York already boasted a rather superior 'German town', east of Central Park, where professors, bankers and musicians talked high culture and consumed *haute cuisine*. Now, the city's Lower East Side, where the passenger steamers delivered their human cargo, was fast becoming a replica of Naples with its street singers, pasta houses and its laundry lines strung between the tenement blocks.

Giuseppe Giacosa, the Italian dramatist (and librettist to Puccini), visited America in 1898 and later described the bustle and squalor of the

Italian settlements he found there. 'Ragged, thin men,' he wrote, wander from shop to shop or gather around the entrance of saloons where they are served 'the bitter dregs' of beer bottles, while the women 'suckle their children, sew, clean the faded greens which are the only substance of their soup (and) wash their clothes in greasy buckets'.

Yet for all its poverty, New York's Little Italy also proved a springboard for many into a better world. As the city underwent a building spree, Italian labour provided skilled masons and stucco workers. Italians entered the service industries, too, working as barbers, fruit dealers, waiters or chefs. Some found their way as entertainers, perhaps in the boxing ring or baseball diamond or signing up as chorus members in one of America's theatres. If you had a voice, this could provide a conduit out of the slums and into the mainstream of the American dream. To many Italian Americans, an ideal role model was provided by Enrico Caruso, a product of the Neapolitan slums and now a celebrated opera singer.

***

There was poverty in America in the years after the Civil War. But also great wealth, especially in the industrial North where many felt their way of life had been vindicated by their victory. After the financial downturn in 1873, a market-based business economy soon began to boom. Big money begat even bigger money: Harriman and Vanderbilt accumulated immense fortunes from railroads, Rockefeller from oil, Andrew Carnegie with his steel company and JP Morgan from a vast financial empire with tentacles reaching into every sector of industry. This was truly a 'Gilded Age' in which unprecedented riches seemed to be available to anyone with the talent and energy to pursue it. The economic jungle was harsh; even its most predatory denizens acknowledged that. But since we are human beings and not animals, it was right and proper for the rich to give some of their wealth to help their less fortunate fellows and soften the edges of the human condition. Thus, the Scottish-born Carnegie founded a network of public libraries and charitable trusts while Rockefeller endowed a Foundation devoted to the promotion of the arts and sciences and, in particular, research into medicine and public health.

There was another thing, too, that you could do with your wealth. You could buy culture. That meant European culture. 'We'll read *Faust* together … by the Italian lakes,' muses Edith Wharton's epitome of new American money (whom she even names 'Newland' Archer) as he contemplates his lady love at the opera in the opening chapter of *The Age of Innocence*. Willa Cather picks up the same theme. 'I'd like to go to Germany to study, some day,' says Thea, the aspirant young singer in *The Song of the Lark* as she echoes the words of her teacher, the mysterious and omniscient Professor Wunsch (Professor 'Wish'), 'it's the only place you can really learn'. Thea, a tense, self-obsessed young woman ill-at-ease in small-town Colorado, uses her voice as a passport to escape her stifling background and go East, initially to Chicago and thence to Europe, returning to become one of the great *prime donne* at the New York Metropolitan. She makes few close relationships, but she eventually marries Fred, of whom Cather reports that 'When he was in Chicago or St Louis, he went to ball games, prize-fights, and horse-races. When he was in Germany, he went to concerts and to the opera.' Fred is something of a *bon viveur* and gastronome. When in Germany, 'he scarcely knew where the soup ended and the symphony began.'

Germany was the source of high culture, of *Kultur* – especially of music, that pre-eminent cultural form that, not dependent upon verbal or pictorial representation, travelled most easily. To many German Americans, music was not a branch of entertainment but something more ennobling, educational, moral almost, that the more earnest among them felt it their duty to disseminate. It was in this quasi-missionary spirit that the Mainz musician Felix Volbach applied to become conductor of the Cincinnati Symphony Orchestra, saying in his awkward way that he wanted to bring the 'rich treasures of our masters … to the world of the future and help that they conquer the world'. To Volbach, the music of the old homeland was a cultural legacy which would help ennoble the new.

He was not alone. During the latter years of the 19th century, America's German émigré community set up dozens of amateur music groups and choral societies, while in the major cities a string of new symphony orchestras appeared, most of them conducted and substantially manned by first-generation German American musicians. All were keen to bring the benefits of high art – and that meant the German classics – to the ignorant hinterland. 'But Mr Bergmann,' someone told the conductor of the New York Philharmonic, 'the people don't like Wagner.' 'Den dey must hear him till dey do!' Bergmann is said to have replied.

To a remarkable extent, the supposedly ignorant hinterland proved receptive to the message of the missionaries. Touring orchestras were often asked to put on a free concert in front of the local 'opery-house' and local newspapers could be sure to report on the glamour and genius of the latest

German musician in town. When Johann Strauss, the waltz king, appeared in America in 1872, it was reported that he speaks only German 'but he smiles in all languages'. Theodore Thomas and his orchestra were once on tour and the train carrying them had to change engines in a cattle town in Colorado. As the musicians stretched their legs on the platform, a collection of local cowboys congregated and demanded a concert there and then or they wouldn't let the train proceed. Eventually, Thomas himself pulled out his violin and lulled them, Orpheus-like, into acquiescence and a Wagnerian soprano in his party sang to them – after which (said a local newspaper) 'there was loud cheering and hurrahing, and as the train pulled out the enthusiastic cowboys fired a hundred guns into the air.' Meanwhile, back in urban America, middle-class families were buying their first pianos and their daughters learning to play *Für Elise* and the Wedding March from *Lohengrin*.

***

The New York Metropolitan Opera, which opened in October 1883, was the product of greed. As Gilded Age America poured new wealth into the pockets of steel and railroad magnates, bankers, financial wizards and shyster politicians, the *nouveau riche* craved the trappings of traditional status: membership of New York's elite clubs, mansions on Fifth Avenue, dinner at Delmonico's – and boxes at the opera. But the antebellum Yankee aristocracy who owned the boxes at the Academy of Music had no desire to share their privileges with parvenu millionaires. And even if they had, there were simply not enough boxes to go round. So when Mrs Alva Vanderbilt applied for one, she was turned down.

The Vanderbilts were among America's wealthiest. When the railroad king, Commodore Cornelius Vanderbilt, died in 1877, he bequeathed to his son William some $100m. With this colossal fortune at his disposal, 'Billy' Vanderbilt was not used to being gainsaid. So when Alva was refused a box at the Academy, her husband took up the cause. Not only Mrs Vanderbilt but others among New York's newly wealthy, too, wished to grace the opera with their presence. The outcome was that they pooled resources to found a new theatre of their own: the New York Metropolitan.

When the Met opened (further uptown once more, on Broadway between 39th and 40th Streets, just below what became Times Square), everyone remarked upon its boxes: 122 of them spread over four tiers, seating a quarter of the entire 3500-strong audience. Here, opulently

The Metropolitan Opera on 39th Street and Broadway.

arrayed for all to see, was the new wealth – and by implication the new power elite – of New York and therefore of America.

***

There had been plenty of opera in America before the opening of the Met in 1883. But this combination of German and Italian immigration, allied to the cultural appetites of Gilded Age wealth, gave it a more secure foothold. For opera to have a permanent presence, however, it needed to increase its reach and popularity. This is where technology came to its aid.

By the end of the century, many people were already becoming familiar with the camera and telephone and were reading mass-distribution newspapers. Soon, they would be going to picture palaces to relish the latest moving pictures and perhaps dreaming of buying that much-discussed product of Mr Henry Ford's inventiveness and entrepreneurship, the automobile. They were beginning to listen to gramophone recordings too, and perhaps, reading about the Italian émigré physicist Guglielmo Marconi whose experiments looked set to make possible the 'wireless' communication of sound.

Everywhere, it seemed, the technologies of communication – of words, ideas, images and sounds – and of the transportation of the people who produced and consumed them, were being transformed. As one century ended and a new one began, people talked of a new age dawning, an era of 'art nouveau', of the 'New Woman', of 'novelties'. Almost as if to stamp the end of an era, Queen Victoria, that great embodiment of a passing age, died in January 1901. A week later, that other great octogenarian symbol of *his* nation, Giuseppe Verdi, passed away in his Milan hotel room just up the road from La Scala. The following year, in another room in that same Milan hotel, the young Caruso was prevailed upon by Fred Gaisberg of the Gramophone and Typewriter Company, to make his first recordings.

The earliest advocates of these new technologies were often blind to their long-term applications. Edison's recording cylinders, for example, were at first regarded by many as possible enhancements to the modern office, while Marconi argued that wireless technology might prove useful for security purposes. The last thing most people envisaged in the early days of radio or recording was that these should become instruments of entertainment and lead to the mass marketing of music. Several top *fin-de-siècle* singers refused at first to record, fearing that the availability of the phonograph would keep potential audiences at home instead of coming to hear them in the opera house. 'Whenever we approached the great artists,' wrote Fred Gaisberg recalling the period around 1900, 'they just laughed at us and replied that the gramophone was only a toy'.

He soon proved them wrong. The enormous success of Gaisberg and his colleagues was keenly observed from across the Atlantic. Perhaps operatic recordings, well marketed, would sell in America after all; here was where the biggest potential market lay. It was the Victor Company that took the initiative. They set up a factory in Camden, New Jersey, and signed up many of the great European operatic stars, among them Caruso, Melba, Plançon, Calvé and Destinn. In order to hear these voices, people had to buy not only the records but the machines on which to play them. Victor found a way of encasing everything – phonograph, turntable and acoustic horn – inside a four-foot mahogany cabinet (a 'Victrola') which it marketed as an essential addition to every elegant living room. Records and reproducing equipment did not come cheap. At a time when a dollar bill could buy a multi-course restaurant meal, a star-studded record of the

Lucia Sextet could set you back by $7, while the Victrola was marketed at a cool $200. Yet demand for records and machines on which to play them repeatedly outstripped supply and the Victor Company's assets, $2.7m in 1902, had risen to $33.2m by 1917.

No wonder they could afford to pay their recording stars astronomical fees. In his biography of his father, Enrico Caruso Jr quotes a 1913 exchange between the tenor and a friend who had asked him how much he earned from his records.

'Guess,' replied Papa.

'$10,000,' the friend said tentatively.

'Right,' he answered. 'Only I make that monthly you know.'

In due course, the advent of recording helped increase the public appetite for the real thing; once people became accustomed to enjoying the disembodied voices of Caruso, Melba and the rest, the urge grew to see them in the flesh.

As Caruso made his first recordings (and was tempted into the film studios), Puccini bought his new cars and, after the Great War, Nellie

Enrico Caruso (1873-1921).
In addition to being one of the great singers of his time, Caruso was a talented cartoonist. Here he portrays himself making one of his early recordings. And note the witty parallel image he has included: the trade mark of the recently created gramophone company depicting a dog listening to 'His Master's Voice'!

Giacomo Puccini (1858-1924) in his car.
Puccini loved all things modern: the motorboats on which he could sail around the
lake near his home and the steamships on which to cross the Atlantic, the emergence
of recording, film, wireless. And all the latest automobiles which he loved to drive.

Melba made the first operatic broadcast and the world of opera found itself presented with a plethora of challenges and opportunities by which, in due course, it would reach a vastly bigger audience than anyone before could have imagined. When I was first in the USA in the early 1960s and would ask any ageing opera lovers I met what first drew them to opera, chances are they'd recollect early memories of listening to the Met Saturday matinee radio broadcasts.

These began in 1931 at the height of the Depression. In the 1930s, too, the Met Guild was established: a 'Friends' organisation that helped elicit much-needed money and support. And right through until the 1980s, the Met went on an annual tour, many Americans recalling with misty eyes the day their parents took them to, say, a *Walküre* in Cleveland with Flagstad and Melchior.

The first full-length, live opera broadcast from the stage of the Metropolitan Opera, New York, was *Hänsel and Gretel* on Christmas Day, 1931. But it was not the first operatic event to be broadcast. In England in June 1920, Melba visited the Marconi plant in Chelmsford, Essex, and sang a few items that could be heard not only in London some forty miles away but on the continent; Tetrazzini did much the same a few months later from her hotel suite in New York, aiming at 'ships within a radius of 400 miles'.

Before long, broadcasts of complete operas or (more commonly) opera highlight concerts were being relayed across America, some of them introduced by a 25-year-old part-time singer named Milton Cross, later to become famous as presenter of the Met broadcasts. The number of people with radios was rising rapidly: just over half a million radio sets were sold in America in 1923, a figure that had quadrupled two years later. By 1928, 12 million sets were broadcasting to some 40 million listeners. In spring 1925, the newly created 'NBC National Grand Opera Company' inaugurated a regular weekly broadcast of abridged versions of operas under the conductor and arranger Cesare Sodero.

By 1931, when the Met's live relays went on air, America was deep in economic depression. Following the stock market crash of 1929, Met box office revenues dropped drastically and emergency steps had to be taken if the company was to survive. And that meant appealing to a broader potential audience. Nobody knows exactly how many people heard that first Met broadcast in 1931, but the excitement soon spread. A week later, on New Year's Day 1932, Gigli was singing a matinee performance of *La bohème*. During the afternoon, a woman rushed up to the Met box office asking if there was a ticket for sale. She was told there was – but didn't she know that the performance was half over? Yes, she said breathlessly; 'I've been listening to the first two acts on the radio, and it's so wonderful I want to see the rest!'

For others, the Damascan moment might have been a visit to the cinema. From the earliest years of film, famous opera singers, such as Caruso and Geraldine Farrar, starred in silent movies: surprising to us, perhaps, but remember that film showings were often accompanied not just by a piano but in larger cinemas by a full orchestra. When the glamorous Farrar made a *Carmen* movie in 1915 directed by Cecil B DeMille, she became a nationwide celebrity.

With the advent of the talkies came a host of feature films that included music and starred attractive actors such as Nelson Eddy or Jeanette MacDonald with operatic-style voices. Sometimes, an aria or two might be introduced into a film to give it a bit of class, or to help 'place' one of the characters. If Eddy and MacDonald (like Howard Keel later) were actors with good voices, there were also successful films featuring that even rarer breed, top opera singers who looked good and could act: the Met's star baritone, Lawrence Tibbett, received an Academy nomination for his dashing presence in *The Rogue Song* while Risë Stevens, the Met's captivating Carmen, starred opposite Eddy in *The Chocolate Soldier*. But perhaps the most famous opera movie of the period was one that satirised it: the Marx Brothers' 1935 movie *A Night at the Opera* which culminates with a spectacularly sabotaged performance of *Il Trovatore* in which everything that can possibly go wrong at an operatic performance duly does so – all in the interests of humiliating an arrogant tenor and bringing professional success and true love to his rival.

As new ways of transmitting reproduced images and sounds became widespread in the early decades of the 20th century, opera was a major beneficiary. For the existence of recordings, radio relays and opera on film seems to have fed but not to have sated the curiosity of those who consumed them. The lady who rushed to the Gigli performance at the New York Met having caught the first half on the wireless may have been exceptional. But only in the extent of her zeal.

***

After the war, with the economic upsurge of the 1960s and 1970s, the existing roster of opera companies in America was joined by a string of additions so that, by 2000, there were over one hundred of them, many in the rapidly growing conurbations of the South and West. In Miami, Houston and Los Angeles (as in 19th-century Munich or Milan), opera came to be something of a civic badge of honour, alongside museums, art galleries and other cultural and educational amenities. Contrary to myth, the US government subsidised opera – not, as in many European countries, via direct grant but by enabling those who supported opera to claim tax exemption on their donations. The decision, in other words, was left to the individual, and it was up to the opera companies to persuade potential donors that this was where they should direct their largesse. This proved one of opera's strengths, enabling it to claim (at least when times were good) that it thrived not because it was placed there by princes or governments but because people chose to support it. Today, with the advent of recession, many US opera companies are facing crisis as donations tumble. But that's a story for another time ...

The ROH Collections

(Covent Garden Archives)

In addition to contributing a number of articles to the Royal Opera House
website, I was invited in 2011 to investigate their entire archive collection
– which, I concluded, contained much that was of potential interest to the
general historian.

(H)e shuffled & told all sorts of lies – I have heard bad things of (him)
& now find him a devil incarnate – the most dreadful rascal with the
smoothest face & manner I ever in the whole course of my life met.

Not the sort of thing, one trusts, that today's top London theatre executives
write about one another. But it's what Covent Garden's manager Frederick
Gye wrote in his diary in 1851 after a series of failed negotiations with his
rival Benjamin Lumley, manager of Her Majesty's in the Haymarket.

Gye ran Covent Garden for nearly thirty years (he died in 1878) and
throughout his time at the top kept detailed diaries. These have survived
and are lodged on semi-permanent loan from the Gye family in the
archives of the Royal Opera House. I had periodically used the ROH
archives (or 'Collections') from the early 1980s, and again while working
on my book *The Gilded Stage* in the early 2000s. Among countless other
sources (including international operatic archives), I often returned to the
Gye diaries, especially while investigating the Covent Garden fire of 1856
and its repercussions (see above, pp. 202–205). And after the book was
concluded, I returned to the Collections and wrote a number of feature
pieces for the new ROH Website: on the broad history of opera, the voice
types most commonly used by operatic composers and performers and the
historically shifting role of operatic librettos and librettists.

One day I received an email from Deborah Bull, the former ballet dancer
and by now the Creative Director in charge of all the interests and activities
of the ROH other than those taking place on the main stage. It seemed the
management was keen to produce a substantial document outlining and
assessing the ROH Collections as a whole, the national and international
importance of the various elements they contained and, perhaps, comparing
the ROH archives with similar collections internationally. Would this be a
project I might be interested in undertaking? I set to work with a will, looked
through all the archive material in house as well as the ROH collections
stored elsewhere (notably in Egham) and in due course produced a document

that included broad outlines of all the variegated materials contained by the Collections and the many purposes they were able to fulfil.

What I discovered was a veritable goldmine of historical data – yet a largely unknown one, I would guess, to most researchers other than those specifically concerned with opera or ballet. Over the years, I had been lucky enough to extract glittering ore from the occasional seam, but had now, like a greedy prospector, had the opportunity to sample a far wider range than hitherto. For all my explorations, and those of others, much in this incomparable Yukon of theatrical history remained to be examined and assessed.

***

Formally established in 1969, the ROH Archives were primarily a collection of documents (written and printed) and photographs. After a period of rapid expansion, including the addition of many designs, staging models and costumes, they were renamed the 'Collections'. The holdings from the period of the first Covent Garden theatre (1732–1808) were and remain mostly of secondary sources: press and legal reports and the like, plus some original playbills and posters. The second theatre opened in 1809, but it was not until it became established as the 'Royal Italian Opera' in 1847 that more systematic managerial and artistic records seem to have been kept. Some of these survived the 1856 fire and the inauguration of the third theatre (the one we know today) a couple of years later. But it is only after 1946, with the reopening of the house after the war and the establishment of permanent opera and ballet companies, that the holdings became more comprehensive.

That said, the Collections contain a dazzling array of superb materials that rival those of any theatre in the world and include programmes, libretti, musical scores, production files, architectural records, business and personnel files, artist files, press cuttings, photographs, props, costumes and audiovisual records. Most of these concern professional matters of a more or less public nature. But a close reading reveals a host of personal touches, such as in the Gye quote with which I began, or when we catch Ninette de Valois, in high-Madam mode, arguing with her boss Sir David Webster or (in one letter) with a hapless designer.

There is a touching handwritten note (in English) from the Italian baritone Tito Gobbi to Ken Davison, founder of the Friends of Covent Garden, thanking Davison for a condolence letter sent on the death of

Gobbi's wife, while the Collections also reveal why, some years earlier, Gobbi was sacked from the role of Iago (correction: released from the necessity of singing this role!) after missing a pivotal rehearsal.

The Collections serve a variety of clients. In house, press and publications mine them for material about scheduled productions and artists while those on the artistic side often seek out details of previous productions. Senior management use them to check legal, financial, insurance or broadcasting precedents while some of the most successful merchandise in the Covent Garden shop is derived from objects in the Collections. From the outside world, the Collections team receive requests for information about particular performances and performers or about friends and forebears who worked at the theatre. Other requests come in from film and TV companies or publishers about the use of images. Audiences clearly enjoy the exhibitions of costumes and photographs regularly displayed in the theatre's foyers and corridors, though these tend to be glanced at only cursorily by people about to have a quick drink or retake their seat, and I am surely not the first person to yearn for some kind of permanent on-site museum (e.g. in what at the time of writing was the unused courthouse opposite).

Outside researchers, too, use the Collections. My own experience is probably typical. When starting work on *The Gilded Stage*, I contacted the ROH's Head of Collections, Francesca Franchi. After an initial chat about the kind of records that interested me, she invited me to look at the Gye diaries. To anyone interested in the financial and political complexities of mid-Victorian London, let alone its rich musical and theatrical history, much that lies in these still unpublished volumes remains largely unexamined as Gye struggles to balance the conflicting demands of political and social acceptability, artistic excellence and economic solvency.

***

The ROH Collections are obviously an indispensable source to anyone interested in the history of opera and ballet. But, potentially at least, their intellectual resonance goes far wider and the Collections could, I think, be of value to a rather larger constituency than at present.

It is revealing, for example, to see how successive managements strove to stay on good terms with power, status and wealth. An encouraging word from the monarch (especially the opera-loving Queen Victoria) could often be translated into money. After the death of Prince Albert in 1861, the Queen dropped her visits to Covent Garden and the management turned increasingly to her son, the Prince of Wales (and future Edward VII) for patronage, agreeing to change operas at the Prince's request – often so he could see and hear a favourite soprano. A book maintained by the keeper of the Royal Box logs every royal visitor to the theatre from 1892–1908, while the influence of various well-connected *grandes dames* (Lady de Grey, Lady Snowden etc) is much in evidence in the Collections. The records leading up to and immediately following the establishment of the permanent companies in 1946 document the links, often through Keynes, between the theatre and the political elite of the day.

There is legal history, too, buried in the Collections. In the 1850s, Covent Garden went to court against Her Majesty's theatre in a famous case over which had a prior claim to the services of the soprano Johanna Wagner (niece of the composer), while in the 1860s much of Gye's time was taken up with a succession of cases filed against him by Colonel Knox, a former colleague who had helped him obtain the original Covent Garden lease and now demanded that he should be paid out of the profits of the new theatre. Not everything is contentious. Thus, the Collections plot the often complex and convoluted but usually successful negotiations between the Bedford Estate and the theatre's many lessees.

Opera and ballet are expensive art forms to produce and the Collections are packed with economic data concerning recruitment and payment of everyone from solo performers (sometimes ruthlessly exigent) to members of the orchestra, chorus and corps de ballet and a plethora of backstage and front-of-house personnel. A document from 1930 lists salaries ranging from the stage manager (£1200), through the stage doorkeeper (£182) to the messenger boy (£65). In our own times, the theatre has been, in effect, a factory with anything up to 1000 people on its payroll, and this has involved complex negotiations with agents, trades unions, the Arts Council and a wide range of donors and sponsors. Ticket pricing has always been a crucial issue: if you reduce prices too much, you may have full houses but gross revenue may fall – but raise them too sharply and you risk alienating your audience base. This was dramatically illustrated when the second Covent Garden theatre was virtually immobilised during the first few weeks of its existence in autumn 1809 by the vociferous 'OP [Old Prices] Riots'.

Before the establishment of permanent in-house companies, Covent Garden was frequently sub-leased: for example, to a showman called the 'Wizard of the North' who had been promoting a rather *louche* masked ball the night the second theatre burned down in 1856. Fund-raising was more genteel by the 1920s when a batch of colourful invitations and programme books reveal a succession of daytime dances and evening balls featuring famous bands of the day (any historian of social dance, incidentally, would do well to investigate the use of the theatre as a *palais de danse* during World War II). More recent schemes to raise funds (and the public profile of the ROH) include the establishment of the Friends of Covent Garden, the development of gift-aided donations and a multiplicity of educational and 'meet-the-artist' events, foreign tours, retail sales and such popular events as raffles, tea dances and playing host to the annual BAFTA ceremony.

There is much in the Collections for students of social history to chew over. Documents illustrating the careers (and fees) of leading female performers show how, at a time when women were not yet allowed to own property and marital failure condemned many to penury, opera held out the possibility of genuine female liberation from gilded cage to gilded stage and beyond. The social profile of audiences, too, is richly documented, with clues suggesting a clientele increasingly augmented during the later 19th century and early 20th by members of an emerging middle class. This can be inferred from the names and titles of subscribers and box-holders, the level of ticket prices, the kind of food and drink on sale and such matters as the ads in the programmes (a rich and under-researched source).

Dress codes could be a further indication of socioeconomic status. In 1853, Gye was visited by an irate customer who had been refused admission to the theatre 'because the cut of my dress coat was not what it ought to be according to the ideas of the doorkeeper'. By the later 20th century, board minutes suggest a determination to make the house and its activities more 'democratic' and 'accessible', for example through education and 'outreach' programmes or by linking the amphitheatre to the rest of the house during the 1997/9 rebuild – while at the same time retaining the goodwill of the wealthy, the powerful and the titled. The contrast is nicely encapsulated in the Collections which reveal that, whereas the mid-Victorian manager Frederick Gye resented not receiving a knighthood, today's chief executive has a peerage but rarely uses his title.

Covent Garden calls itself 'A World Stage'. It always was. With a legacy going back nearly three centuries, the archives are richly endowed with written and visual material illustrating the successive technologies of theatrical history: the development of lighting schemes in front and back of house, for example, from candle to gas to electricity to modern digital lighting, or various advances in stagecraft, from ropes and pulleys to the most modern lifts, hoists and revolves. Covent Garden was long one of the most important theatres in Europe, its reputation for offering high fees attracting top international performers. Gye, knowing his bargaining power, embarked upon frequent talent-scouting expeditions and his travel diaries throw much light on events on the continent. In autumn 1860, he found himself in Italy on the eve of unification and the diaries are dotted with personal encounters (with a Habsburg naval officer on his way to inspect Austrian gun installations, and a boatman who once ferried Garibaldi) of interest to any historian of the *Risorgimento*. During the early decades of the 20th century, the theatre housed Diaghilev's Ballets Russes and regular seasons of Italian and German opera, while the globalisation of our own times has internationalised opera and ballet still further.

***

The Royal Opera House is a great institution that trades in part on its continuities with the past, and much of that cultural heritage is preserved in the Collections (and increasingly online). But don't all rush! Research space at the theatre is limited: there is only room for one independent researcher at a time, and much that is retained in the Collections, including props and costumes, is stored elsewhere. One day (who knows?) the whole thing may be kept on a single site, with adequate research facilities. But until that day comes, and if you know the kind of thing you are looking for, try contacting the Collections team. If they can accommodate your request, I know they'll do their best.

Callas as Catalyst

Memories of Maria Callas to mark her centenary.
OPERA Magazine, January 2024.

During the late 1940s and early 1950s, I had been to a number of operas, mostly taken by my father at the treasured theatre of his own pre-War youth, Sadler's Wells. Covent Garden had to wait until, in autumn 1952, an opera-loving schoolfriend and I took advantage of the half-term holiday to mooch around the great opera house and wondered how we might obtain a glance of its legendary interior. There, guarding the portals, was the stolid, begowned and often top-hatted figure of Sergeant Martin, doorkeeper extraordinaire. Was there anything we young boys wanted? Well, yes there was, we answered with all the chutzpah of intrepid not-yet-14-year-olds, and told him we loved opera, sang it together, and would give anything to see inside his great theatre.

Sergeant Martin took pity on us and said that, yes, he could sneak us into the theatre. But there was a rehearsal going on so we must promise to sit very quietly and keep out of everybody's way.

On stage, wearing a wide, full-length rehearsal dress, was a pleasantly rotund red-haired young lady and a small, older lady all in black. They were evidently working on a succession of duets, to piano accompaniment, while getting used to the basic moves: through a doorway ('La porta?', I heard the younger singer ask at one point), across to the other side of the stage or wherever they were instructed to go. The opera was Bellini's *Norma* and the man in charge, beating time from the pit, was the conductor Vittorio Gui. The 'Producer' (as we used to say) was Gui's son, Gianfranco Enriquez. The older lady to the left of the stage was the famed Italian mezzo Ebe Stignani and the plump youngster a Greek American soprano about to make her Covent Garden debut. Her name, I learned, was Maria Meneghini Callas (born 2 December 1923).

For a couple of hours or more, my friend and I sat enthralled, close to the stage, as Callas and Stignani, working cooperatively together under guidance from Gui, sang and re-sang one of the most powerful duet scenes in all opera ('Mira, o Norma' from Act 2). Callas's debut at Covent Garden was still a few days away; this morning was mine.

A year later, when Callas returned to Covent Garden, I wrote asking for her autograph. I had long been an avid collector and had by now accumulated the signatures of hundreds of my heroes, among them Gigli, Martinelli, Galli-Curci, Toscanini, Sibelius, Vaughan Williams et al.

This could be tricky territory. VW wrote to advise me not to bother to collect autographs ('it's worse than collecting stamps!') but signed his letter nonetheless. Back in 1862, Verdi was in London and wrote to a friend complaining about people sending him letters through the post and enclosing a stamped envelope addressed to the person to whom he was asked to send his signature when he had no idea who they were! At least '*GVerdi*' had a shorter name to sign and shove into the return envelope than my latest heroine.

Callas replied, signed the photo I had enclosed (almost invisibly against its dark background) and added – with a further signature – that she would send me a presumably better photo. In both signatures she used her full three-word married name, Maria Meneghini Callas.

Letter to Callas, signed.

Of course, I never received that further photo Callas had promised as she moved rapidly from young singer on the make to celebrity to superstar. By then she had slimmed down almost beyond recognition. And a few years after that, she was no longer Meneghini. The legend had begun ...

***

In addition to that legendary *Norma* (in which an even younger soprano, one Joan Sutherland, sang the minor role of Clotilde), Callas went on to star in a number of productions at Covent Garden, among them *Aida*, Cherubini's *Medea*, *La Traviata* and an overwhelming *Tosca* with Tito Gobbi as Scarpia. Wherever and whatever she performed, Callas was able to draw upon not only a rich vocal lyricism but also whatever dramatic intensity the particular role and libretto required. Like Gobbi and Jon Vickers (who sang Jason to her Medea), Callas was one of the great singer-actors of her day: perfect for the richly evocative productions by contemporaries like Franco Zeffirelli and Luchino Visconti.

Personal problems ate into her professional life and at times her vocal power and agility, and Callas gradually retired from the operatic stage, resorting to occasional concerts and helping coach younger singers. People loved to read about the supposedly wild, fiery prima donna, the 'diva', and Callas soon entered popular mythology as much for walking out of a performance attended by the President of Italy or spitting in the face of a warrant-server as for the quality of her singing. Many of history's celebrated songstresses had tried to combine marriage and career, with variable results, and Callas was not the first singer to cancel an occasional performance as a result of illness. But my memories are that, given the intense public and private pressures she underwent and the artistic heights to which she aspired, Callas was generally as professional, conscientious and courteous to colleagues as she was able to be. And that, once on stage, 'Doctor Theatre' invariably took over.

***

I saw Callas at both the beginning and the end of her UK career. Having caught the chubby young redhead rehearsing *Norma* for her Covent Garden debut in early November 1952, I was also present in late 1973 as the elegant former diva passed her 50th birthday and bade farewell to her British admirers in a concert at London's Royal Festival Hall with tenor Giuseppe di Stefano (and pianist Ivor Newton).

230

By now Callas had nothing like the mesmeric vocal and dramatic flair that had characterised her earlier performances. Indeed, as the evening progressed I remember thinking that I was here to celebrate someone I immensely admired, not for what she was but for what she had once been. I thought back to the occasion when, as a student at Cambridge, I had gone to watch Winston Churchill, by then nearly eighty-five, who had come to dedicate the ground on which Churchill College would one day be built. The old man stumbled over part of the speech he had to read to the assembled crowd, but I revered him nonetheless. And most of the arias Callas sang to us in 1973 (after a not particularly suicidal *Suicidio* from *La Gioconda*) were relatively undemanding, the range often remaining within barely an octave or so (e.g. *O mio babbino caro* from Puccini's *Gianni Schicchi*). Meanwhile the ever-caring di Stefano supported her in the duets they sang together and kept away from the fiery show-off arias with which, under other circumstances, he could have wowed the audience.

It saddened me, less than half-a-dozen years later, to read that Callas had died. Let's be sure to celebrate the centenary of her birth!

Composers: Handel, Verdi, Wagner and Puccini

One day in 2012, I received an invitation to attend an exploratory meeting at the Victoria and Albert Museum, London, at which members of the V&A and Royal Opera House management teams would explore the possibility of a major exhibition on the history of opera. The meeting took place on 9 August and was chaired by the V&A's recently appointed Chief Executive, Martin Roth. I was evidently invited on the strength of my book The Gilded Stage *and, as those around the table discussed the possible scale and style of such an exhibition, costs, visitor numbers and whether and where it might tour after London, I found myself – the only 'unattached' person present – advocating the widest historical focus: not merely a collection of memorabilia of great composers and singers, but something about the cities and theatres in which opera took place, audiences and ticket prices.*

In due course – and I like to think I had some influence over this – the plan was for the exhibition to concentrate on seven European cities, each of which had hosted an historically significant operatic premiere:

> *Venice (Monteverdi's* L'Incoronazione di Poppea, *1642/3)*
> *London (Handel's* Rinaldo, *1711)*
> *Vienna (Mozart's* Le nozze di Figaro, *1786)*
> *Milan (Verdi's* Nabucco, *1842)*
> *Paris (Wagner's* Tannhäuser, *Paris version, 1861)*
> *Dresden (Strauss's* Salome, *1905)*
> *St Petersburg (Shostakovich's* Lady Macbeth of Mtsensk, *1934)*

The aim was to examine each of these through three perspectives:

> *– the broader social/cultural history of the city concerned*
> *– more specifically, the theatrical and operatic context*
> *– the particular composer and featured work*

The exhibition opened in September 2017 in the V&A's new wing on Exhibition Road which had only recently been inaugurated. Originally intended to remain in London for three months, it was later decided that the exhibition warranted a longer residence at the V&A, remaining there through the new year until the end of February 2018, after which it was intended to travel abroad to a number of cities over the course of the next two or three years.

During the run-up to what was clearly intended to be a major international exhibition, I found myself not only called upon periodically as opera historian/consultant but also invited to undertake a twelve-week course of lectures to accompany the exhibition from September–December 2017. Meanwhile, the publishers of The Gilded Stage, *evidently impressed at the potential marketing opportunities all this provided, decided to do whatever they could to add further foreign language editions of the book to those already obtained (Italian, Spanish and Chinese) in good time for the show's journeyings across the map of Europe.*

In addition, I agreed to write one of the principal essays for the exhibition catalogue: that on Handel, Rinaldo *and the London of the early 18th century.*

A year later, in October 2018, the Royal Opera House mounted a much later work by Handel: his oratorio Solomon – *the piece famous for the orchestral 'arrival of the Queen of Sheba'. Back in 1711 when* Rinaldo *had had its premiere Handel was in his mid-twenties (and there was no theatre at Covent Garden until John Rich opened his in 1732). By the time* Solomon *appeared in March 1749 Handel was approaching his mid-sixties and well over a dozen of his works, operas as well as oratorios, had already been performed there.*

In 2018, with the premiere of Solomon *approaching, I was invited to write an introductory article for the ROH programme. Having done a piece for the V&A catalogue to mark young Handel's arrival in England and his 1711 operatic premiere, it seemed only fitting to write another by way of welcoming the old man once again and, this time, his 1749 oratorio.*

Handel: Introduction to *Solomon*

ROH programme, October 2018.

One of the things people nowadays tell visitors to Halle, a small town just a couple of hours' drive from Berlin, is that in the years since German reunification many of its brightest youngsters have left to seek fame or (at least fortune) elsewhere. It is a story prefigured by Halle's most celebrated citizen, Georg Friederich (or George Frideric) Handel, who was born there in 1685 but died nearly seventy-five years later in his elegant home in London.

Halle could not hold Handel, his prodigious talent demanding a larger stage. He went to Hamburg where he played in the opera orchestra, then on to Italy where he absorbed the musical culture of Florence, Venice, Rome and Naples, befriending not only influential composers such as Corelli and the Scarlattis, but also the aristocratic and ecclesiastical magnates who supported them. Handel returned to Germany in 1710, armed with recommendations to several of the most brilliant courts, notably that of the Elector of Hanover who took the gifted young man into his service. Soon, Handel requested and obtained permission to visit that great commercial hub of the musical world and of much else besides – London.

***

London was the biggest city in Europe: a vast, sprawling, bustling metropolis of well over half a million, a great capital whose port and river provided a gateway to and from the wider world. Here, financial speculation and peculation dwelt cheek by jowl, alongside every gradation of wealth and poverty, industry and idleness, puritanism and licentiousness, coffee house and whorehouse. There was a sense of freedom in London unmatched on much of the continent where monarchs and churches had traditionally kept strict control over forms of cultural expression. In England, by contrast, the monarchy had undergone a series of formidable trials each of which had further weakened its powers and ambitions. Some monarchs – Charles II, for example, or Queen Anne – enjoyed patronizing the arts but were in no position to control them. Music and the arts, like everything else, responded to the invigorating and sometimes chilly market economy. Looking back, we celebrate the theatrical imagination of Congreve and Wycherley, the satirical pen of Defoe and Swift, the portraiture of Kneller and Lely, the buildings of Wren and Hawksmoor and the music of Purcell. But there were as many snakes as ladders awaiting the unwary.

Take, for example, the ill-fated venture into theatre management by that formidably talented soldier, playwright, architect and landscape gardener John Vanbrugh. Vanbrugh had a vision: he would design, build and run a new theatre – The Queen's Theatre in the Haymarket – and make it the first in Britain to be devoted to the presentation of all-sung opera. Not opera alone, but a mixed season including semi-opera and stage plays, the latter presumably making sufficient profit (he must have calculated) to finance the former. It was probably a madcap idea from the outset, as Vanbrugh discovered within weeks of embarking upon the final chapter of his ill-judged venture in January 1708. As the books began to slide into the red, he applied to Queen Anne for a subsidy to help finance his losses but was turned down, transferred management of the Queen's Theatre to one Owen Swiney and went off to busy himself with the construction of Blenheim. Meanwhile, the presence in the company of a number of expensive Italian singers, notably the castrato Nicolini, doubtless helped raise artistic quality and audience size while helping plunge things further into debt.

For several years, one hapless manager after another wriggled awkwardly between the conflicting demands of popular entertainment and high finance. In 1710, Swiney quit the Haymarket, ceding control to William Collier, an ambitious MP, who went on to hand day-to-day management to a young man called Aaron Hill. Hill was ousted less than a year later – but not before he had mounted *Rinaldo*, an opera for which Hill himself had drafted a text (based on Tasso) and for which the music was provided by the 25-year-old Handel, recently arrived in London. Handel is said to have written the score in a fortnight, not as remarkable as it sounds for the work contains some fifteen numbers previously composed for other occasions.

***

The production of Handel's *Rinaldo* at the Queen's Theatre in February 1711 aroused considerable attention. Just as Hill had promised, the show was designed to please not just the ear but also the eye with a series of spectacular stage effects as Armida enters in a chariot drawn by dragons, magic gardens and castles materialise and men sail across turbulent oceans and climb mountains that, with a stroke of a wand, are deemed to disappear. Particularly impressive was the presence of Nicolini in the title role. Nicolini, we are told, could act as well as he could sing (which possibly helps explain the huge fees he demanded).

Then as now, satirical journalists had no difficulty making fun of opera and its (to many people) exaggerated pretensions. Thus, you may imagine the kinds of gossip that went the rounds – and continued to do so for many a decade – about the cult of the castrato: the jokes, cartoons and general giggly gossip about 'who can do what and with what and to whom'! As for all those 'Scenes and Machines', the editors of the original *Spectator* magazine, Joseph Addison and Richard Steele, lambasted what, for all Hill's protestations, seemed to them like an overblown, over-expensive, over-elaborate and essentially alien form of art. Addison poured his amused wrath upon the extravagance of *Rinaldo* and of Italian opera in general. He reported how he had encountered a man in the street carrying a cage full of birds evidently destined for the opera and had naughtily imagined the birds making an entrance 'in very wrong and improper Scenes, so as to be seen flying in a Lady's Bed-Chamber, or perching upon a King's Throne' – not to mention the 'inconveniences' the birds might drop upon the heads of those in the audience.

***

To most people, opera was of little account. On a good night, the theatre on the Haymarket held an audience of perhaps 600 in a city with a population a thousand times the size, and the audience would have been almost entirely composed of 'the quality', i.e. people choosing to pay for an expensive evening of what we would now call 'elite' entertainment, the vast majority of people living in London being far too poor to afford tickets to the opera or to have any interest in it. By the end of the season, the opera company at the Queen's Theatre was in dire straits. Box office receipts proved scarcely enough to pay the basic expenses of all involved, Handel himself receiving only £186/7/11 of an agreed payment of £430. Opera, people sniffed, was foreign: it displayed overblown, effete emotions, was performed in a language ordinary British people did not understand and was sung by Italians (which meant Catholics), among them those ludicrous but tragic half-humans, the castrati.

In June 1711, Handel returned to Germany, increasingly confident of his artistic powers and reputation and determined to come back to London – which he did toward the end of the following year. But he found things theatrical continuing to lurch from crisis to crisis, while the political and financial uncertainties generated by the death of Queen Anne in 1714 and the subsequent Jacobite rebellion did opera no favours, and the whole enterprise soon juddered to a complete halt. Thereafter, no Italian opera was produced in London until 1720.

***

Several things saved Italian opera in London, at least for the time being. The first was the accession to the British throne of George I, a somewhat perplexed German Protestant who scarcely spoke or understood English. He did, however, have a reasonable understanding of Italian and loved Italian opera, attended it frequently and contributed financially to its revival.

It did not hurt that the foremost composer in London was the King's former *Kapellmeister*. By now, Handel was receiving an annual pension of £200, granted by Queen Anne shortly before her death, and living in Burlington House in Piccadilly where he encountered many of the principal patrons and players in London's musical and artistic worlds. Given the parlous state of the Haymarket theatre (now renamed the King's), Handel gave little attention to opera during the first few years of George's accession.

All that was to change in 1719 with the creation of the Royal Academy of Music: a joint stock company, established by royal charter and financed by subscription (and a modest royal grant) set up in order to place opera production at the King's Theatre on a secure footing in the hope of producing a healthy return. One of the first things the Academy did was to send Handel off to the continent on a talent-hunting expedition (he was especially asked to secure the services of the great castrato Senesino, who made his London debut in 1720). On his return, Handel composed *Radamisto* which was premiered to great acclaim in April 1720. Handel was at the acme of his powers. So, as it happened, were some of the most famous Italian opera singers of the age, many of whom he engaged for the Academy and for whom he went on to compose what became some of their most famous roles. During its brief life, the Academy – fuelled by the attentions of an opera-loving monarch and a composer of genius – provided a framework for some of the most magnificent works and performances of Italian opera seen until that time. But it, too, proved to be yet another financial catastrophe, going bankrupt by 1728.

***

1728 was also the year of *The Beggar's Opera*, an arrangement of well-known ballad tunes set to new words by the poet John Gay and stitched together to create an engaging show about a highwayman and his girlfriends. *Beggar's* was produced by that highly entrepreneurial actor-manager John Rich, not in the posh theatre on the Haymarket but at the more popular Lincoln's Inn Fields theatre. Unlike Italian opera, with its elevated sentiments of ancient gods and monarchs and the like, *Beggar's* parodied Whig politics, Italian opera and much else while featuring the thrills and spills of the lowest of London's lowlife. It even included a spat between two loud-mouthed women, and everyone would have recognised in Lucy and Polly, the two inamoratas of the highwayman hero Macheath, a parody of the operatic *prime donne* of the day.

Beggar's proved far more popular than anything ever achieved by Handelian opera seria. It ran for over sixty performances and John Rich was able to use the proceeds to build an entirely new theatre: the first of three to occupy the north-eastern corner of the Covent Garden piazza where today's Royal Opera House now stands. Rich opened his theatre to great acclaim in 1732. It was not an 'opera house' as we might use the term. Indeed, it opened with a play, Congreve's *The Way of the World*. Soon, however, Rich turned to Handel and in 1734, just two years after the opening of the first Covent Garden theatre, and persuaded him to compose what proved to be a succession of Italian operas for the new house. *Oreste* was premiered at Covent Garden in 1734, followed by *Ariodante* and *Alcina* in 1735, *Atalanta* in 1736 and three more the following year culminating with *Berenice*.

Handel continued to compose further operas. However, the taste for Italian opera was by now clearly on the wane, and the composer soon found himself turning more and more to English-language texts whilst also looking away from stage works towards the great oratorios of his later years. Many of these, too, were launched at Covent Garden, among them *Samson*, *Semele*, *Judas Maccabeus*, *Theodora* and *Jephtha*. And, in 1749, tonight's great work, *Solomon*.

'Viva Verdi!'

OPERA Magazine, January 2011.

This year, 2011, saw the 150th anniversary of Italian statehood, an event with which the name of Verdi is forever associated. His music – especially the patriotic choruses of his early operas – acted as an inspiration to his compatriots as they yearned to overthrow oppression and create a nation of their own.
True or false?

At the premiere of *Nabucco* at La Scala in 1842 (wrote Verdi's Italian biographer Franco Abbiati, quoting from a Milanese press report), the audience gave 'Va pensiero' such an enthusiastic reception that an encore had to be given despite strict Austrian rules to the contrary. Raymond Grew, the American historian of Italy, said much the same; at the *Nabucco* premiere, according to Grew, Verdi's great chorus:

> ... had to be sung again (as it has been ever since), despite police orders against such encores ...

Grew added that when Verdi died in 1901, 'the crowd at his grave softly and spontaneously sang it, and so did a chorus of 800 at official ceremonies a month later'. And here is an entry from the Internet History Sourcebooks Project on the website of New York's Fordham University:

> 'Va pensiero' became the Italians' song of liberation, for, in the oppressed Hebrews, they found a symbol of their own longing for reunification.

This chorus, says the entry, became an 'underground "national hymn"', and it goes on to tell how Verdi's name came to be used as a political acronym (Vittorio Emanuele Re D'Italia), 'a reference to the sole native dynasty in Italy and the focus of nationalist hopes for unity'.

It has long been popular currency to cite 'Va pensiero', with its yearning for a 'patria perduta', as having become a virtual national anthem of the Risorgimento, the movement for Italian independence, and to tell of a forest of 'Viva VERDI' signs held defiantly aloft by Italian patriots in the face of their Austrian oppressors. And what could be more moving than the idea of a vast crowd mourning the loss of their beloved leader and spontaneously intoning his most famous composition?

Verdi's sympathies with the broad aims of the Risorgimento are not in doubt. But how far did he and his music actually contribute to its success? Research by Roger Parker and others has severely modified the popular image. For example, having scoured reports of early performances of *Nabucco* (1842–4) across the Italian peninsula, Parker finds that most took place within fifty miles of Milan (and none south of Rome), and that:

> ... the number of occasions on which 'Va pensiero' is singled out for particular praise (or mentioned because of the notable enthusiasm it aroused) is embarrassingly small ...

Nabucco and its great chorus certainly became popular; but probably no more so than some recent works by Bellini or Donizetti, or others that Verdi himself was shortly to write. Nor was *Nabucco* more politically incendiary than, for example, Bellini's *Norma*, an opera about an oppressive foreign occupation (of Gaul by the Romans) with its powerful chorus calling for 'Guerra! Guerra!'. As for the encore of 'Va pensiero' at the opening night, Parker has shown that the review Abbiati cites in fact makes no such claim.

In 1848 a rash of revolutions broke out across Europe, and in May the citizenry of Milan managed against all odds to oust their Austrian masters during the course of five delirious days (the 'Cinque Giornate'). Verdi, who had been working in Paris, came back to Milan to exult in the news. But for all his enthusiasm, he soon left Milan to oversee the purchase of his new farmlands at Sant'Agata near his old home town of Busseto, and by the end of May was back in Paris. There, he composed a new, overtly nationalistic work, *La battaglia di Legnano*, which was produced in republican Rome in January 1849 (the Pope having fled) and which opens with a chorus proclaiming 'Viva Italia!' But the revolutions of 1848–9 were soon snuffed out, and in his next operas Verdi eschewed political themes, turning instead to personal conflicts between love and honour, and to family relationships.

Then, in 1860, the dream of Italian nationalists was speedily and somewhat surprisingly fulfilled. In October Garibaldi, whose forces had wrested Sicily and southern Italy from its Bourbon monarchy, handed over his conquests to the constitutional King of Piedmont-Sardinia, Vittorio Emanuele – the 'VE' of the 'Viva VERDI' signs (which had no more than a brief vogue). The Italian peninsula – most of it at least – was at last united, and the King's chief minister, Cavour, set about establishing the formal trappings of a new nation state. First, a parliament needed to be elected, and in January 1861 Cavour wrote to Verdi pressing him to offer his services as a Deputy.

Verdi, by now more a farmer than a composer (or so he liked to say), followed political events with a keen eye but from a distance. Like many educated northerners at the time, Verdi had long dreamed of some kind of Italian politico-cultural resurgence. But his was a somewhat passive patriotism, not that of the barricades. Even at the height of the revolutions of 1848–9, Verdi had never showed any sign of wishing to become directly involved in politics (unlike Wagner, for example, who became an active revolutionary in Dresden). And it was much the same in 1860 when, from the more or less safe haven of Sant'Agata, Verdi enjoyed reading about the flamboyant military achievements of Garibaldi and the more subtle politics of his special hero, Cavour. When Cavour's letter arrived on his desk, it amounted to an offer he could scarcely refuse. He went to Turin, met Cavour, and duly became a Deputy in the first all-Italian parliament. Cavour (to Verdi's deep distress) died shortly afterwards, and Verdi never became an enthusiastic or active politician.

The composer lived for a further forty years. On his death in January 1901, he was eulogised as a national treasure, one parliamentarian describing him as having been:

> … the symbol of the heroic era of our Risorgimento because of the mystic fusion of his music and the longed-for, prayed-for unity of our nation.

It is a reputation that has clung to his name ever since. But Verdi's adoption into the political pantheon occurred more gradually – and later – than is popularly imagined.

***

In pre-1848 Vienna, the capital of the most multi-cultural of empires, Chancellor Metternich was more concerned with maintaining political control over the far-flung Habsburg lands than whether Italians (or Czechs, Hungarians or Poles) were dancing their traditional dances or speaking or singing in their local languages. From the perspective of Vienna, Austrian Italy doubtless looked like some kind of political unity, at least on the map.

On the ground, however, regional and local differences abounded. If a young Parmigiano like Verdi had wanted to visit his librettist Piave in Venice, he would have needed a passport and crossed a series of customs barriers, while an ordinary peasant from Parma or Lombardy would have found the dialect of someone from the Veneto (let alone a Neapolitan) almost incomprehensible. Language became an increasingly resonant issue as intellectuals and aesthetes, seeking the outlines of a genuinely national identity, argued about which regional dialect was the most 'correct' form of Italian, the consensus being that it was Tuscan, the language of Dante. Music, too, became a potent embodiment of aspirant national culture. As the early operas of Verdi, with their rousing choruses, began to appear across the peninsula they came to provide one of the few shared experiences linking Italians everywhere – a vital link between Italy being merely (in Metternich's dismissive phrase) a 'geographical expression' and its eventual unity and statehood.

It is tempting to see composers such as Verdi incorporating into his early operas an element of subtle political opposition, from the *Nabucco* chorus about the desire to regain our *'patria perduta'* to the Roman general in *Attila* attempting to keep out the invading Huns by saying 'You have the world; leave Italy to me!' But if Verdi periodically ran into difficulties with the censors, these more often concerned the religious than the political content of his operas.

Any new theatrical work at the time had to be passed by the censors before it could be performed (as continued to be the case in Britain until 1968). Verdi's early work *I Lombardi*, a celebration of *Italianità* set in Crusading times, included a patriotic chorus not unlike that in *Nabucco* and a scene in which (as in *Norma*) the chorus cries out 'Guerra! Guerra!'; in the Verdi opera this was in response to a feverish proclamation from our hero that 'The Holy Land will be ours!' But what exercised the Cardinal Archbishop of Milan was a scene in which a converted heathen becomes baptised, and it was only after an 'Ave Maria' became a 'Salve Maria' that the work was allowed to be produced. Furthermore, the nature of the censorship Verdi encountered varied from one part of Italy to another. Religious censorship was particularly stringent in Papal Rome and political censorship in Naples (where the opera house was part of the royal palace), while the Habsburgs in the north were relatively lenient. *Nabucco* may have been about Hebrew slaves; but it was dedicated – as was *Lombardi* – to a Habsburg duchess.

During the decades following the Napoleonic Wars, a host of new opera houses sprang up across Italy and old ones were renovated. By the time Verdi was setting out on his career, the opera house was almost as ubiquitous as the cinema a century later, and fulfilling many of the same functions. Opera was often the only show in town, the only popular diversion in a country where there were as yet few museums, libraries, choral societies or clubs (let alone chamber ensembles or symphony orchestras). Here the local citizens could relish lavish entertainments that reflected back to them their own sense of social and economic advancement. And what did they see on stage? Noisy choruses advocating war and patriotism, to be sure; but also earnest advocacy of such archetypally bourgeois virtues as honour, loyalty, duty.

The impresarios who produced these operas knew their market, and prudent self-censorship usually ensured that a new work contained little the authorities need worry about. No one, after all, went into the business of opera with the intention of having his house closed down. Capitalism, not subversion, was the spur. Nor did governments like to shut down a theatre, a step far more likely to exacerbate than to silence political rumblings. Even in the immediate wake of political unrest, the first thing a restored ruler would often do was to reopen the opera theatre, preferably with shows that would prove popular, and be seen visiting the theatre smiling and waving to his subjects. Once Milan was securely back under Austrian control in the wake of the 1848 revolutions, the authorities chose to put on Verdi at La Scala, just as they did in Naples where revolt had recently been suppressed right outside the San Carlo theatre itself. If audiences purred with satisfaction at the end of the evening (and loyally applauded the monarch or minister if he chose to attend), everybody went away happy and those in government could be confident they had little to worry about.

***

After independence, things were different. No all-Italian government, probably, could have fulfilled the miracles expected of it, and a series of bad harvests and stock-market failures in the 1870s led to widespread economic and social distress. Emigration from Italy accelerated, especially from the impoverished south, while industrialization stubbornly refused to take off and Mafia corruption increased.

Operatically, too, Italy became something of a desert as a succession of beleaguered national administrations tightened or abolished traditional subsidies. Some opera houses closed down; many were forced to reduce their seasons. As for the new generation of composers, few measured up. Verdi was such a giant that, other than emulate or imitate him (out of the question), they had little option but to try to bypass him. Many turned to foreign influences, at first French and later wagnerismo. 'Here is the tomb of the greatest composer of the century!' wrote Toscanini on a postcard to a friend in 1899; the card was sent from Bayreuth and showed the grave of Wagner.

Verdi himself felt increasingly estranged from the younger musicians and artists then emerging. No crusty old antiquarian, he appreciated the genius of Wagner (and outdid all his supposedly modern-minded contemporaries with *Otello* and *Falstaff*). But Italian composers, he felt, could not move forward unless they had a thorough grounding in the music of their own national past. As he put it in a famous letter: 'Let us turn to the past; that will be progress.'

Like many ageing celebrities, Verdi was not above a little mythmaking. In 1879, in the course of a brief autobiographical sketch, Verdi told the story of the origins of *Nabucco* in general and of 'Va pensiero' in particular. He had run into the boss of La Scala, Bartolomeo Merelli, in Milan. Merelli greeted the young man and took him to his office. La Scala, it seems, was due to present a new opera; the libretto had been written but the composer had pulled out. Merelli pressed the text into Verdi's hands, inviting him to set it to music. Verdi was in no mood to comply. Now in his late twenties, he had made a faltering start as a composer and had endured the multiple tragedy of losing both of his children and then his wife. Merelli was persistent, Verdi recalled, so he took the wretched libretto home and flung it down on a table where it fell open at the lines 'Va pensiero sull'ali dorate'. Verdi was transfixed. Before long, he tells us, the music of *Nabucco* was racing through his head: the opera that made him famous. The story was hugely dramatized and embroidered. But the way Verdi told it did no harm to his reputation in a demoralized nation thirsting for heroes.

During Verdi's final years, Italy underwent further crises. Agrarian unrest in Sicily was put down by martial law, a colonial war in Ethiopia led to humiliating defeat at Adua in 1896, and in 1898 troops ordered to quell labour unrest in Milan left scores of protesters dead. In 1900, the Italian king was assassinated. To the elderly Verdi, it must have seemed as if the noble dream of a liberal-minded, united Italy was descending into a tailspin of regional and sectarian self-destructiveness.

Verdi was buried in Milan's Cimitero Monumentale. A month later, his body was reinterred (with that of his wife) in a special tomb at the Casa di Riposo, the home for retired singers Verdi himself had recently founded. Huge crowds poured into the streets of Milan to pay their last respects. Before the cortège left the cemetery for its journey across town, Toscanini conducted a choir of over 800 in 'Va pensiero', a deeply moving moment that led to reports that the onlookers had launched into the piece by a kind of spontaneous combustion. The mythmaking about Verdi's pivotal role in the forging of Italian unification and identity, already under way before his death, evidently went into overdrive soon afterwards. And the famous picture of the 'Viva VERDI' signs? It dates from 1901.

'VIVA VERDI!'

Winifred Wagner
A Life at the Heart of Hitler's Bayreuth

Brigitte Hamann, translated by Alan Bance (Granta Books, 2005).

Review from *Opera Now*, September/October 2005.

Thirty-six years ago, in October 1969, I spent a cold, blustery week in out-of-season Bayreuth with Wagner expert Geoffrey Skelton. My mission was to record for BBC radio Skelton's conversations with Bayreuth's formidable dowager-in-retirement, Winifred Wagner. Each morning, we would walk across town to *Wahnfried*, the Wagner family compound, and sit bewitched by the tales this powerful old woman had to tell. By then in her seventies and speaking her native English through the patina of an acquired German accent, Winifred was unstoppable. Would she like to take a break, I asked politely one day after a solid couple of hours of unashamedly vivid Hitleriana? No, she was happy to keep going. As Geoffrey gently reminded me, dyed-in the-wool Wagnerians, inured to *Götterdämmerung*, were used to sitting still for hours at a time. A few years later, Winifred famously poured out her stories at even greater length for the filmmaker Hans-Jürgen Syberberg.

Winifred Wagner, an English girl doubly orphaned as a small child, was raised by elderly German foster parents and went on to become chatelaine of Germany's most revered temple of the arts and one of the earliest and closest friends of Hitler. After the war, she was formally denazified but was excluded from the Bayreuth Festival which passed to her sons Wieland and Wolfgang. Hers is an extraordinary story, a gift to a would-be biographer. But 'gift' is the German for poison, and Brigitte Hamann, experienced historian that she is, sips from the chalice with due caution. The basic story is narrated in a series of graphic chapters broken up by bite-sized subsections. We read how the girl's kindly foster father took her as a teenager to Bayreuth where she met Wagner's widow Cosima and went on to marry her 46-year-old son Siegfried. The marriage, despite the age difference and Siegfried's homosexuality, produced four children. Not surprisingly, perhaps, Winifred was forever falling in (apparently unconsummated) love with others, most famously Adolf Hitler to whom, on his imprisonment after the failed Beerhall *putsch*, she offered aid and comfort and the writing paper on which he penned *Mein Kampf*. In 1930, Cosima died, rapidly followed into the hallowed *Wahnfried* soil by Siegfried. As in 1883, the

Bayreuth Festival fell into the hands of a young Wagner widow. Winifred proved a tough, tireless administrator capable of dealing on equal terms with such giant artistic egos as Toscanini and Furtwängler. Her resolve was greatly strengthened (as in due course were Bayreuth's precarious finances) when Hitler became Chancellor. Under Winifred, Bayreuth was bedecked with swastikas.

Yet she was no blind ideologue. To Winifred, artistic and personal integrity were what counted, retaining for a while several friends and colleagues who were Jewish or homosexual even while at the same time giving increasing preference to artists of 'Aryan' background. And she never hid or denied her friendship with Hitler, claiming she saw in him a visionary and a statesman holding at bay such philistine henchmen as Göring and Goebbels.

The Winifred who emerged from the catastrophe of the Third Reich remained an astonishingly independent-minded woman, a 'Valkyrie of imposing dimensions and imposing insolence' in the words of Klaus Mann (son of Thomas) who interviewed her in June 1945. She acknowledged her friendship with Hitler, as she did to Skelton and myself a quarter century later and to Syberberg later still, in a manner Mann described as 'shamelessly honest' – a phrase Winifred quoted thereafter with pride. She scorned those cowering Germans who, after the war, falsely presented themselves as having been secret resisters, just as she resented the occupying powers for being, as she saw it, bent more on vengeance than on justice. And she continued a time-honoured Wagner tradition – in evidence to this day – by presiding over internecine family warfare reminiscent of the House of Atreus.

Brigitte Hamann tells the story well and, true to her title, keeps a disciplined eye on the main theme. For all the book's admirable concentration on Winifred, I didn't quite feel by the end that I had got the full measure of its principal protagonist. In what ways did Winifred's bizarre upbringing help mould the confident mistress of 1930s Bayreuth? Did this passionate woman really 'love' (or mourn) her oddly ineffectual husband? What was the nature of her serially unfulfilled romantic longings? How far did she really believe in the tenets of Nazism and the relative innocence of Hitler for its worst excesses? Hamann sometimes approaches such questions only to move abruptly on, rather as if her editor had told her to cut the analysis and get on with the narrative.

The book ends with Winifred's death and burial in 1980 with little attempt to assess the impact of her notorious regime on the subsequent history of Bayreuth. Its author, it seems, has been afflicted by the perennial Curse of the House of Wagner: the closer you look, the more critical the treasures you are denied – notably, in this case, the papers of Siegfried, Wieland and Winifred herself. For the full story, and its longer-term implications, we evidently need to wait until the present regime at Bayreuth finally passes on the keys to next generation.

Wagner

Compass magazine, 2012.

In 2012, in anticipation of a tour for Cox & Kings to Bayreuth, and to mark the forthcoming bicentenary of the birth of Richard Wagner in 1813, I wrote an introductory essay about the great and controversial composer for COMPASS *magazine.*

What is it about Richard Wagner that arouses such a powerful response? Some people hate him with a passion, finding both man and music equally repulsive. Others – vastly more – go into ecstasies at the mention of his name and pack the world's opera houses whenever there is a chance to encounter his superheroes and villains, his erotically-charged and/or self-sacrificing maidens and his woeful or triumphant mariners, mastersingers, knights and Nibelungen.

I have been trying to track Wagner down for over half a century and still struggle to get a firm grip. The first time I attended a Wagner opera, I was swept away by what felt like its almost cosmic ambition and intensity. True, the evening was very long, and I remember thinking guiltily once or twice that there were scenes that might have benefited had Wagner tightened them up a tad. But I realised that the great musico-dramatic climaxes were all the more overwhelming for the fact that you had been made to wait for them. Wagner knew exactly what he was doing: more than any other composer before or since, he took personal control over all aspects of this most multimedia of art forms as he strove to create a fully integrated theatrical experience.

But there is a dark side to Wagner, too. Not everyone relishes the prospect of sitting through an earnest, epic five-hour music drama. And the man himself could be vain, arrogant, a serial borrower of money he never got round to repaying, a seducer of friends' wives, nauseatingly obsequious to those in authority – and crudely anti-Semitic. Fifty years after his death, Germany came to be ruled by a leader, Hitler, who proclaimed himself to be inspired by the Master of Bayreuth. The first time I visited the little Franconian town where Wagner finally settled and where he built his famous Festival Theatre, was back in 1969. I was in Bayreuth to record a series of BBC interviews with Winifred Wagner, the composer's English-born daughter-in-law. Winifred was living in 'Wahnfried', the villa built by Wagner in which he and his wife Cosima lived out their final years.

Winifred, the widow of the Wagners' son Siegfried, ran the Bayreuth Festival throughout the 1930s and was one of Hitler's closest personal friends.

Today, Wahnfried is a museum and the Festival is run by a duo of Wagner great-granddaughters, Eva and Katharina. But if Wagner himself has long receded into history, and even Bayreuth's Nazi past is fading from living memory, one of the town's greatest jewels is older still: the richly Baroque 'Margravial' Theatre that attracted Wagner to Bayreuth in the first place. One look at this 18th-century theatre, even from the outside, made it obvious to Wagner that it was far too small to house the forces required for his vast music dramas. But it remains a salutary reminder that Bayreuth was home to high culture long before Wagner came onto the scene.

This is even more obviously true of other great German cities with Wagnerian associations. Nearby Nuremberg, for example. Today, as you enter through its turreted city walls and stroll past the elegant A-frame buildings, across the Pegnitz river and perhaps visit the historic home of the painter Albrecht Dürer beneath the castle walls, it is easy to forget that Nuremberg was also the home – historically as well as operatically – of the 'mastersingers' and other craft-based guilds. Until, that is, you encounter the wonderfully expressive statue of one of Nuremberg's great heroes, the cobbler and poet (and 'Meistersinger') Hans Sachs, the central figure of what is surely the most upbeat of all Wagner's great works.

Then there's Munich, the Bavarian capital in which *Die Meistersinger*, *Tristan und Isolde* and two of the *Ring* operas all had their world premieres. Any Wagner lover visiting Munich will head for the Nationaltheater, the very house in which – courtesy of 'Mad' King Ludwig of Bavaria – these premieres were mounted. Ludwig was besotted with Wagner and plundered the state coffers to help support the composer. You get a good insight into the King's opulent tastes from his absurdly extravagant state coach, now on show at the Nymphenburg Palace (in which Ludwig was born).

There are other attractions in Munich, too, which even the devoted Wagnerite might want to visit: not just the city's astonishingly rich array of art galleries, but the beautiful Baroque 'Cuvilliés' theatre, nestling within the royal 'Residenz' complex. It was here that Mozart's *Idomeneo* was first staged in 1781, and in the Residenz too that Wagner and King Ludwig first discussed the idea of a 'Festival Theatre' to be devoted to the works of Wagner.

Munich, like Nuremberg and Bayreuth, has its darker associations. It was a major centre of Nazism (and scene of Hitler's abortive 'Beerhall *Putsch*'), while Nuremberg, that archetypally 'German' city, hosted the infamous Nazi rallies and later the post-war trials of Nazi leaders. Much of what you see in both, including Munich's National Theatre, was reconstructed after severe wartime bombing. The footsteps of Wagner are at times hard to locate, or squelchy with the mud of a sometimes deeply disreputable history. Yet whenever I find myself embarking on the trail of the man who gave us *Tristan*, *Meistersinger* and the *Ring*, I reflect once again that anyone so stupendously talented must surely be worth pursuing!

At home with Puccini
Torre del Lago

Opera Now, May/June 1999.

My first Puccini opera was La bohème, *which my opera-loving dad took me to see at Sadler's Wells theatre on 13 December 1947.* Bohème *was also the first opera I saw at Covent Garden when my parents took me there on 4 November 1953. That occasion marked my fifteenth birthday and also, I learned, the 250th performance* Bohème *at the Royal Opera House – by a composer who had died less than thirty years earlier. I loved* Bohème, *and got to know and relish most of Puccini's other operas over the years that ensued.*

But it was only after I started visiting his birthplace in Lucca and his long-term home in Torre del Lago that I really felt I knew the man, understood his life and times and appreciated the genius that had so enriched my life. For something like twenty years, well into the 2000s, I led a succession of cultural tours to Lucca and the annual Torre de Lago Festival (and met Puccini's granddaughter Simonetta a number of times), and in 1998 presented a five-part series about Puccini and his work for BBC Radio 3's 'Composer of the Week'. The following article, based on a feature originally written for Opera Now *in 1999, was slightly edited and updated over the years since.*

Puccini statue in Lucca.

Halfway along the motorway between Florence and Pisa, and mercifully less frequented than either, lies the ancient walled city of Lucca. Stroll through its narrow cobbled streets, up the via San Paolino, past little *pasticcerie* and cafes and some of the town's many churches, and your route will open into a modest piazza. On a plinth is a statue of a man sitting in relaxed comfort looking nonchalantly down upon the passing world. And in the tiny side street behind, up a couple of flights of stairs, is his birthplace.

Giacomo Puccini was born in Lucca on 22 December 1858. Four generations of Puccinis before him had all been musicians. Giacomo's father, Michele Puccini, wrote learned treatises on harmony and counterpoint and was organist and choirmaster at Lucca Cathedral, and died when Giacomo was five. From then on, throughout his childhood, adolescence and young adulthood, his life was very much dominated by his widowed mother, Albina Magi, who died when Giacomo was twenty-five.

Today, Lucca is in many ways much as Giacomo Puccini must have known it during his childhood and adolescence. A few yards from the family home, the city opens into a great piazza (on the site of the old Roman forum) which is dominated by the church of San Michele. Would Giacomo uphold the family musical tradition? It was unlikely from the outset that he would ever become a church organist, though he seemed happy enough to attend Sunday services and perhaps join the choir. But it is said that, during the respite from singing, he and his teenage pals would occasionally slip out with one or two of the surplus organ pipes lying around, try and sell these and spend the cash on cigarettes. In any case, the defining moment of his adolescence seems to have been a performance of Verdi's new opera *Aïda* in Pisa in 1876 (which Puccini is said to have walked to in order to attend). This evidently confirmed Verdi as his god and opera as his vocation.

In due course, Puccini managed to obtain a grant to pursue his studies at the Milan Conservatoire where he shared a room with Pietro Mascagni. Their teacher, Amilcare Ponchielli (composer of *La Gioconda*), thought both young men showed promise and encouraged them to enter a competition sponsored by the Sonzogno music publishing company. Mascagni won with a short work entitled *Cavalleria Rusticana* though Puccini's *Le Villi* went on to be performed and its score printed without charge by the all-important publishing company Ricordi.

Looking back, it is easy to see Puccini's flat-sharing with a fellow student as being not unlike the student garret he so vividly portrayed in *La bohème*. As his career developed, Puccini tended to avoid the historic grandees Verdi had so often featured. A contemporary of the so-called *'Verismo'* school of composers (Mascagni, Leoncavallo, Cilea, Giordano and others), he tended to gravitate towards the 'realistic' passions of ordinary people: students in and out of love, an American sailor who has an affair with a Japanese girl, desperadoes in goldrush California and a bargee on the Seine whose wife is unfaithful.

While still in Lucca, Puccini developed an affair with Elvira Gemignani, the wife of an old schoolfriend and neighbour, and had a child, Antonio, with her. Elvira (who already had a daughter from her marriage) moved in with Puccini. Giacomo's youthful escapades were well enough known to his friends, but the social implications of 'adultery', 'living in sin' and producing 'illegitimate offspring' did not go down well in small town, late-19th-century Lucca. Puccini's next opera, *Edgar*, found its hero torn between the sacred love of 'Fidelia' and the profane love of 'Tigrana'. Wonderfully evocative names. But the opera was not a success. By now, Lucca no longer gave Puccini the tranquillity he needed to compose. It was time to move.

In 1891, the family went to Torre del Lago, initially for the summer but this became their permanent home for some thirty years. And it was here that most of Puccini's greatest works were created. To get there nowadays from Lucca you have to drive westwards along the road to Viareggio and then, just before you reach the coast, left towards Pisa. Within the imaginary triangle is a shallow, reedy inland lake, Lake Massaciuccoli. And nestling alongside the western edge of the lake, with its stocky little tower as a phoney talisman, is Puccini's beloved Torre del Lago. Here, Giacomo and Elvira took lodgings and, with the onset of the composer's increasing fame and wealth, built a villa on the lakefront.

Again, little has changed. But a piazza was built after Puccini's death in front of the house, pushing the lakeshore back some fifty metres, and a statue of the composer in characteristically languid pose stands among the trees. The boats lolling lazily against the water mostly await tourists nowadays, while the ducks are a lot safer than when Puccini and his cronies would go out on the lake to shoot them. And just up along the shoreline is a large open-air theatre – location for many years of the annual Torre del Lago Puccini Festival. If you stand on the stage of this of this 3,500-seat arena you can just see, through the trees on your left, the memorial plaque on the wall of Puccini's villa, something singers are daunted or comforted by, according to temperament.

As for the house itself, which now includes a room packed with Puccini's guns and stuffed wildfowl, it remains much as Puccini would have known it (except for the addition of a little mausoleum where the composer, Elvira, Tonio and his wife Rita dell'Anna are buried). An element of added authenticity might have come your way if you had visited when the composer's granddaughter Simonetta was there to show you around. Simonetta (daughter of Tonio) died in December 2017, and she too is now buried within the villa.

You enter through a small front garden, walking along gravel pathways between blocks of opulent cultivation – a flowing palm tree here, a rich hydrangea bush there – and into the house through a bow-shaped solarium. The large reception room is packed with portraits and photographs of the composer, his family and his celebrity friends. There is a large fireplace and, opposite, Puccini's heavy upright August Förster piano, including candelabra in the 19th-century style. Immediately to the left of the piano is Puccini's desk, part of it jutting forwards so that he could swivel between piano and desktop to write as he composed. This was where, often in the dead of night, Puccini created *La bohème, Tosca, Madama Butterfly, La fanciulla del West, La rondine* and the *Trittico*.

By the early 1900s, Puccini and Elvira, long his mistress, now his wife, had settled down to a kind of marital stalemate. Puccini must have been a difficult man to live with. He used to say that, whenever he was composing, he'd fall in love – and that didn't just mean with the fictional women he was creating. He also had a weakness for the latest technological toys: glamorous cars, motorboats and the like. Indeed, this local Mr Toad landed in serious trouble one night in February 1903 when he ran off the road and was found unconscious beneath his automobile. Photographs taken over the next few months show him convalescing in a wheelchair.

Work, as ever, was a consolation. Puccini would manoeuvre himself over to the piano and *Madama Butterfly* was completed by the end of the year. At least nobody could accuse him of laziness! Vanity, perhaps: for the rest of his life this fashion-conscious man walked with a limp – which people said he tried to disguise by putting weights in his trouser leg.

The Puccinis often had problems with staff, Elvira hiring and firing with tedious regularity. But she seems to have been happy at first with a young local girl, Doria Manfredi, who came to work for them in 1903. For some years, all went well. Then, Elvira began to suspect an affair between Doria and her husband. She'd scream at the girl and creep down the stairs at night into Puccini's work room or into the garden to try and catch the supposed lovers. She told everyone in the village that Doria was a slut and a whore, that she'd kill that girl. Doria, bewildered, eventually sacked, returned to her parents. But Elvira's shrill accusations merely increased. Eventually, the poor girl took poison and, after several days of agony, died. A post-mortem showed that she had been a virgin. Maybe there had been intimacy of a kind between Doria and the composer, if not fully sexual. Perhaps Doria had simply provided a kind of solace to Puccini all too evidently not available from his wife. Who can be sure? The immediate consequence was that Elvira was sued, and initially sentenced to prison, though the case was eventually dropped after an out-of-court settlement. But the Doria incident hovered like a dark cloud over Puccini's life for years – and, of course, made it difficult for him to concentrate on his music.*

Puccini's first composition after the Doria affair was his Gold Rush opera *La fanciulla del West*. A triumphant premiere at the New York Metropolitan in 1910, with Caruso in the cast and Toscanini in the pit, did much to restore his confidence after the traumas of recent years. Puccini adored America, land where everything seemed possible. Puccini loved all things modern. The steamships on which he could cross the Atlantic, the latest automobiles, wireless, film. He first visited the USA in 1907 to attend the New York Met premiere of *Madama Butterfly* after which, over a celebratory drink, he made a little thank you speech that was recorded. If you get a chance to hear the recording, note Puccini's final words: 'America Forever!' – which his tenor, Pinkerton, proclaims in Act I of *Butterfly* to the tune of *The Star-Spangled Banner* (soon to become the US National Anthem).

While composing *Butterfly* Puccini was keen to hear something of genuine Japanese music, and Chinese music later on when he embarked upon *Turandot*. By now he could borrow or buy gramophone recordings of the music he needed and imbibe something of the neo-oriental style he went on to incorporate into his work. For all his widespread reputation as a composer of romantic weepies, Puccini was throughout his career a brilliant, open-minded musician capable of listening to the latest creations of Debussy, Stravinsky and Schoenberg and learning from their musical insights as he developed his own, inimitably and irresistibly theatrical style.

Was Puccini something of a plagiarist? Some have thought so, and he often seems to have built on operatic works previously initiated by others.

---

* Many years later, newly discovered documents revealed that it was not in fact Doria but her cousin Giulia that Puccini was involved with. Doria had acted as a go-between, carrying letters to and from Puccini and her cousin.

Thus, his first major opera, *Manon Lescaut* was produced in 1892 just a few years after Massenet's *Manon*, both of them based on the novel by the Abbé Prévost. Then, a few years later, his friend Leoncavallo mentioned that he was beginning to work on a possible opera based on the *Scènes de la vie de bohème* by Henri Murger (1851). Puccini beat him to it and his opera proved much the more successful. Sardou's play *Tosca* was originally assigned to the opera composer Alberto Franchetti before it was reassigned to Puccini. Plagiarism? Far from it. Which of us has not learned from what others have assayed and tried to improve upon it?

***

Puccini travelled far and wide, in mind and body. And he loved doing so. But his heart remained in Torre del Lago. This remained home for some thirty years until, in 1921, he and Elvira moved to Viareggio. A peat factory had been erected near his villa, and Puccini was irritated by the noise from the dredging, not to mention the smell. And perhaps he needed a new environment to help stimulate his creative imagination as he embarked upon what was to prove his final opera, *Turandot*.

Looking back over the large number and wide range of Puccini's works, are there any particular themes that run through his output as a whole? It is hard to generalise, whether dramatically or musically. Are they all (or any of them) 'Verismo'? 'Realistic'? Hardly. Unlike (say) Mascagni's *Cavalleria Rusticana* none of Puccini's operas is placed among the people of Italy in or around his own times. Some are set in France during earlier periods (*Manon Lescaut, Bohème*) or Italy a century before (*Tosca*) or the American West during the Gold Rush, while *Suor Angelica* takes place in a 17th-century convent and *Gianni Schicchi* is a comedy derived from Dante. Then there are the Viennese-inspired *La rondine* and the Chinese-based *Turandot*.

But dig a little deeper (and look back over Puccini's personal life and times) and it can be revealing to examine the women who feature prominently in so many of his works. To put it over-simply, some are attractive young girls, sweet and honourable, who fall in love, sacrifice everything for the man of their dreams and finally, when things go wrong, are doomed to die for their principles. More subtly perhaps, as a Puccini opera unfolds, the humble young girl often develops into a woman with a strong personality within which are embedded powerful principles. Thus, the sweet little seamstress Mimì in *La bohème* or pretty young geisha girl Cio-Cio-San (aka 'Butterfly') become formidable, independent-minded adults able to move on from an early love life and, if necessary, to sacrifice themselves on the altar of female independence. No-one is going to tell Minnie, the Girl of the Golden West, how to run her life. She knows that, if she plays her cards right, she will get the man she fancies; if not, she (or he) will probably die. Manon dies at the end of her opera, as do Mimì, Tosca, Butterfly, Angelica and, in the final operatic scene Puccini completed before his own passing, Liù.

Many of the men, meanwhile, have perhaps been using (or abusing) the women they hold in their sights: from Scarpia and Pinkerton to Michele in *Il Tabarro*. It's the women who, again and again, are the heroes. Or heroines. Often the tragic heroines.

It is not hard to see elements of Puccini's life and loves in the romantic relationships that blossom and collapse in so many of his operas. The author Mosco Carner, in his biography of Puccini, suggested that the composer, raised from childhood by his all-powerful mother, may have felt an element of subconscious guilt, or betrayal, when developing a sense of love for other women. Or even fear, perhaps. Again and again, his operas contain a sweet, innocent young girl who goes on to suffer and perhaps die – a Doria figure, perhaps. And also a number of women whose growing, almost maternal authority will brook no male opposition. And in his final opera, Puccini created both kinds of woman: the sweet, honourable Liù who is prepared to die for her love and the authoritative Princess Turandot who has no qualms about beheading the men who fail to answer her questions correctly. Puccini's long-time companion, his mistress-become-wife Elvira, clearly embodied elements of both.

***

Early in Puccini's career, as Italy's great hero Verdi sank into decline and old age, many opera lovers (including George Bernard Shaw) found themselves thinking that Puccini might have the wherewithal to become the 'heir to Verdi'. Puccini's first real success, *Manon Lescaut*, was premiered on 2 February 1893 just a week before Verdi's last opera, *Falstaff* while *Bohème* and *Tosca* followed soon afterwards before Verdi's death in 1901. But the differences between Verdi and Puccini, as both men and musicians, were immense. For a start, Verdi was not primarily concerned in his operas (or his life) with the rise and fall of romantic love affairs in the ways that preoccupied Puccini. But the greatest difference was in the political preoccupations (or lack thereof) between the two great composers.

Verdi, as discussed above, was a thoughtful, sophisticated but not over-demonstrative supporter of the idea of Italian unity. And he was honoured when invited by Italy's first Prime Minister, Cavour, to become a Deputy in the nation's first parliament and agreed to accept the invitation, at least for a while. But what Verdi primarily cared about was the development of a cultural, linguistic Italianness, or *italianità*, that would bring Lombards and Venetians, Neapolitans and Sicilians all closer together with a communal feeling that they had outgrown the dominance of their former Habsburg, Papal or Hispanic rulers. The sort of thing the author Alessandro Manzoni had tried to evoke in his celebrated 1827 novel *I Promessi Sposi*. Manzoni was one of the few cultural figures of pre-united Italy whom Verdi genuinely admired (and in whose memory he composed his *Requiem*).

As for the content of Verdi's operas, many of them certainly contained patriotic choruses and invocations of war, honour, loyalty and the rest. But these, and the political and military leaders who often led the casts, were often just the standard stage characters in the grand operas of the day. If there was a personal theme running through many of the operas of Verdi (whose two children and then his wife had all died while he was still in his twenties), it was perhaps a poignant relationship between a parent and child: think *Rigoletto, Traviata, Trovatore, Aida* et al.

Puccini, for all his personal adventurousness and open-mindedness, seems to have been pretty bereft of Verdi's political sensitivity, in his life or in his operas. *La rondine* was originally commissioned in 1913 to be premiered in Vienna. By the time this supposedly Viennese operetta was completed in 1916, Italy had joined the Great War alliance fighting against Austro-Hungary, so it was simply decided to present the new Puccini in Monte Carlo instead.

When Mussolini and the Fascists came to power after the war, Puccini was made an honorary 'Senatore'. Was the great composer thrilled? Or shocked? Neither. He just liked to joke that Mussolini, the 'Duce', had made him a 'Sonatore' (i.e. someone famous for the noises he made!).

One of the results of the advent of fascism to Italy was that a cool distance developed between Puccini and his former friend and colleague the adamantly anti-fascist conductor Arturo Toscanini. After Puccini's death of throat cancer in 1924 (he was a relentless smoker throughout his life) he had still not quite completed his opera *Turandot*. Having reached the suicide of Liù, he had said he hoped someone would finish it for him if that became necessary. The composer Franco Alfano completed the piece with a nice, pseudo-romantic ending and a premiere was arranged in 1926 which Toscanini would conduct. Word was received that the Duce would personally be attending and that, on his insistence, the evening would open with the Fascist anthem, the *Giovinezza*. This Toscanini resolutely refused to do and the Duce stayed away. And when the performance reached the death of Liù, Toscanini put down his baton, turned to the audience and said that this was where the opera ends because at this point the maestro died.

***

If you want to see the piano on which Puccini composed *Turandot* you must return to the house in Lucca. Where Torre del Lago gives an impression of the life Puccini led at the height of his career, the apartment in Lucca is a museum. Here you will find memorabilia from previous generations of Puccinis, and some of Giacomo's earliest scores. There are letters in his almost illegible handwriting to and from family, friends and colleagues, including one sent from London's Claridge's Hotel to his son around the time of the Doria affair and, most moving, his pathetic scribbles ('Elvira, povera donna') as this compulsive smoker approached death from throat cancer in Brussels in November 1924. Selections of his medals and other honours and a magnificent cashmere coat are on display, plus a superb *Turandot* costume donated by Puccini's favourite soprano, Maria Jeritza.

As you stroll through the piazzas and narrow streets of Lucca, or lazily along the Torre del Lago lakeside, you breathe the air that Giacomo and Elvira, Doria Manfredi and Tonio and his wife breathed not so many years ago. And when I used to go there, their shadows would still stalk the streets and cafes as locals would discuss the latest rumours and controversies. Have you heard, asks one, bushy eyebrow raised knowingly, about how Communists in the Viareggio Council plan to block funds for the Torre del Lago Festival? A couple of drinks later, someone would be sure to bring up the various high-profile court actions by which the composer's resolute grand-daughter Simonetta had been attempting (with considerable success) to wrest control of the Puccini legacy. Torre del Lago is not Bayreuth and Puccini was no Wagner. But, in a smaller, homelier, more Italianate way, the ghost of Puccini continues to provide something of the frisson, at least for locals, that has transfixed generations of Wagnerians. Long may it continue to do so. For if there was one thing Puccini (like Oscar Wilde) could not stand it was not being talked about.

Life and Times:
Past, Present and Future

Pepys and Covent Garden

This article is based on a lecture originally delivered to the Samuel Pepys Club in London (June 2023) and later adapted as introduction to an all-day tour of the Covent Garden piazza undertaken for the Institute of Historical Research (May 2024).

On Friday, 9 May 1662, Samuel Pepys recorded in his diary that he went with a friend 'into Covent Garden to an alehouse'. But he wasn't only in search of a drink. Pepys also wanted to see a picture that was displayed for sale at the alehouse and, deciding against buying it, he moved on 'to see an Italian puppet play that is within the rayles there'.

Pepys recorded that this was 'very pretty, the best that ever I saw' – and noted that the area was a 'great resort of gallants.' In this brief extract Pepys tells us, or at least suggests, a great deal about what was, in effect, the first formal public square in England.

***

Throughout much of his life Pepys lived near the Thames. After all, he was Chief Secretary to the Admiralty under both King Charles II and King James II. And Covent Garden was even nearer the river then than it is now: just up from the Watergate that opened up onto the Thames. The Watergate was built in 1626 by Inigo Jones and is still there. Nowadays it's on the north side of Victoria Embankment Gardens. But back in the days of Inigo Jones and Pepys the river flowed in a loop all the way up towards the Watergate and it was only in mid-Victorian times that it was redirected further south.

So Pepys's beloved Covent Garden was just a short walk north of the Thames. In earlier times the area had been fields: arable land and orchards walled off for use by Westminster Abbey as 'the garden of the Abbey and Convent' and officially known as the 'Convent Garden'. Seized by Henry VIII when the monasteries were dissolved in the 1530s, the gardens were later (1552) granted to the Earls of Bedford.

In 1630, the fourth Earl of Bedford was given permission by Charles I to redevelop the land and build on it. Bedford's aim was to create 'houses and buildings fitt for the habitacions of Gentlemen and men of ability'; the new buildings would be Italianate, neo-Renaissance in style, the standard being set early on by St Paul's church at the west end of the square. This was designed by Inigo Jones and completed in 1633, the year Pepys was born.

It was the first important new church to be built in London since the Reformation and dissolution of the monasteries a century earlier. The Earl was said to have asked Jones to put up just a simple church that need be 'not much better than a barn', to which the architect replied 'Then you shall have the handsomest barn in England!' In designing it, Jones made strict use of Vitruvian rules of proportion and symmetry, following recent models in late-Renaissance Italy by Andrea Palladio and others.

By the time Pepys visited, 'CoNvent Garden' or 'Covered Garden' (as it was variously called) was developing into a self-consciously Italianate, arcaded square: a 'Piazza' known for its Palladian church, Italian puppetry and much else. But not just Italian. It became a centre of interest to artists of all kinds from across Europe, among them the painters Peter Lely and Godfrey Kneller, the Dutch-born sculptor and wood carver Grinling Gibbons and the Bohemian map maker Wenceslaus Hollar.

Immediately to the south of the Piazza was the 'Strand' and beyond

Wenceslaus Hollar portrait of Covent Garden piazza, c.1647.

that the Thames, both of them providing a direct link between the City to the east, where the great majority of London's population resided, and that elite enclave of political and ecclesiastical power, the West Minster. So the Covent Garden piazza was in a perfect position for access to both, and the London *eleganti* soon began to move into the square (especially on its south side) and its immediate surrounds. In the 1660s three factors greatly increased this movement.

***

The first was the Restoration of the monarchy in 1660. King Charles II sailed from the Dutch coast to Dover and in May entered London in triumph. Pepys was one of those who, under the aegis of Edward Montagu, 1st Earl of Sandwich, accompanied the King on his return. Sandwich on his mother's side was the first cousin of John Pepys, the father of Samuel Pepys. On the King's return, and wherever he appeared thereafter, large crowds turned out to celebrate his presence. And that included in and around what came to be thought of as Central London: the Covent Garden area.

The Restoration of the monarchy heralded a huge spate of social and cultural novelties. For example, it was within a short time of arriving here as King that Charles II revived the theatre (mostly closed since the outbreak of the Civil War in 1642), granting Royal patents to the Duke's Company (Dorset Gardens) under William Davenant and the King's Company (Drury Lane) led by Thomas Killigrew. 'Drury Lane', an ancient, narrow road once known as Via de Aldwych, ran between St Giles and the modern-day Aldwych, derived from *aldwic* meaning 'old settlement'. It was named after Sir Thomas Drury who had a large house at the Strand end of the lane. By the time of the Restoration it was an upmarket, fashionable place (which for a while had even included Oliver Cromwell among its residents). By now, coffee had arrived in London from the Ottoman world and from around the 1660s it seems coffee was coming to be sold in Covent Garden 'in almost every street'. A Covent Garden barber was prosecuted 'for making an evil-smelling liquor called coffee to the greatest nuisance and prejudice of the neighbourhood'.

Two further factors contributed to Covent Garden's growth, one of them being that the district largely avoided the Plague of 1665, which was far more severe immediately to the East in the overcrowded City of London. By October 1665 Pepys described the City as a ghost town only populated by the sick and the poor: 'How empty the streets are and melancholy, so many poor sick people in the streets full of sores, and so many sad stories overheard as I walk…' Many in the City who could afford to do so soon moved out of London, westwards where the Plague was in general less severe.

Eventually, as winter drew on and the weather got colder, mortality rates began to drop. By new year 1666, a few shops in and around Covent Garden were beginning to open up again, and by February the King and his court returned to London from Oxford where they had decamped the previous summer. But it wasn't until autumn 1666 that the Great Plague was deemed all but over.

And then, during the first week of September 1666, another tragedy befell the City: the Fire which once again led many of its denizens to flee Westwards to Covent Garden and beyond. The Fire got as far west as Fetter Lane. But tens of thousands of Londoners lost their homes and many of the great, the good and the wealthy escaped from the City and fled westwards to relative safety along the river. Once again, the first realistic place to disembark was immediately to the south of Covent Garden.

Only the better-off could seriously contemplate living in the newly developing square, or renting (or buying) a new home. But as they began to do so, shopkeepers and, indeed, anyone with anything to market, tried to set up their businesses. And with some success. Fashionable folk from all around came to shop and to be entertained, to see and be seen, to exchange news and gossip.

***

In the decades following the Restoration the piazza filled up, gradually becoming ever more crowded. There were fine houses, restaurants and much-frequented taverns; places like the Rose Tavern where Pepys says that on Christmas Eve 1667 he drank 'burnt wine' (probably some kind of mulled wine). Many former members of the Long Parliament chose to reside here, as did current political figures and some of the prominent artists of the time. Lady Castlemayne (aka Barbara Villiers, one of Charles II's special friends!) was painted by Peter Lely, an artist of Dutch origin most of whose career was spent in England where he became portrait painter to the court. Lely lived within the Covent piazza for some thirty years, was knighted in 1679 and died soon afterwards while at his easel in Covent Garden and was buried at St Paul's Church.

Another of the local ladies painted by Lely was Nell Gwynn. Pepys notoriously had an eye for the ladies – all the more so if, like 'Pretty, witty

Nell', they showed off their assets in the theatre. On 1 May 1667, he reports that he 'saw pretty Nelly standing at her lodgings' door in Drury-lane in her smock sleeves and bodice, looking upon one: she seemed a mighty pretty creature'.

Covent Garden was packed with artistic and cultural figures during Pepys's time and he personally got to know many of them. The poet and playwright John Dryden was an old friend from college days while, among painters, not only Peter Lely but also that younger immigrant from Europe Godfrey Kneller who was born in Lübeck in 1646 and became court artist to monarchs from Charles II to George I. He too lived for many years in the Covent Garden piazza as did Thomas Killigrew, the man appointed to build and manage the original Theatre Royal – the King's Theatre – in Drury Lane.

As the *eleganti* settled in to their new homes on the fashionable new piazza, they were followed by anyone and everyone with something to market: fruit and vegetables, coffee and ale, wigs, dresses and greatcoats and every kind of luxury the wealthy denizens might like to buy.

Just on the north side of the Covent Garden piazza was Long Acre, known for supplying the latest, most elegant coaches. On 30 April 1669, Pepys visited his coach-maker and was 'vexed to see nothing yet done to my coach, at three in the afternoon'. He hung around for several hours, and 'saw the painter varnish which is pretty to see how every doing it over do make it more and more yellow; and it dries as fast in the sun as it can be laid on almost; and most coaches are, now-a-days done so, and it is very pretty when laid on well, and not pale, as some are, even to shew the silver. Here I did make the workmen drink, and saw my coach cleaned and oyled.' Anything to get the work done!

Pepys notes that, while hanging around waiting for the coach to be ready and 'staying among poor people there in the alley, [I] did hear them call their fat child Punch, which pleased me mightily that word being become a word of common use for all that is thick and short.'

In and around the piazza was every kind of theatricality. Much of it we might today think of as busking: singing, dancing, juggling, tightrope walking – and, above all, Italian-style puppetry. Mr Punch began life as 'Pulcinella', one of the stock characters from Italian *commedia dell'arte* that often also included Pantalone (the dirty old man), the lovers (Arlequino and Columbina) and a wily servant. Pulcinella, or Mr Punch (or Piero – or Pagliaccio in the Leoncavallo opera) was the outrageous clown, a sad but subversive simpleton with a squeaky, pinched voice produced by a reed retained at the back of the puppeteer's mouth known as a swazzle. Punch was characteristically quick to irrational bursts of anger and carried a big stick (or 'batone') with which to hit his opponents.

Commedia dell'arte, emanating from the environs of 16th- and early 17th-century Naples, rapidly became a popular genre of entertainment adopted by masked actors or peripatetic puppeteers who peddled their wares up across Italy and much of Europe to wherever they thought they might find a market – notably that which rapidly built up in and around London's Covent Garden 'piazza'.

***

In the years following the Plague and Fire, Covent Garden became an increasingly popular centre of theatre and theatricality of all kinds. Not only the puppetry and street theatre in and around the piazza but also the popular performances at the new King's Theatre in Drury Lane where, for the first time, high-profile actresses were permitted to strut their stuff publicly, on stage. During the years following the Plague and Fire a whole new crowd of people would descend on and around Covent Garden seeking a more colourful night life. At the theatre and afterwards. And that, for many, meant sex.

Prostitution, already rife in nearby spots like Drury Lane, soon spread to the Piazza itself. There were large numbers of women for hire, often nicknamed 'Covent Garden nuns' or 'spells'. Some solicited openly outside the theatre, others used the side streets or the colonnades. Some of the flower-sellers – the forerunners of Bernard Shaw's Eliza Doolittle, who insisted she was 'a good girl' – changed roles after dark, and no doubt earned a greater income by so doing. Brothels thrived just near the new theatre: in Long Acre, Bow Street and Brydges Street.

Everything interconnected. If you were hoping to have sex – or simply live healthily and in some degree of hygiene – you had to have ways of washing yourself. And that too did not escape the attention of those seeking to make money from the ever-growing market. In 1681 the first bath house opened in Covent Garden, its Italian title 'bagnio' taken from those in Venice which had in turn been inspired by the 'Turkish Baths' of Constantinople.

***

Pepys loved visiting the Covent Garden piazza throughout much of his adult life. Indeed, if you walk south of the Piazza today, just across the

Strand and down Buckingham Street towards the Watergate, you'll pass a plaque testifying that Pepys, long-term Chief Secretary to the Admiralty, came and lived on a site right here throughout much of the 1680s.

Pepys died in 1703. A few years later, a young German composer named Handel turned up on these shores and was soon commissioned to write an Italian opera for the delectation of the upper classes. *Rinaldo*, starring an Italian castrato known as Nicolini, opened in London's 'Hay Market' theatre in February 1711. Meanwhile, in the nearby Covent Garden piazza, a man called Martin Powell put on a puppet show.

Richard Steele, one of the co-founders of the original Spectator magazine, decided to sample both - and pretty similar he found them. By the 'squeak of their voices', he said, the heroes of both the opera and the puppet show were evidently eunuchs. He added, somewhat sniffily, that the wit in both pieces was 'equal', but 'I prefer the performance of Mr Powell because it is in our own language!' – or, as we might say today, more 'accessible'. I suspect Pepys might have felt the same way!

***

A few years later, opera came to Covent Garden for the first time (as we saw above, p. 238). In 1728, John Rich produced a new show in nearby Lincoln's Inn Fields, the hugely successful *Beggar's Opera*, and with the resulting profits he built a new theatre overlooking the Covent Garden square where the present opera house (the third on the site) stands to this day. Rich remained in charge of his new theatre from its opening until his death in 1761.

Meanwhile, the Drury Lane theatre, a block away from the Covent Garden theatre, was run for many years by another well-known actor-manager, David Garrick (who lived in Southampton Street), while others whom you might have encountered in the piazza in the 1700s ranged from Voltaire to Samuel Johnson (who first met his biographer James Boswell here), to Hogarth, the poet and playwright John Dryden, the novelist and magistrate Henry Fielding and the aspiring young artist JMW Turner.

Covent Garden continued to thrive as a market throughout the nineteenth century and well into the 20th. Rich's original theatre burned down in 1808, as did its replacement in 1856 (see above, pp. 202 et seq), the latter being replaced two years later by the opera house that, with various subsequent renovations, is the one we know today.

Virgins: A Cultural History
Anke Bernau (Granta Books, 2007).
Rape: A history from 1860 to the Present
Joanna Bourke (Virago, 2007).

History Today, October 2007.

We all know what is meant by virginity, how greatly it has been valued by some and that its loss is irreversible. Mary, mother of Jesus was a virgin (*the* Virgin, indeed); so was Queen Elizabeth I, her virginity celebrated in the establishment of that 'virgin' territory, later an American state, named in her honour. Rape, too, is easily understood. In ancient times, the Sabine women were raped, as was Lucretia; that is, they were taken sexually by force and against their will. In recent times, a successful charge of rape dispatched the boxer Mike Tyson to jail. But on closer examination, neither virginity nor rape is as easily defined as we might have thought, each concept coming down to us loaded with centuries of accrued anatomical, theological, legal, social, psychological and cultural baggage. It is this complex historical legacy that Anke Bernau and Joanna Bourke attempt to unpick.

Bourke has carved out for herself an enviable reputation as expert on the cultural history of topics many find nasty yet irresistible, among them war, killing and fear. Bernau is a medievalist who also has an interest in film. Both authors concentrate on western history, Bernau including material from across medieval Europe, Bourke augmenting her primarily British and American sources with data from Australia. Although both books have the word 'history' in the subtitle, their authors have opted for a thematic rather than a chronological approach and include much present-day material. Both books contain a handful of poorly reproduced (and inadequately sourced) black-and-white illustrations, and each volume is encased in a pale, delicately coloured cover.

Virgins, the slighter of the two, is really a series of five essays on different aspects of virginity: its variegated physical definitions, the theology of virginity, virginity in literature (the longest chapter), virginity and politics (e.g. the importance of pre-marital virginity in the arrangement of dynastic marriages) and a final chapter about the revival of premarital sexual abstinence in modern America. Bernau calls upon a wide variety of sources, from Galen, St Ambrose, the *Roman de la Rose* and Chaucer to today's wide-eyed apostles of born-again virginity, and her narrative includes some gruesome tales of punishment meted out to women who fell short of the virginal ideal – especially those in religious orders. When the 12th-century Nun of Watton became pregnant by a young monk, she was whipped and tortured by her fellow sisters and forced to castrate her lover, after which his genitals were stuffed into her mouth 'foul and bloody and just as they were'.

Rape also provides deeply uncomfortable reading at times, especially at the beginning of chapters when Bourke recounts a vivid story to highlight a particular topic. A chapter entitled '"No" means "Yes"' starts with a British instance in which an RAF man out drinking with his buddies in 1973 told them how his wife loved pretending to be gang raped – an implied invitation duly taken up by his friends which eventually led to a series of court cases. Bourke's starting point, she freely acknowledges, was anger that so few accusations of rape end in conviction. The anger recurs periodically throughout the book, Bourke sometimes adopting the mien of social reformer rather than historian. She is no simplistic ideologue, however, dismissing the cliché that all men are potential rapists and confronting such tangled topics as marital rape and the rape of males by females. More than anything else, her book is a typology in which every aspect of a complex topic is meticulously outlined and analysed. From her initial adoption of a deliberately wide definition, Bourke considers the commonly held myths about rape (e.g. that it's physically impossible if the woman really doesn't want it), the relationships between sexuality and identity, the psychopathology of rape, some of its principal locations (the home, the prison, the war zone), the adequacy or otherwise of the law, and feminist attitudes towards rape. During the course of a substantial tome, we encounter the relationship between sex and social status, sex and race, sexual relationships between parents and children, the legal problems of proof and victim credibility, and a catalogue of human viciousness, ingenuity, bestiality and vulnerability. By the time I had finished the book, I found myself sharing much of Bourke's anger. *Rape* may not be a 'history' book in the conventional sense. But, like *Virgins*, it brings a degree of valuable historical perspective to a sensitive topic that remains highly controversial.

Pole Positions
The Polar regions and the future of the planet

From the Foreword to the book (Hodder & Stoughton, 1993).

In 1988 I produced a series of BBC radio documentaries about Antarctica, presented by Bernard Jackson. Bernard and I had recently made a lengthy and extensive visit to the far South with the polar scientists from the British Antarctic Survey. The BBC project, which we entitled South of Sixty, *proved a great success, and a year or so later I was invited by the Australian Antarctic Division to join them on a similar visit to the more easterly side of the continent.*

Stimulated by these experiences, I went on to undertake what became a five-week multi-programme Radio 4 Festival covering all aspects of life – and science – in the other end of the world, the Arctic. For this, I made a number of journeys to the far north, spending time in Alaska, Arctic Canada, northern Norway and the Russian Kola peninsula. The Northern Lights *Festival was broadcast in early 1992.*

Over the course of the following year, I wrote a book about the Arctic and Antarctic, my experiences there and what I had learned from the polar scientists. The book was, I believe, the first to contain substantial material about the imminent dangers of climate change. What follows is taken from the Foreword to the book.

Pole Positions *cover.*

A thousand and more years ago, as the first millennium drew towards its close, prophets of doom proclaimed the imminent end of the world, and a paler version of this kind of *fin de siècle* fatalism has tended to recur at the end of each century since. As we approached the year 2000, there were many candidates for legitimate concern: nuclear holocaust, world population explosion and accompanying famine, an international epidemic or pandemic, genetic manipulation and abuse, and global warming resulting from the so-called greenhouse effect. These were large issues, united by a feature highly characteristic of our times: the fear that our scientific and technological temerity had gone too far and aroused the ire, and might perhaps produce the nemesis, of nature. It is science – global, macro-science – that excites and frightens people today.

None of those fears is trivial, but of them all the most awesome are those that concern not just the people on earth but the globe itself. After all, if we manage to avoid blowing ourselves up, keep world population within manageable limits, find a cure for pandemics and breed responsible geneticists, this would count for little if we bequeath to our heirs an earth that is uninhabitably hot or cold, wet or dry. Thus, environmental issues are rapidly coming to assume ever higher priority, and governments until recently oblivious of the dangers of chlorofluorocarbons or leaded petrol are now keen to appear 'Green'. My contention is that the governments and peoples should also learn to think 'White'. For it is in the vast but little-known polar regions that the key to the future of the planet probably lies.

The Arctic and Antarctic are two of the greatest deserts on earth, the least known and most vital to our survival. They are in many ways, as well as literally, polar opposites. The High Arctic is a sea surrounded by land, Antarctica a mountainous continent surrounded by ocean. The Arctic sustains an indigenous population of 'Eskimos' (Inuit) and others; nobody except a few scientists with extended supply lines can survive for long in Antarctica. Politically, the Arctic is largely controlled by the nations whose land it includes; the Antarctic is neutral, demilitarised territory, subject to an international treaty with to date some forty signatories. There are polar bears only in the North and penguins only in the South.

In a deeper sense, however, the poles meet. The Arctic and Antarctic act together as the earth's refrigerator, helping to drive the world's weather system and controlling nine-tenths of its stock of fresh water. Both contain clues, moreover, hidden beneath a thick layer of permafrost in the North and an almost impenetrable ice sheet in the South, about the early history

ABOVE LEFT *Approaching Antarctica.*

ABOVE RIGHT *In Arctic Canada.*

LEFT AND BELOW *Penguin colonies in Antarctica.*

of the planet and perhaps thereby of mankind. There are undreamed-of riches in the polar regions for the meteorologist and geologist, the biologist and palaeontologist; tempting opportunities, too, for the military strategist and mineral speculator, both of whom have been at work in recent decades in the North but whose activities have been restricted in the South by the workings of the Antarctic Treaty.

For centuries the poles have exerted a powerful fascination on the minds of the curious and the predatory and have often, Siren-like, lured the unwary to their deaths. Today, the paths are better trodden, the stakes more clearly defined, the dangers better known – and the potential rewards greater than ever.

My own journeys around the top and bottom of the world have been by many forms of transport, among them dog teams and skidoo (or snowmobile), ship, dinghy, plane, train, and helicopter. I have met polar people – native northerners, and the scientists, engineers and others who come out from warmer climes. I have encountered something of the economics and working conditions of the Far North and Far South, come across examples of the ways in which mineral resources have been both used and abused around the Arctic and learned of the new environmental concerns in Antarctica, including the decision to ban mining. From economics and environmentalism the focus moves to polar science, particularly its contribution to our understanding of climate change and the large questions about the interrelationships between global warming and polar ice. Finally, circumpolar politics. Both polar regions have provided the setting for competing sovereignty claims and national rivalries in the past, yet both seem at present to be in some ways models of international cooperation.

Throughout, whether we are considering the economics or the politics of the polar regions, the science or the indigenous peoples, one theme constantly recurs: the beauty and fragility of the polar environment – and its fundamental importance to the future of our planet and all it supports.

One result of my book was the emergence of the concept of 'Nominative Determinism': a hypothesis (first proposed in 1994 in the magazine *New Scientist*) that some people seemed to gravitate, perhaps subconsciously, towards areas of work that reflected their names. 'Snowman' on the Arctic and Antarctic seemed to prove the point (as did, for example, the urologists Splatt and Weedon). Fun. But utterly wrong in my case certainly – and no doubt, too, in that of Britain's former Lord Chief Justice Igor (Lord) Judge!

21 Lessons for the 21st Century

Yuval Noah Harari (Jonathan Cape, 2018).

Denial: The Unspeakable Truth

Keith Kahn-Harris (Notting Hill Editions, 2018).

The Jewish Chronicle, 1 August, 2018.

Don't read these two books if you are of a nervous disposition and find yourself inconsolable about the world we seem to be entering: a post-Brexit, post-Trump world, a 'post-truth society' of social media and 'fake news' in which opinions – and lies – can be forcibly expressed and made universally available via Facebook and Twitter.

But if, like me, you are seriously concerned by current trends and wish to understand them better, Harari and Kahn-Harris both make compelling reading. Harari, an Israeli professor of history, is currently one of the world's most widely read and respected thinkers about the past, present and future of life on this little planet of ours, while Kahn-Harris has written on everything from British and international Jewry to popular music, youth culture and much else. Both take off from the recent past and plunge into the strange, uncomfortable world of today and tomorrow.

Not so long ago, we were threatened by Nazism, then by Soviet Communism and possible nuclear annihilation. Mercifully, Nazism was defeated, Cold War anxieties disappeared with the dissolution of the USSR and, for a while, the hope and the expectation, at least throughout the West, was that the nations of the world would aspire to live under the tenets of a liberal democracy in which truth, goodwill, rational argument and the mutual exchange of goods and services would prevail to the benefit of all. Today, however, we appear to live in a world in which, as Kahn-Harris shows, verifiable truths can sometimes be not only disputed but categorically denied: about the Holocaust, for example, or climate change. Harari, meanwhile, tells us we are on the edge of two major revolutions: one technological and the other biological. Between them, he says, biotech and infotech look ready to hand power to remotely controlled digital algorithms capable of manipulating us into holding pre-programmed opinions, a world in which disembodied robotic powers invested with Artificial Intelligence (AI) seem likely to replace mere humans as Masters of the Universe. Farewell, then, to rational, human intelligence. Welcome, instead, to Denialism, and AI.

Kahn-Harris attempts to enter the spirit of the deniers. How and why might someone deny the existence of the Holocaust, or the evidence for anthropogenic global warming or the efficacy of demonstrably beneficial forms of vaccination? In the past, you and I might have thought the best way to convince someone of the truth of something they were denying was to present them with further facts. But in today's divided and angry world, 'denial' has become almost a badge of honour among those united in their detestation of the people (the 'elite', so-called 'experts' etc) who trumpet the so-called 'truth'. Denial is no longer a question of logic, of the rational assessment of supposedly verifiable data. Rather, it is becoming for some a psychologically comforting state of mind which Kahn-Harris dubs 'Denialism'.

Harari takes things further, into a digital age in which not just our voting patterns or shopping preferences are controlled by electronic algorithms of which we are not consciously aware, but our very being. Our bodies as well as our minds. Every 'decision' we make, including whether to scratch our nose, laugh at a joke or cross the road, will be instantly registered and assessed as part of our digital profile. The very idea that we humans have a degree of 'free will' or the capacity to 'decide' will be rendered obsolete. And all this at a time when humanity faces genuine existential dangers such as possible nuclear elimination and a planet rendered incapable of supporting human life as a result of global warming.

Can humanity come together and find viable ways of dealing with the supreme challenges our time? Our authors hold out a few hopes (Harari suggests a touch of Buddhist meditation can help). But the overwhelming feeling left by these two books is one of despair. Informed, intelligently and engagingly chronicled despair.

Obituary

In April 2006, after another extensive lecture tour of Australia and New Zealand, I took a long, tedious overnight flight from Auckland across the Pacific and the international date line (and Equator) to Los Angeles. During the lecture tour, several people had suggested I update the personal profile on my website and, to pass the time on the flight to LA, I found myself starting to draft what I mischievously thought of as a kind of third-person 'obituary'. Every now and then over the years that followed I added further brief edits.

Daniel Snowman will best be remembered as the author of *The Hitler Emigrés*, a study of the cultural impact of the refugees from Nazism, and a book about the social history of opera entitled *The Gilded Stage*. An accomplished writer, broadcaster and public lecturer, Snowman's greatest strengths and weaknesses arose from his versatility. By his own admission a jack of many trades and authentic master of none, he authored over a dozen books on topics ranging from American history and Plácido Domingo to the people and politics of the polar regions, produced (and latterly presented) a string of memorable BBC radio programmes and developed into a much sought-after speaker on the British (and international) lecture circuit. A would-be cosmopolitan character, Snowman was at heart a cultural historian, a gifted communicator keen to share his concerns and his passions with all who would listen.

DS was born in London on 4 November 1938. Both his parents came from well-known Anglo-Jewish families, and Daniel was raised in suburban Edgware in a secure, happy and conventionally Orthodox environment alongside a brother, Julian, who was six years his junior. Much that Daniel learned from his parents' home, notably a love of opera, stayed with him for life. A questing and questioning mind led to an Open Scholarship and a Double First in History at Cambridge – and also to the rejection of traditional Jewish observance. Keen to widen his own window on the world, Snowman joined the Cambridge University Music Society (beginning a fifty-six-year career as choral singer, most of it with the London Philharmonic Choir); he also became chairman of a university society promoting Britain's entry into the Common Market. When his degree work required him to make a special study of 'Anglo-Irish relations, 1916–21', he went to Dublin and sought – and obtained – an interview with the aged Éamon de Valera.

Some frontiers were not so painlessly breached. The wisdom and tolerance of his parents were strained to the limits when Snowman's first serious girlfriend (at Cambridge) proved to be a blond, blue-eyed beauty from Germany. A few years later, Snowman married a non-Jewish American girl he had met while doing post-graduate work in political science at Cornell (the marriage was later dissolved).

At Cornell, during the Kennedy years, Snowman researched the dynamics of US presidential decision-making (under Clinton Rossiter). An MA thesis on Truman's decision to drop the atomic bomb led Snowman to seek out Truman himself and, at a meeting at the Truman Library in Independence, Missouri in 1963, the old ex-president took time out to tell the young Englishman about a decision which (Truman insisted) was 'no decision'! Snowman later wrote up this encounter in *The Times* in 1995, the 50th anniversary of the Hiroshima bomb, and later in his memoir, *Just Passing Through* (published in 2021).

While Snowman's fellow-postgrads struggled towards their doctorates, he was invited by Asa Briggs to return to the UK to join the faculty of the new University of Sussex as Lecturer in Politics and American Studies. Relishing the avowedly interdisciplinary ethos of Sussex, Snowman moved easily between the Schools of 'Social Studies' and 'English and American Studies', was soon contributing to popular journals and broadcasts, and writing his first book, a history of 20th-century America. In 1967, he was phoned by Lord Archie Gordon of BBC Radio's Talks and Documentaries Department. Would Snowman be interested in bringing his American expertise to the BBC, initially for a six-month period during the run-up to what promised to be the tempestuous 1968 US presidential election? He went to consult Asa Briggs, his boss and a leading historian who, as it happened, was also undertaking the history of British broadcasting. 'I think you'd enjoy the BBC,' said Briggs – adding with great generosity that he'd keep the Sussex post available if Snowman wanted to return.

He didn't. Having been a bit of a 'media' don, Snowman felt at home at the highbrow end of broadcasting where his senior colleagues in (what was still) the Third Programme included the poet George MacBeth, the Brecht expert Martin Esslin, the musicologists Hans Keller, Lionel Salter and Basil Lam and the film critic Philip French, all presided over by PH Newby, a weekend novelist who became the recipient of the first Booker Prize. As time passed, Snowman received mixed signals from BBC management as he struggled to straddle the academic and broadcasting worlds. A year teaching in California enabled Snowman to write the bulk of *Kissing Cousins*, a pioneering work comparing attitudes and values in Britain and the USA. Back at the BBC, Snowman's essentially freelance temperament was unlikely to project him to the top of the corporate hierarchy, suiting him rather to the creation of ambitious broadcasting projects, several of which later materialised in book form. These included *The Long March of Everyman* (Snowman produced half of this twenty-six-part series), programmes (on TV as well as radio) with Domingo, a Radio 4 Festival of the Arctic and, in the run-up to the Millennium, a series (and book with Asa Briggs) about previous turns of centuries entitled *Fins de Siècle*. During his years in the BBC, Snowman helped develop the skills of many who went on to become well-known public broadcasters, among them Aled Jones, Susan Hill, Norman Lebrecht, Robert Lloyd, Edward Seckerson and Lucie Skeaping.

At the end of 1995, Snowman left the BBC to concentrate on his freelance career and, in particular, to write what were to become his most important books. *The Hitler Emigrés* described and attempted to assess the impact of refugees from Nazism on British cultural life: in art, architecture, music, film, broadcasting, publishing, the academic humanities and sciences and much else. A richly textured and thoroughly researched book, *The Hitler Emigrés* pulled together the work of such luminaries as Pevsner, Popper, Gombrich, the Amadeus Quartet, the artistic founders of the Glyndebourne and Edinburgh Festivals, the cartoonist Vicky and several generations of Freuds. When the book was published in May 2002, BBC Radio 3 devoted an entire evening to the subject which Snowman presented. Later that year, he went on a two-month round-the-world lecture tour, promoting the book in some thirty lectures and interviews across Hong Kong, Australia, New Zealand and North America (a similar tour followed in 2006).

This was merely the latest in a more or less decennial pattern of especially testing and lengthy journeys of mind and body to which Snowman liked to submit himself. In the early 1960s, while a post-graduate student in the USA, he visited over forty States (and spent a month as 'Limey-in-residence' on the local newspaper in Amarillo, Texas). A year in California ten years later was followed in 1981–2 by a three-month tour (for a BBC series on world economic development) through many of the poorest parts of Asia. In the late 1980s and early 1990s, Snowman sailed on extensive voyages to both Eastern and Western Antarctica while also visiting much of the circumpolar Arctic; during these trips, he learned much about polar science and politics from those in the front line, and went on to write and broadcast about global climate change well before the subject became common currency. Meanwhile, he also undertook countless briefer trips to continental Europe, North America and Australia, often for the BBC but usually enabling Snowman, *à la fois*, to further his freelance interests and, in particular, his love of opera.

A man capable of considerable social energy and charm, Snowman felt most at ease in small groups, or one-to-one. Impatient at over-lengthy meetings (or late dinner parties), he often preferred to eat alone in his office than to brave the hordes of the academic common room or BBC canteen. But, with a captive audience, he developed into a highly accomplished public speaker. A decade after his polar adventures, by the early years of the new millennium, Snowman – now a freelance – rapidly became one of the most highly regarded (and best paid) lecturers for the National Association of Decorative and Fine Arts Societies, sometimes giving as many as fifty lectures in a year for NADFAS and similar organisations. When NADFAS – and then Cox & Kings, Martin Randall, ACE and other travel companies – invited Snowman to lead music tours to some of the great opera capitals of Europe and beyond, it was an offer Snowman couldn't refuse and he went on to lead over fifty such tours.

In 1975, Snowman married Janet Levison and they had two children, Ben (b. 1977) and Anna (b. 1978) – able and attractive youngsters who, like their parents, retained strong bonds of family friendship while pursuing their own lives and interests. 'An expanding universe' was how Snowman referred affectionately to his immediate family in the Foreword to *The Hitler Emigrés*. During the early 1990s, Snowman developed a serious relationship with the well-known musician and broadcaster Lucie Skeaping, an intimacy that both partners felt enriched their lives while inevitably casting broad shadows of sadness. Some two decades later, in 2013, Lucie and Daniel each brought their respective marriages to an end and, in due course, set up home together. In this, as in much of his life, Snowman, from the secure base of a happy and fulfilling childhood, characteristically seemed to feel the need to stake out his own territory, often going further afield – both physically and psychologically – than many more conventional 'rebels'.

***

What led him to go – literally – to the ends of the earth, to try to master so wide a variety of topics, to pursue special relationships beyond the point of acceptable respectability? What, if anything, linked Snowman's love of opera, his interest in history and his visits to the faraway places of the earth? One answer is that, throughout his life, Snowman always seemed to be striving to find out what it was like living in another time or place, or to imagine what it must be like being someone else (it was thus entirely characteristic of him to draft his own obituary!). As a teenager, he took a postal course in Roman Catholicism, not because he was thinking of converting but because he was curious to know what it was like believing in Catholicism. When on a US civil rights project in the early 1960s, while staying with poor black sharecroppers, Snowman marched into the 'Freedom Store', a segregationist bookshop in the heart of the Mississippi State capital, Jackson, and, trusting that his English accent would carry him through, chatted up the local white supremacists and bought some of their poisonous literature. Visits to India, Nepal and Bangladesh, like those to the Arctic and Antarctic, cast Snowman's own life in wider perspective, just as *Rigoletto*, *Tristan* and *Otello* drew him towards the emotional heart of worlds that his own life merely touched upon.

Perhaps it was his fundamental seriousness of mind. There was an earnestness to Snowman which led him, in a world of cheap popular culture, easy options and soundbite solutions, to seek moral and intellectual integrity in complex circumstances (sometimes of his own making). That, at least, was how in more reflective moments he liked to characterise himself. And, as one of his BBC bosses gently put it, he had a tendency to turn every project into an entire industry. Snowman himself would shrug off the accusation of workaholism, laughing that 'one had to find something to do to pass the embarrassing interval between birth and death'. When asked when and whether he ever took a holiday, he was prone to reply, with a touch of defiance, 'all the time!'. Just occasionally, however, his demeanour would take on a darker hue as he would talk, in all seriousness it seemed, of the need constantly to distract oneself from the fundamental meaninglessness of life.

Like many people, Snowman found himself returning to early influences during his later years. Although his own family background, like that of much of Anglo-Jewry, traced back to the Eastern European Pale rather than Central Europe, his impetus to write about the 'Hitler Emigrés' was undoubtedly fuelled in part by his lifelong attempts to link his own Jewish and secular cultural legacies. An historian by training and temperament, Snowman was a frequent contributor to *History Today*, edited the magazine's 50th-anniversary anthology *PastMasters*, and wrote a quarterly feature for several years on the life and work of leading historians, a series of essays later published in a single volume as *Historians*. In 2004, he was appointed to a Senior Research Fellowship at London University's Institute of Historical Research, an appointment that was regularly renewed thereafter. In 2010, he delivered the IHR Annual Fellows' Lecture, and in 2015/16 and again in 2016/17 organised and chaired a series of public seminars at which panels consisting of some of Britain's top historians debated the often controversial ways in which people in the present were prone to use – and abuse – the past.

Snowman returned to another early love when commissioned to write a book about the social history of opera, a project which, with attendant lectures, articles and broadcasts, preoccupied him throughout his later sixties and early seventies. *The Gilded Stage*, first published in 2009, was a bold attempt to bring together two hitherto largely separate approaches to the past: social history (which rarely touched on the 'high' arts), and opera history which, mostly written by musicologists, had tended to concentrate on composers and works while giving minimal attention to their wider historical context. Snowman's was the first comprehensive history of opera from its beginnings to modern times that emphasised not only the supply but also the demand, not just the production of opera but also its consumption. Thus, *The Gilded Stage* touched on the patronage and financing of opera, the kinds of people who entered the opera professions (and the opportunities it offered women), the changing nature and behaviour of audiences, and the impact of war and peace and of such innovations as copyright law, the introduction of electric lighting and the invention of recording.

The book proved a great success. It was translated into several languages, led not only to countless invitations to lecture to arts groups and opera houses around the UK and beyond (e.g. New York's Juilliard School and Metropolitan Opera Guild) but also to Snowman's active involvement, from the outset, in the establishment of a major exhibition on the history of opera at Britain's Victoria and Albert Museum which opened in autumn 2017. He contributed an essay to the V&A catalogue and agreed to undertake the lecture course accompanying the exhibition (and many subsequent lectures on a variety of topics at the V&A over the next few years). As in so much of his work, all this represented an attempt by Snowman to find links between mutually exclusive intellectual territories. It also represented a further example of his lifelong attempt to bridge the academic and media worlds and find acceptance in both.

In March 2020, much that Snowman had known and loved was suddenly curtailed by the onset of a potentially lethal global virus, initially called Coronavirus and in due course Covid-19, that threatened the lives of everyone on the planet. This worldwide plague was the worst since the onset of 'Spanish flu' over a century earlier and, in effect, meant that Snowman and his ilk had to stay at home indefinitely (except for an occasional masked visit to a nearby shop or park), and give up any thought of visits to friends, restaurants, theatres, lecture venues or hotels while seeking out anti-virus vaccinations as soon as these became available. Depressed like many others by the 'locked down' domesticity, the ever-active Snowman knew that the best way of passing through the indefinite period of inactivity ahead was to undertake a succession of home-based projects, among them a new online course of lectures for the V&A, many individual lectures via 'Zoom' and a mountain of time-consuming but ever welcome commissions to write more articles, book reviews etc.

But the largest project Snowman undertook in his early eighties was to look back over his life and write what proved to be a substantial memoir. Rather than simply produce a traditional autobiography his aim was to say something about the wider world – 'From the War to the Virus' – via a series of vivid literary vignettes. Starting with a Jewish child's memories of the war and VE Day, the book included colourful accounts of life in Cambridge and across JFK's America, the revolutionary 'new map of learning' with Asa Briggs at the University of Sussex, the heights (and depths) of the BBC in its heyday and the hopes and fears of the 21st-century world. The text was packed with action, extended journeys to the hottest and coldest places on the planet, celebrities in close-up (Churchill making his last public speech, talking to Harry Truman about Hiroshima, a week in Bayreuth with Wagner's daughter-in-law, meeting Pope John-Paul II, Domingo, the 'Hitler Emigrés' etc.), while the whole thing was held together by a powerful central theme: the exciting if dangerous experience of questioning and crossing all sorts of supposedly sacrosanct boundaries – personal, religious, cultural, intellectual, political, institutional, geographical et al. The book was published in

September 2021 and entitled *Just Passing Through: Interactions with the World, 1938–2021*. Its final paragraph was taken from this obituary, as follows:

By the time he entered his eighties, Snowman at his curmudgeonly worst would fulminate eloquently against the historical and cultural shallowness of the world and its leaders, not to mention electorates capable of opting for 'Brexit' and President Trump. But when in more benign mode, which was most of the time, he remained an engaging conversationalist, peppering his thoughts with insights garnered from a rich and varied life that had enabled him, more than most, to enter the spirit of other people, places and times and find links between them. Although a long-term pessimist (convinced that human life on earth would eventually succumb to the interaction between population increase, global epidemics and climate change), Snowman generally seemed to possess a fundamentally placid temperament, a legacy perhaps of a secure childhood. And, as he readily acknowledged, he was a member of the 'Lucky Generation', born in the right time and place to have enjoyed the best that life had to offer while avoiding the privations of war and want. Like many who enjoy excellent health, Snowman always claimed to be unselfconscious about ageing and unafraid of death (so long as it was reasonably painless). He knew he had had a good innings.

Afterword

The essays included in this anthology were originally drafted, written and most of them published over the course of many decades, from as long ago as the 1970s to earlier this year (2024). In order to compile the collection for re-publication I read my way through hundreds of articles, reviews and essays from a wide range of academic journals, specialist and popular magazines, books, newspapers and websites which, between them, were aimed at every kind of readership. Once I had begun to home in on possible or probable inclusions in the new volume, I contacted as many of the previous publishers as I could, all of whom agreed that I could go ahead on condition that the original publication details were identified. Which, in every case, I have done. A punctilious reader might spot one or two carefully considered overlaps between the content of one essay and another, while I have tried to make it clear that some articles have been slightly edited and updated. The collection as a whole is far from comprehensive, and I have excluded all but a handful of the countless reviews of books and operas and much else that I have published over the decades.

All due diligence has been exercised in ensuring that every word in the book is my copyright (except for occasional, brief and clearly identified quotations from other authors). The same applies to the illustrations, almost all of which are from my own collection except where another source is acknowledged or the source is unknown, unobtainable or, to my knowledge, copyright free. In the unlikely event that any copyright material has inadvertently been used, the author and publishers trust this will be drawn to their attention in the hope that formal permission may be obtained and acknowledged in future editions.